• • • • •

RE-MADE IN JAPAN

• • • • •

RE-MADE IN JAPAN

EVERYDAY LIFE AND CONSUMER TASTE
IN A CHANGING SOCIETY

EDITED AND WITH AN INTRODUCTION BY JOSEPH J. TOBIN

YALE UNIVERSITY PRESS   NEW HAVEN AND LONDON

Published with assistance from the foundation established in memory of Philip Hamilton McMillan of the Class of 1894, Yale College.

Designed by Nancy Ovedovitz and set in Times Roman type by Rainsford Type. Printed in the United States of America by Vail-Ballou Press, Binghamton, New York.

Library of Congress
Cataloging-in-Publication Data
Re-made in Japan : everyday life and consumer taste in a changing society / edited and with an introduction by Joseph J. Tobin.
  p. cm.
Includes bibliographical references and index.
ISBN 0-300-05205-7
1. Ethnology—Japan. 2. Japanese—Ethnic identity. 3. Consumers—Japan—Attitudes. 4. Japan—Economic conditions. 5. Japan—Social life and customs. I. Tobin, Joseph Jay.
GN635.J2R36 1992
306′.0952—dc20   91-46611
                                        CIP

A catalogue record for this book is available from the British Library.

The paper in this book meets the guidelines for permanence and durability of the Committee on Production Guidelines for Book Longevity of the Council on Library Resources.

10   9   8   7   6   5   4   3   2   1

• • • • •

CONTENTS

CONTENTS

• • • • •

ACKNOWLEDGMENTS

This book, which began as a session at the American Anthropological Association meeting in 1988, took on much of its present shape at a conference held at the University of Hawaii in the summer of 1989. This conference was made possible by support from the Office of the Summer Session at the University of Hawaii and from the university's Japan Endowment Committee. A second Japan Endowment grant helped defray prepublication expenses. I am especially grateful to Victor Kobayashi, dean of the University of Hawaii Summer Session; Patricia Steinhoff, director of the Center for Japanese Studies; and Keith Brown, director of Asian Studies, University of Pittsburgh, for their help at the early stages of the project. Takada Masatoshi, Ueda Atsushi, Tsukada Mamoru, Aikawa Kayōko, Yoshino Shōji, Katagi Atsushi, and Sakudo Yotarō also participated in the conference and made valuable contributions.

Gladys Topkis, my friend and editor at Yale University Press, once again expertly guided me through the arduous task of turning an idea into a book. Thanks also to Karen Gangel for her excellent editing and to Brad Goda for the photography used on the jacket and in the introductory chapter.

The contributors to this book have been imaginative, diligent, patient, and open-minded. For this, and for their excellent chapters, I thank them.

• • • • •

NOTE ON NAMES

Many Japanese customs have changed since contact with the West, but not the order of names. Thus in both the text and the reference sections of this book the names of Japanese are cited with the family name preceding the given name, with no comma in between. The names of Japanese Americans, Japanese fashion designers working in the international arena, and Japanese authors writing in English, however, follow the usual Western practice.

As a decolonizing gesture, writers in Hawai'i insert an apostrophe between the last two letters to reflect Hawaiian pronunciation and to remind readers that Hawai'i has a meaning that precedes and transcends its identity as a state and a tourist destination. We have followed this convention in this book, except in the case of institutions with established names, such as the University of Hawaii and the Hawaii Visitors Bureau.

· · · · ·

1

INTRODUCTION: DOMESTICATING THE WEST

JOSEPH J. TOBIN

For more than a decade we've been inundated with studies of Japan's prodigious productivity. This book, in contrast, is about Japanese consumption. Yes, the Japanese work hard, export aggressively, and save assiduously. But they also spend their money, time, and energy with panache, enthusiasm, and even, at times, abandon. If it is true that in Japan students study hard and workers work hard, it is equally true that pleasure seekers play hard and consumers consume hard.[1] And much of what they play with and consume is Western in style and spirit, if not in country of manufacture.

The West is unmistakably present in Japanese daily life. Contemporary food, clothing, household furnishings, and leisure are a pastiche of traditional Japanese and borrowed Western elements. Hamburgers, motorcycles, and rock and roll are consumed by the Japanese young; coffee, double knits, and televised baseball by the middle-aged middle class; and haute cuisine, haute couture, and golf by the urban elite.

These manifestations of the West strike Westerners as an unlikely and at times unsettling combination of the familiar and the exotic. For American tourists in Japan the smell of temple incense, the feel of tatami, the starkness of Nō plays, are expectedly exotic. But when tourists stumble upon a pizza parlor in the Ginza, Japan becomes unexpectedly familiar. When they discover that the special for the day is

squid pizza, Japan becomes unexpectedly, peculiarly exotic. The chapters in this book attempt to deexoticize and depeculiarize Japan by explicating the meanings Japanese attach to Western things and practices. It is our hope that after reading this book, once-unlikely cultural artifacts, including squid pizza, will begin to make sense.

The Japanese are known to themselves and to others as an imitative people. The way this story goes, the Japanese, unable or unwilling to create, borrow. The genius of the Japanese lies not in invention but in adaptation—of Korean pottery, tombs, and textiles, Chinese script and scripture, Dutch science and medicine, French education, English colonialism, German militarism, and American egalitarianism, corporate efficiency, and popular culture.

Such stories tend to produce unflattering views of the Japanese either as passive victims of first Chinese and then Western cultural domination or, alternatively, as active, underhanded agents of cultural plagiarism. The chapters in this book speak to, but also against, these stories of

3

imitation by viewing the Japanese as engaged in an ongoing creative synthesis of the exotic with the familiar, the foreign with the domestic, the modern with the traditional, the Western with the Japanese. The chapters are about Japanese importation rather than Western exportation. The book is about not the actual West but about those aspects of the West (real or imagined) that the Japanese have made part of their culture.

I have chosen the word *domestication* as the central theme of this introduction to indicate a process that is active (unlike westernization, modernization, or postmodernism), morally neutral (unlike imitation or parasitism), and demystifying (there is nothing inherently strange, exotic, or uniquely Japanese going on here). *Domesticate* has a range of meanings, including tame, civilize, naturalize, make familiar, bring into the home. This book argues that the Japanese are doing all of these things vis-à-vis the West.

The term *domestication* also suggests that Western goods, practices, and ideas are changed (Japanized) in their encounter with Japan. Japan is unmistakably westernized, and yet Westerners who visit Japan do not necessarily find what they see familiar. Mary Yoko Brannen's chapter argues that Tokyo Disneyland is not an imitation or a replica of the Disneyland in Anaheim but a recontextualization of an exotic cultural form into the world of Japanese history, politics, and semiotics. James Stanlaw argues forcefully against applying the "borrowing metaphor" to English loanwords used in Japanese as he provides examples of how "English-inspired vocabulary items" often have meanings in Japan that are inventive, playful, and uniquely Japanese. Stephen Smith notes that in the postwar period beer and whiskey have dramatically increased their market share at the cost of traditional Japanese beverages but suggests that these Western drinks are marketed, purchased, and consumed in ways Jack Daniels and Augie Busch would find surprising.

It is tempting to see in contemporary Japanese consumption the playing out of familiar Western social, economic, and political theory. But is it appropriate to describe changes in Japanese everyday life as modernization, westernization, or postmodernism?

Quantitative analyses of Japanese consumer preferences and behavior can be used to show that over the past century Japan has become more Western and modern—Western in the sense that traditional food, clothing, furnishings, and forms of entertainment have been displaced by imported goods; modern in the sense that the Japanese have become dramatically more urban, educated, mobile, and technological. The

story of Japan's past 120 years can be presented as a transition from fish to meat, silk to synthetics, rice to wheat, tatami to carpet, sake to whiskey, and extended households to single-family dwellings. The sense of progress in this story can be quantified using statistics like Engels's coefficient—the percentage of household income spent on food. In Japan this percentage has declined dramatically, from 37 percent in 1966 to 33 percent in 1974 and 25 percent in 1988.

A sense of progress is implicit in the term *modernization* and in a related Weberian term popular in Japan—*gōrika* (rationalization). As William Kelly (1986) has observed, "For almost forty years *gōrika* has proved an ideologically potent and semantically slippery rubric for reform of everything from work rules and school texts to kitchen design, traffic flow, and dietary habits" (606). From the 1920s through the Occupation and on into the 1960s there was an intense interest in explaining Japan's economic, political, and moral successes and failures in terms of modernization theory.[2] Japanese and Western theorists struggled to place Japan somewhere along the road Karl Marx and Max Weber suggest runs from feudalism to industrial capitalism. Just as China remains the most problematic exception confronting Marxist scholars (how can a country be a true Communist society without passing through Marx's stages of capital development?), Japan is the most compelling problem to modernization and postmodernization theorists, who ask and then attempt to answer the question: How could Japan have become the preeminent postindustrial society without going through the stages of preindustrial development in an orderly way?

The American and Japanese versions of this debate have different central concerns: since the expedition of Commodore Matthew Perry, Americans have wondered paternalistically how to expedite Japan's modernization and integration into the world economy. The answer has been "Americanization"—of schools, factories, houses, leisure, and so forth. For the past century Japanese intellectuals and government leaders have posed the question of Japan's modernization somewhat differently, as they have wondered how to become as strong as the West while avoiding the social and cultural costs that success in this venture could bring. Recently America has turned to Japan for ideas on how to modernize and rationalize industrial production, management styles, and education, and yet the Americanization of Japanese everyday life has continued. Government and business leaders on both sides of the Pacific seem to agree that the answer to the trade-deficit problem lies chiefly in the Japanese becoming more like Americans in their tastes, spending, and leisure.

Scholarly interest has shifted of late from Japan's modernization to its postmodernity. Modernization accomplished, Japan now appears to intellectuals as the prototypical late-capitalist, postmodern, mass-culture, information-based consumer society. Employing Ernest Mandel's (1978) notion of late capitalism and Frederic Jameson's (1984) definition of postmodernism as a combination of commodity reification, superficiality, simulacra, and the waning of affect, Western and Japanese avant-garde critics both criticize and celebrate Japan as the first truly postmodern land. In their introduction to *Postmodernism and Japan* (1989), Masao Miyoshi, and H. D. Harootunian cite Alexandre Kojève's observation that for over three hundred years Japan "experienced life at the 'end of history.' " Depicting the Japanese as a precociously deconstructive people, Harootunian's *Things Seen and Unseen* (1988) and David Pollack's *Fracture of Meaning* (1986) suggest that Japan anticipated the West's belated discovery of an unbreachable gap between the

sign and the signified. In a celebrated discussion with Jacques Derrida, Karatani Kōjin argues that the postmodern sense of meaninglessness that is considered new and radical in the West is old stuff to the Japanese (Ivy 1989). In *Empire of Signs* (1982), a work that can be read as either an offensively or a satirically naïve ethnography of Japan, Roland Barthes finds the postmodern condition everywhere he looks in Japan: in the "decenteredness" of sukiyaki; in geisha played by male actors in kabuki ("the Oriental transvestite does not copy Woman but signifies her"); in (of course) Zen ("the whole of Zen wages a war against the prevarication of meaning"); and (shockingly) even in the Japanese eyelid ("the Japanese face is without moral hierarchy; it is entirely alive, even vivid . . . because its morphology cannot be read 'in depth' ").

The chief problem with applying the concepts of westernization, modernization, and postmodernization to Japan is that Japan comes out as either just another example of a general panhistorical, global process or as the exception that proves the rule, the antipode, the enigmatic nation that inscrutably refuses to conform to our theories. If we begin with a notion of modernization or late capitalism developed in the West and then apply it to Japan, the central questions inevitably become, Why is Japan an exception to the rest of the world? Why didn't Japan become Christian? Why wasn't it colonized? How could it industrialize so fast? What features in Japanese society can account for its unnaturally rapid development of a mass-culture, late-capitalist economy?

Yoshimoto Mitsuhiro is critical of Japanese and Western theorists who attempt to analyze Japanese society from the perspective of global arguments such as modernization or postmodernism:

> The problem with this global argument is that it ignores local differences which can never be reduced to local "variations" of a total system. Although I do not deny that the increasing permeation of multinational capital is now fundamentally transforming a number of non-Western countries, I do not think this fact can be used as an excuse for Western critics to claim that the multifariousness of the world is finally unified into a single totality under the name of postmodernism. Postmodernism . . . becomes nothing more than a catchword for Western critics' last-ditch effort to reclaim the lost hegemony of the West at least in the intellectual field. (1989, 8)

The contributors to this volume take no single position on this problem. Most are concerned in some way with the question of Japan's postmodernity, but none views Japan as just another case of a totalizing theory or as an exception to it. As a whole, the book aims for a middle ground: we try to avoid seeing contemporary Japanese consumer behavior and domestic life, including the domestication of the West, as either a universal story or a unique process (Sakai 1989). As a group, the chapters in this book, mostly by anthropologists, emphasize contextualized cultural description over decontextualized grand theory.

Most studies of work life in Japan tell us that Japanese locate their identities primarily in their productive, professional roles as lifetime employees of large companies (E. Vogel 1963; Rohlen 1974), farmers (Embree 1974 [1939]; Bernstein 1983), craftspeople (Singleton 1989; Kondo 1990), or housewives (Salamon 1975; S. Vogel 1978; Imamura 1987). In contrast, the chapters in this book suggest that in a changing Japan, what people consume may be as important as what they produce in shaping a sense of self. Japanese social planners are concerned about survey data indicating that younger workers are rejecting the notion that the central meaning of their lives lies in the workplace. The conclusion of these surveys is that young workers may be less interested in expanding their companies' market share or in making their country strong than in shopping.

Production and consumption in Japan, as elsewhere, are complexly linked. In consumer electronics, for example, the competitiveness of the Japanese domestic market pushes Japanese manufacturers to develop state-of-the-art products, which, in turn, are marketed for export. Profits generated by these exported goods eventually trickle down to create increased buying power among Japanese consumers. This, at least in theory, stimulates consumption of both domestic and imported goods. As a result of this prosperity, wages rise, industrial jobs are lost to the newly industrialized economies of Korea, Singapore, Taiwan, Hong Kong, and the domestic Japanese economy shifts toward hyperconsumerism. Thus the massive trade surplus of the 1970s and 1980s that made Japan the preeminent producer in the world is being cashed in for a new identity in the 1990s as the foremost consumer. Having neutralized the once-formidable economic power of the West through production and exports, the Japanese now are domesticating the suddenly vulnerable West by buying it.

Some of these purchases of the West, such as Kansas farms, Wyoming ranches, West Virginia steel mills, and Honolulu shopping malls, are best explained as rational capital investment. Others seem to have less to do with economic calculation than with cultural prestige and conspicuous consumption. Purchases in this category range from golf courses and condominiums in the United States and Australia, to French paintings, perfume, and handbags, to the services of American jazz musicians, baseball players, and ex-presidents brought to Tokyo to perform for Japanese fans. Chapters in this book describe how Japanese domesticate the West by consuming Iowa beef and Maine lobsters at a French restaurant in Hawai'i, by bringing home high-status souvenirs from trips abroad, by incorporating romantic English lyrics into their popular songs, and by spending a day in the Old West of Tokyo Disneyland.

The contemporary Japanese consumption and domestication of the West can be viewed as testimony to Japan's successful movement from the periphery to the core of the world economic system (Wallerstein 1979). Dorinne Kondo documents this movement in her description of the changing global flow of designs, fabric, and piecework in the world

9

of haute couture, as does Marta Savigliano in her analysis of the Japanese importation of the tango as one small piece of a world economy of passion.

One reason that consumption in Japan and elsewhere has received less scholarly attention than production is that consumption is associated with the sphere of women. In Japan as in the West, domestic consumption—the purchase and use of home furnishings, appliances, clothing, and food—is highly gendered. In this volume Nancy Rosenberger explains the gendered subtleties of furnishing a contemporary Japanese living room. William Kelly tells us of the discomfort experienced by an elderly man who is forced to perform the unfamiliar and, to his mind, feminine task of answering the telephone when the women of the home temporarily abandon their posts. Diana Bethel describes how important it is to the women in a Hokkaido home for the elderly to have appropriate treats to serve guests in their rooms. Dorinne Kondo analyzes the refiguring of gender in contemporary Japanese men's and women's clothing.

When ten of the contributors to this volume first met as a group in Honolulu in 1989, we discussed the dangers as well as the advantages of using the gendered terms *domestic* and *domestication* in our project. We view the Japanese consumption of food, clothes, and home furnishings as highly gendered, but we do not mean to suggest that in Japan it is men who produce and women who consume. As ethnographies like Ezra Vogel's *Japan's New Middle Class* (1963) describe, there are families in Japan in which men and women live separate lives—the men at work, the women at home; the men earning, the women spending. But we must avoid the sexist assumptions implicit in some accounts of separate spheres and female domesticity, which depict women as the conspicuous spenders of their husbands' and fathers' money.

The reality for the majority of Japanese families is that female members of the family also produce and males also consume. An overemphasis on studying the white-collar employees of Japan's largest companies has obscured an appreciation of women's productive work. Most Japanese women are employed. The holiday gifts purchased in department stores are sold and wrapped by armies of female salesclerks. The neighborhood stores selling everyday Western goods, ranging from toiletries to breakfast cereals, are generally run by women. Many of the small factories where bread is baked, ball bearings are manufactured,

10

and shopping bags are lettered with English sayings are staffed largely by women. Kondo describes the key productive roles women play in the global high-fashion industry. When Japanese women buy Western goods, they are usually spending their own hard-earned cash, as Fumiteru Nitta describes in his discussion of "*OL*" (office lady) souvenir shopping in Honolulu.

And Japanese men consume. The men in Bethel's old-folks home have ingenious ways of purchasing and smuggling in liquor bought in town. Similarly, Smith explains that the consumption of Western spirits is overwhelmingly a male phenomenon. William Kelly shows that tractors are not just utilitarian machines; they are fetishized consumer goods to the men who purchase and operate them.

The Japanese domestication of the West is a gendered issue in another sense. During the Meiji period, when the West enjoyed the power to force unequal trade agreements on Japan and other Eastern nations, the Western colonial powers were situated in the masculine position, and Japan and its nearby Eastern countries were in the position of feminized, violated victims. This feminization of Japan is represented metaphorically by the figure of Cho-Cho-San (Madame Butterfly), who is desired, taken, and then abandoned by her Western lover.

But in the contemporary period these gendered international dynamics have grown more complex (Kondo 1990).[3] The Japanese now have the power to penetrate Western markets with their exports and to consume the West at bargain-basement prices. With dramatic shifts in wealth come shifting patterns of intercultural intimacy: in the mid-1980s the number of Japanese men marrying Western women for the first time surpassed the number of Japanese women marrying Western men (Nitta 1988). In red-light districts of Tokyo, where just thirty years ago GIs and other foreigners purchased the sexual services of Japanese women, Japanese men now are being served by foreign (mostly Southeast Asian but also North and South American) women. As Savigliano's paper on tango suggests, Japan now has the desire, wealth, and power to import and consume passion in many forms from the West.

How does the West enter Japan? As Japan's power has grown and the West's has waned, the Japanese have shifted from being the desperate consumers of a superior Western culture to functioning as brokers of the West's diminishing resources. In the early years of contact, the West often entered under the cover of direct or implied force, producing

11

explicit and subtle resistance. Missionaries, for example, first entered Japan as the religious vanguard of colonizing powers. The Christianity they introduced was sporadically embraced but in the end rejected. The Japanese, once viewed as the most likely Asian converts, have neutralized generation after generation of Catholic, Protestant, and Mormon missionaries. Ignoring Christian dogma, the Japanese have domesticated select Christian artifacts and customs, leaving little that Western missionaries would find familiar or attractive. Many contemporary Japanese couples are married in actual or simulated Christian services, either in Hawai'i, as Nitta describes, or in Japanese wedding halls that artfully blend Christian and Shinto architecture, ceremonies, dress, and foods (Edwards 1989). Millie Creighton (1991) describes the successful merchandizing of Christian holiday customs and paraphernalia in a country that remains, after hundreds of years of proselytizing, only 1 percent Christian. Christmas cakes, sold in Japan the week before Christmas and eaten on Christmas Eve, are such a formalized tradition in contemporary Japan that the term *kurisumasu kēiki* has become a sarcastic expression for an unmarried woman over twenty-five, who, like a Christmas cake on December 25, is rapidly losing appeal (Stanlaw 1988).

A second route of entry of Western goods and practices is as *omiyage,* objects of value carried home from sacred or exotic places. As Nitta explains, the word *omiyage,* which now means a souvenir gift, historically referred to amulets and talismans brought home from faraway shrines. In addition to collecting religious artifacts, travelers brought back foods and handicrafts characteristic of the regions they visited and *miyage banashi,* tales of the wondrous things they experienced and learned on their journeys.

This tradition of traveling to sacred places and returning with goods and stories served as a modus operandi for the Japanese who traveled to Europe and the United States at the turn of the century in search of the wonders of the West (Kato n.d.). From the Meiji era on, the overseas sojourn has been a favored mode for importing and domesticating the West.

To expedite and organize the process of learning from the West, the Meiji government sent the best and the brightest scholars and government leaders abroad on fact-finding missions. In addition to meeting with foreign diplomats and heads of state, tour members studied Western agriculture, industry, education, banking, trade, government, arts, and routines of everyday life. The five-volume, two-thousand-page report of the most ambitious of these tours, the Iwakura Mission, served for many years as a blueprint for westernization (Mayo 1959).

During the Meiji period there were also many unofficial trips—personal pilgrimages to the shrines of Western power and knowledge. A trip abroad became a rite of passage for the Meiji elite, a finishing school of worldly tastes and Western life-style. While official delegations went West in search of rationality and efficiency and came back with plans for postal systems and irrigation projects, civilians journeyed in search of sophistication, adventure, and self-actualization.

By the 1920s Japanese sojourners were bringing home low- as well as high-European culture. Edward Seidensticker (1990) relates the founding in 1929 of Tokyo's first European-style review, the Casino Folies, by a pair of brothers who had frequented the Casino de Paris and the Folies Bergère during their stay abroad. Savigliano tells us about Baron Megata, the "father of Japanese tango," who, as a young aristocrat traveling abroad in the 1920s, fell in love with the beauty and passion of the tango while living in Paris. The baron brought the tango back to Japan, where it was embraced by the aristocratic *mobo* and *moga* (modern boys and girls) of the Tokyo jazz age. The tradition of living in New York, London, or Paris to acquire cultural capital continues to this day. Washizu, the chef described in Jeffrey Tobin's paper, wielded the authority of one trained in Paris in his kitchen. Kondo tells of Japanese designers who earned domestic respect by winning acclaim in Paris.

Foreigners living in Japan have been another important conduit for the entry of Western goods and practices. During the late Meiji period there were rapid and spontaneous changes in the quotidian dimensions of Japanese life. In spite of the protests of Buddhists, Confucians, and other traditionalists, many Japanese quickly began to imitate the dress and life-styles of the foreigners suddenly in their midst. The aristocracy, the military, and students in urban areas were particularly quick to adopt the Western material culture they were exposed to through personal encounters or through woodblock prints and magazine and newspaper illustrations. Japanese officers were wearing European-style uniforms (including Western sabers rather than samurai-style *katana*) as early as 1850. Early in his reign the Meiji emperor dramatically changed his attire to have it conform with that of foreign leaders. The emperor's new clothes were Western long before his countrymen had traded in their kimono.

For a while country dwellers and the lower classes resisted following the urban elite's conversion to Western dress and grooming. But by the end of the nineteenth century, less than fifty years after Perry's arrival, the majority of Japanese men owned at least one Western-style suit and hat. By the end of the Meiji era, the term *hai-karā* (high collar) had entered the language as an idiom for "sophisticated" or "high-class."

During the Occupation Japanese daily life once again underwent an intense westernization—specifically, an Americanization. The Occupation authority, under the direction of General Douglas MacArthur, imposed those aspects of the West that the Japanese could not do without. Reforms affecting government, land tenure and inheritance, education, and industry were mandated by the Americans, who would not leave until they were convinced that Japan had been thoroughly domesticated and properly democratized. Again, as in the Meiji (1868–1912) and Taishō (1912–1925) eras, in the aftermath of the war there was an unofficial importation and rapid diffusion of the West accompanying the official importation of technology, capital, and democracy. As Stanlaw describes, the GIs and other Americans who lived, worked, and traveled widely throughout occupied Japan taught a generation of Japanese versions of English not found in English-language textbooks.

In the postwar era radio and movies played an increasingly important role in introducing Western popular and material culture. Elvis Presley and other American rock idols became stars in Japan as the American Top 40 were broadcast across the country on FEN, the Far Eastern version of Armed Forces Radio. American movies and television along with records and radio made American popular culture the rage in Japan in the 1950s. The *nostarujii būmu* (nostalgia boom) that became chic in Japan in the 1980s indicates a rekindling of consumer desire not for traditional Japanese music and dress but for the look and sound of the leather-jacketed hoods and poodle-skirted teenyboppers of that earlier era. Japanese promoters of "nostalgia products" refer to this consumer trend as "neo-nostalgia" (Ivy 1989).

Today, a powerful group of culture brokers orchestrates the importation, diffusion, and domestication of Western material culture. Included in this category are the television, music, and publishing industries, trading companies, advertising agencies, and department stores. As Creighton's chapter describes, department stores are much more powerful in Japan than in Europe or the United States. The major Japanese department stores developed and still own most of Japan's liveliest shopping districts. In some cases department stores opened railway lines to bring customers to their stores, and railway lines opened department stores in their stations to draw riders to their trains. Currently, diversified Japanese companies like Hankyū, in the Osaka area, and Seibu, in Tokyo, dominate Japanese retailing, including the importing, packaging, and promoting of Western things. Creighton describes how department stores market Japanese and Western foods, clothes, and furnishings differently, by displaying them in separate sections of the store and by using individual promotions. The latest approach of the most successful retailers is the mini department store, which carries only trendy Western goods. Although the aging giants like Takashimaya and Mitsukoshi continue to do good business, young shoppers are increasingly turning to such stores as Seibu's Parco, Wave, Walk, and Loft. These stores, like The Sharper Image in the United States, sell not just things but life-styles, what trendy retailers refer to as *mono igai no mono*—things that are not things.

The Japanese advertising industry plays a key role in the contemporary merchandising of the West. Western models and celebrities are paid huge sums to pitch products associated with the West. Such artists and performers as George Lucas, Woody Allen, and Faye Dunaway, who are rarely if ever seen in television ads in the United States, have been featured in Japanese advertising campaigns for drinks, cars, and electronic goods. Western and Eurasian models dominate the Japanese advertising of clothes and cosmetics. Advertising has become so important and salient in contemporary Japan that some *ado-man* and *kopii-raitā* have become celebrities in their own right, commodified performance artists whose campaigns are consumed and critiqued by scholars and intellectuals as well as by the shopping in-crowd (Ivy 1989).

Many of the phenomena discussed in this book are truer of Tokyo and other urban centers than of the Japanese countryside, where hip clothing trends, nouvelle cuisine, and the lambada have lesser powers of penetration. There is an internal circulation of cultural and material capital in Japan: the West most often enters Japan through Tokyo, is domesticated there (made appropriately and uniquely Japanese), and is then repackaged for export to the provincial periphery. To rural Japanese, Tokyo, Osaka, and other megalopoles represent the modern, the Western, the hectic, the decadent, the individualistic, the powerful. Urban and rural in Japan suggest a dichotomy as much of time as of space: Tokyo is the future; rural Japan, the past that was "always already there" (Harootunian 1988, 416). If Tokyo is Japan's West, the countryside is Japan's Japan.

Maruyama Masao (1965) reminds us that the flow of influence and power between urban and rural Japan goes in both directions. Clearly, Japan's core cities powerfully shape the tastes and desires of the countryside. But the rural periphery also holds considerable power over the city, in part because of the peculiarities of Japanese legislative apportionment but mostly because of the migration from country to city. Maruyama explains that each generation of urban immigrants brings with it country tastes and values. Migrants to the city retain a sense of connection to the old paddies for many years, even several generations. Though they may not return to their *furusato* (hometown) as often as they feel they should, urban Japanese take comfort in the knowledge that in the mountains or on the seacoast there are still authentic folk villages where simple people live traditional Japanese lives. Some of these urbanites cling to the dream of moving back to the countryside someday.

We have made an effort in this book to look at the rural as well as the urban versions of the contemporary Japanese consumption of the West. For example, Bethel's study of a home for the aged in rural Hokkaido shows how rural elders' spatial, temporal, and emotional remove from Western practices (including nursing homes) makes their experience of abandonment and shame upon entering the home all the more acute. Kelly's study of farm technology in Shōnai is a tale from the Japanese periphery. Because rural Japanese, whose housing costs are low, tend to have as much cash to spend on travel as their higher-paid but house-poor urban counterparts, the tourists Jeffrey Tobin depicts dining on French food and buying souvenirs in Honolulu are a mix of town and country. Most of Rosenberger's home decorators are urban, as are Smith's drinkers and Creighton's department store shoppers, but the phenomena they discuss can also be found in the countryside. The Latin dance boom described by Savigliano remains very much a Tokyo and Osaka scene, but before long they'll be doing the lambada in Kyushu.

The supposedly homogeneous middle class in Japan is in fact many middle classes (Kelly 1986). At similar income levels there are two- as well as one-income families, blue- as well as white-collar workers, and self-employed as well as salaried earners. We need the same careful study of class, taste, and distinction in Japan that Pierre Bourdieu (1984) has done for France: How does taste, especially taste in Western things, reflect subtle distinctions among the various Japanese middle classes?

Imagine, for example, a neighborhood forty minutes by train from downtown Tokyo. As we move down a street in this neighborhood we encounter a variety of middle-class consumers. Above and behind their camera store lives a *shitamachi* (old Tokyo) family. They are part of the shitamachi middle class not because they live in downtown Tokyo (they don't) but because they identify with a life-style that has been characteristic of Tokyo merchants for several centuries. Urban but not

17

urbane, they are likely to ridicule both Japanese traditionalists, who embrace the high Japanese arts and reject the West, and Japanese yuppies, who have lost touch with their Japanese souls. Propertied but cash poor, they are saving to tear down their old two-story dwelling and to rebuild a more westernized four-story workplace and domicile.

Next door is the Sun Palace Mansion, a six-story, vaguely castellated building containing twenty-four condominium units, most of which are owned by university-educated, white-collar employees of large companies. Having managed to purchase their own homes before prices in Tokyo shot beyond the reach of the middle class, these Japanese yuppies have money to spend on study desks for their kids, Western clothes and furniture, a family car, and trips abroad. Though they may occasionally go to the public bath and may wear kimono once or twice a year, these members of Japan's new middle class have decidedly Western tastes.

Down the street, in a garish, chateaulike two-story house, lives a family of Japan's *nyū ritchi* (nouveau riche). Their wealth derives from a parcel of land on the outskirts of Tokyo that they recently sold for two million dollars to a firm planning to build a combination parking lot and golf driving range. Suddenly rich, this family consumes the West in great chunks: trips to Hawai'i, a Mercedes-Benz, crystal chandeliers, scotch whiskey. Further down the street is a row of *danchi*—three-story walk-up rental apartments. These eighteen-mat (approximately four-hundred-square-foot) "rabbit hutches" are home to blue-collar and lower white-collar workers. Some residents of the danchi are frugal, saving to move into better housing; some are profligate, spending their paychecks and their biannual bonuses as fast as they earn them on projection televisions, electronic toilets, and packaged tours abroad. They are the urban equivalent of the rural *kikkai-binbō*—(machine-poor) farmers who are forever paying off their last tractor loan. Some of these danchi families are more future-oriented, investing heavily in their children's education, hoping, but not optimistic, that this strategy will be a route to their children's economic success.

A few of these families, liberated in their gender expectations, have the same dreams and expectations for their daughters as for their sons; most, however, pursue the older strategy of hoping that their daughters will marry up. One way to increase a daughter's marriage value is to invest in cultural capital: they hope that by giving her good taste in Western clothes, some lessons in English, tennis, and flower arranging, and a degree from a prestigious women's college, they will enable her to find a husband who can offer her a securely middle-class life-style. Ten years ago this ideal mate was captured by the ironic popular expression *ie tsuki, kā tsuki, baba nuki* (a house, a car, and no mother-in-law). The new phrase describing the contemporary dream husband is "the three Ts," for the three *takais* (highs): a graduate of a highly regarded university who has a high salary and is tall.

Another version of the struggling middle class is the *nyū-binbō,* the "new poor" counterparts to the nyu ritchi. The new poor live in shabby homes in shabby neighborhoods, but each weekend they put on expensive foreign suits and take their fancy dogs for walks in Roppongi, Tokyo's chicest and most westernized neighborhood, where they can pretend for a few hours that they are rich. One special figure among the new poor is the "Danchi Princess," a young single woman who lives with her parents in a tiny five-story walk-up apartment (known as a *2DK*—two small tatami rooms plus a combination dining room–kitchen). The Danchi Princess, holding on to the fantasy that she was meant for better things, spends a significant portion of her family's income on trendy designer clothing that belies the humble realities of her lower-middle-class life. Princess Kiko gave hope to a whole generation of these would-be princesses by escaping from a 2DK upbringing to marry Prince Akishino, whom she met at a tennis club in college. Creighton's chapter describes how the Isetan Department Store targets this special group of shoppers with a Cinderella City section where members of the Cinderella Club can purchase expensive upscale outfits using their Cinderella Cards.

For each of these types of Japanese consumers, Western goods play a key role in the negotiation and display of social class. Golf is the preeminent leisure activity of the already powerful and the upwardly mobile. Ambitious businessmen who cannot afford greens fees, much less membership in a club, nonetheless invest in irons, shoes, golfing attire, and lessons. Those who do not even own a set of clubs can try to impress by spending their coffee breaks taking shadow swings in the office hallway. For young Japanese of both sexes, skiing and expensive skiwear similarly function as displays of status.

Several of the chapters in this book are concerned with issues of class and taste. Smith's discussion of drinking, for example, suggests that the Japanese who were once impressed with any foreign import are now very *burando-shikō* (brand name conscious). Having a "keep-bottle" of Johnny Walker Black Label on hand at a bar suggests a certain dis-

tinction. But the guy at the next table may be showing greater sophistication by ordering a single-malt scotch, while the real cognoscenti have
traded in their Western liquor for *shōchū,* the revalorized Japanese
moonshine, or for the current trendy beverage, "beer nouveau." Kondo
gives us a glimpse of the upper end of taste and class in her description
of the world of Japanese haute couture, where sophistication can be
found in an evening gown made of a humble Japanese fabric or in a
kimono-style miniskirt.

The consumption practices of many struggling middle-class families
seem faddish, frantic, and unsatisfying. To borrow a phrase from Bourdieu (1984) by way of Jean Baudrillard (1981), their lives seem driven
by "a rhetoric of despair." They cram their apartments with state-of-
the-art electronic goods and furnishings. Commuting to work six days
a week by subway, they buy cars they are able to use only on Sundays.
Knowing that home prices are rising much more rapidly than their paychecks and savings, they buy desperately, impulsively, whimsically.

The despair that Bourdieu, Baudrillard, and other intellectuals see
in the consumption practices of the French and American middle classes
is associated with a sense of decay characteristic of declining national
fortunes and of the end of eras. As once-great capitalist empires crum-
ble, the middle class hungrily appropriates the cultural capital and style
of the old elite. As the force of sumptuary law and custom fades, the
middle class decorate their modest homes and apartments in the style
of sun kings and robber barons and drive cars named after elegant
eighteenth-century carriages. But for all their ersatz finery and preten-
sions, in their hearts they despair, knowing that the patina of class they
attempt to buy covers over but can never erase a sense of meaninglessness, repetition, boredom (Lefebvre 1947), and a waning of affect
in their lives (Jameson 1984).

Does this story apply to Japan? Japan may share something with
France, but there are also important differences. As a capitalist nation,
Japan is still in its salad days, and consumption often has the feeling
of adolescent exuberance rather than of middle-aged despair. The
new consumers seem less interested in breaking sumptuary laws than in
casting away old notions of taste, hierarchy, and class. Their mood
seems less like despair, more like carnival: shopping on a Sunday on a
pedestrians-only street in Shinjuku, Shibuya, or Harajuku feels like the

Japanese equivalent of Mardi Gras in New Orleans or Carnival in Rio, with money and packages taking the place of music and dance.

In its most profligate and exuberant forms, Japanese consumption transcends our conventional notions of extravagance. To make sense, for example, of one-hundred-dollar cantaloupes, five-thousand-dollar business dinners, or fifty-thousand-dollar weddings, we must set aside our concept of rational economic calculation and even of Veblenian conspicuous consumption and turn instead to the logic of potlatch, the ceremonies of wealth exhibition and redistribution associated with the Indians of the American Northwest (Mauss 1967). As in the potlatch, Japanese gift giving and expense-account entertaining are clearly complex and overdetermined, combining motives of display, power and prestige, repayment, social solidarity, and investment in future favors. And yet, like the potlatch and other exotic forms of consumption and exchange (Appadurai 1986), the extravagance of contemporary Japanese who spend on themselves and others sometimes seems to add up to more than the sum of these familiar intentions. Although "price-is-no-object" consumption is not unheard of in the West, it seems far less common in American than in Japanese middle-class life, where higher-priced goods are often preferred to their lower-priced near-equivalents. In elegant as well as shabby restaurants and drinking establishments, prices are frequently not listed, so that the bill is often a surprise. Though they might well be trapped in the same cycle of consumption as Americans, middle-class Japanese somehow manage to save more regularly and yet to spend with less guilt, less regret, and less ambivalence than their counterparts in the West.

The energy devoted to consumption seems, if not decadent, at least misspent to many older and more conservative Japanese, who remember life in Japan as having once been very different—harder but morally sounder. Alternatively, some Japanese social critics see in this carnivalesque, extravagant consumption a reenactment of the hedonism and selfishness of Japan in the 1920s.

By the 1920s, as the Meiji military and industrial sectors accelerated their imitation of and competition with the technological accomplishments of the Western powers, privileged youth in Tokyo and Osaka were playing out their own version of the nihilistic, hedonistic life-style of the West's jazz age. In addition to emulating the Folies Bergère and

the tango, the westernized, decadent youth of Tokyo embraced jazz, gin, movies, and baseball. Kawabata Yasunari and other popular authors of the time chronicled the adventures of these new moderns as they pursued *ero-guro-nonsensu,* the erotic-grotesque frivolity associated with the West (Seidensticker 1990).

According to Maruyama Masao, ero-guro-nonsensu is a symptom of modernization, which inevitably produces a sense of social and psychological disruption by emancipating the individual citizen "willingly or unwillingly from the communal ties which have hitherto bound him and which have prescribed to him certain traditional behavior" (1965, 494). Maruyama argues that by the early twentieth century, contact with the West had produced an "awakening of individuality," which Natsume Sōseki saw as the "spiritual breakdown which follows modernization" (Arima 1961, 16) and which Robert Bellah has called "the modernization of the soul" (1965, 422). Maruyama suggests that the emerging individualism of "atomization" and "privatization" became the predominant worldview of Japanese intellectuals during the first third of the twentieth century, as, for instance, in the "*watakushi shōtsetsu*" (the "I novels") of the period, whose

> protagonists evidenced precociously the feeling of dull and nihilistic boredom with life or the apathetic attitude of a mere onlooker of society— feelings and attitudes expressed in the "over-matured" culture of Western

Europe after the First World War. Such a literary work could have a wide audience precisely because such types of people, if not predominant, were in fact emerging. The expressions *kootoo-yuumin* [educated loafers] or *hammon-seinen* [agonized youth], which were the fashionable words in the newspapers and magazines of the time, cleverly depicted the trend of PRIVATIZATION and ATOMIZATION of the rapidly expanding group of urbanized intellectuals. (508)

The privatized individualism sweeping the higher classes of urban Japan had consumer as well as literary and political manifestations. The new urban elite's tastes in food, drink, entertainment, clothing, and housing became increasingly westernized and atomized. During this period Japan's emerging middle class began to move out of extended-family households into suburban *bunka jūtaku* (cultured residences). In a passage from a popular song of the time, these single-family homes with red roofs and small gardens were sentimentalized as "my happy, though cramped home" (Maruyama 1965, 518). The bunka jūtaku of the 1920s was reborn in the 1960s as the postwar urban middle-class dream of owning a *mai homu*. In this volume Rosenberger discusses the "romantic couple" version of this privatized mai-homu dream as interpreted in the 1980s. Smith finds that Japanese drinking patterns from the 1930s on have been characterized by a shift toward more individualized servings and more diverse products to satisfy the thirst of an increasingly atomized market. Stanlaw suggests that Japanese singers use English lyrics to communicate individualized feelings—most typically, love and sexual desire. Herbert Passin (1977) argues that the use of the pronoun *mai* (my) in Japanese expressions such as mai homu, *mai kā* (my car), and *mai puraibashii* (my privacy) is indicative of a new social order in Japan that gives "priority to one's family and to one's private realm" (26).

Today (as in earlier eras) one hears complaints that young people have crossed the line from privacy and individuality to anomie and selfishness. Japanese social critics have coined the term *shinjinrui* (the new humans) to describe urban young whose values and life-styles their elders find so bizarre as to suggest another species. The media depict these youth as disrespectful, individualistic, selfish, uncommitted, and materialistic. The songs and novels produced and consumed by the urban in-crowd do little to contradict this image. *Nantonaku, Kurisutaru* (Somehow, Crystal), a best-selling novel of the 1980s, captures this antiethic of hedonistic consumption not only in its description of a Tokyo young elite committed to pleasure and consumption but also in its extensive endnotes, which identify and thus advertise the boutiques and clubs the protagonists frequent (Field 1989).

This new life-style of the urban elite is marked by the words *trendy, self,* and *new.* The last also shows up frequently these days as *nouveau, nouvelle,* or *neo.* The central notion is to create an identity of one's own through enlightened consumption.[4] One purchases not things in themselves but a life-style defined by things. The new ideal is the man or woman who is not self-made but self-consumed.

With these changes, the line dividing the public from the private or domestic sphere is shifting. In the process of importing and domesticating the West, the boundaries surrounding Japanese homes, neighborhoods, and perhaps even the Japanese self have changed. For example, Seidensticker (1983, 1990) blames modernization and westernization for the breakdown of the traditional boundaries between the low and high cities of Tokyo. The tatami-less floors of modern buildings such as department stores, hotels, and city halls contribute to a blurring of the important distinction between inside and outside marked by the ritual of removing shoes.

Several of the chapters in this volume discuss such boundary shifts brought on by rising individualism, modernization, and contact with the West. Bethel describes the struggle of residents of a home for the elderly to find privacy and a sense of familiar (Japanese) domesticity in an environment they perceive as oppressively public and westernized. Rosenberger, noticing the conspicuous absence of elderly parents and children in home decorating magazines that encourage "a couples lifestyle," suggests that the line between private and public is being redrawn within homes and families. Scott Clark chronicles the domestication of bathing, a once-public activity that has become increasingly privatized and domestic. Kelly's essay is a rumination on the privatizing effects of the telephone, television, and tractor on Japanese rural life.

The salience in Japan of the distinction between foreign and Japanese is hard for Westerners to grasp. Japanese things and foreign things are marked as fundamentally different in the way they are advertised and marketed (Ivy 1988); in department stores' use of separate displays (as Creighton describes); in the syllabary used to write about them (Stanlaw, this volume); and, most basically, in the way they are categorized by

the Japanese language as being *wa* (Japanese) or *yō* (Western). The self-evident power of this distinction between Japanese and foreign goods and practices might be compared to our Western common-sense notion of gender difference: before we can evaluate a person's character or social class, we notice if the person is male or female. Similarly, in Japan, before a food, an article of clothing, or a piece of furniture is evaluated as good or bad, expensive or cheap, it is identified as either foreign or Japanese.

The foods served in a Western *resutoran* are *yōshoku* (literally, Western dishes); those served in a Japanese *shokudō* (dining place) are *washoku* (Japanese dishes). The rice served in a European-style restaurant in Tokyo is called *raisu;* the same rice served in a shokudō is called *gohan.* As Bethel points out, a paramount concern of Japanese elders, and a common source of disagreement that the elderly have with their children and household staff, is the elders' preference for foods they consider traditionally Japanese. Clothing is *yōfuku* (Western wear), *wafuku* (Japanese clothing), or kimono (literally, a thing that is worn), which refers specifically to a woman's silk garment but may also refer generally to any traditional article of clothing. Kondo's chapter relates how Japanese haute couturiers are playing with and against the limits of the distinction between wafuku and yōfuku as they create clothes and identities in Tokyo, Paris, and New York.

According to Rosenberger, architecture, interior design, and furniture are similarly marked: a tatami-covered room is a *washitsu;* a carpeted room with chairs and sofa, a *yōshitsu.* A Japanese scroll would be as surprising in a yōshitsu as a Western-style painting would be in a washitsu. A traditional Japanese toilet, over which one squats, is a *benjo* or a *washiki no toire* (a Japanese-style toilet) as opposed to a *toire* (toilet) or, more clearly, a *yōshiki no toire* (a Western-style toilet). The phrase *yōshiki no washiki no toire* (a Western-style Japanese toilet) might mean either a squatting toilet with plumbing or a toilet seat placed over a latrine. Many Japanese consumers are drawn to decorating schemes that artfully mix Japanese and Western features in a style called *wayō setchū* (Japanese-Western eclecticism). As Rosenberger suggests, Western as opposed to Japanese furnishings suggest to young consumers a new, alternative life-style and self-image: a couch is not just a place to sit while watching television but a symbol of Western-style conjugality. On the other hand, Japanese touches give a basically Western room a human feeling that it would otherwise lack.

These boundaries, though vigilantly maintained and universally acknowledged, are continuously shifting. What was marked as foreign and exotic yesterday can become foreign but familiar today and traditionally Japanese tomorrow. Sukiyaki, for example, a dish borrowed from the meat-eating Europeans by the then-more-vegetarian Japanese, has become a traditional Japanese food, usually served by kimono-clad wait-

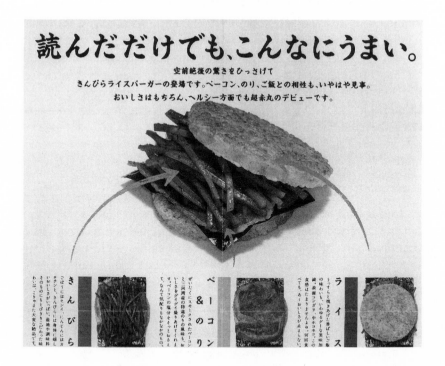

読んだだけでも、こんなにうまい。

空前絶後の驚きをひっさげて
きんぴらライスバーガーの登場です。ベーコン、のり、ご飯との相性も、いやはや見事。
おいしさはもちろん、ヘルシー方面でも超赤丸のデビューです。

resses on special occasions to guests sitting on tatami. At this moment, foods once marked as foreign are being domesticated by young Japanese: perhaps by the turn of the century spaghetti and hamburgers will have lost all traces of their foreign origins. Signs of the domestication of the hamburger can be seen in its inclusion (without bun) in the *okosama teishoku* (the special children's lunch) served in department store restaurants and in the success of McDonald's Japan, whose Biggu Makku and Makku-furai (French fries) have become so thoroughly a part of Japanese life that Japanese tourists in Waikiki and Paris wait in line to order them when they are feeling homesick and want to eat something familiar. McDonald's has been so successful in Japan that it has produced its Japanese imitators, including MosBurger, which features, in addition to the standard versions, a "riceburger" composed of *kimpira* (burdock root), bacon, and seaweed served on grilled rice (*onigiri*) pressed into the shape of a bun.

As the new, the modern, and the foreign become familiar, aspects of daily life previously taken for granted become self-consciously tra-

27

ditional artifacts from a distant and exotic past. As the West is domesticated, once-ordinary Japanese things and practices can become special,
wondrous, and exotic. When Western clothing became common, the
kimono became rare: today, young Japanese women enroll in classes
devoted to the art of the kimono, in which they learn how to put on,
sit down in, and fold this unfamiliar garment. Once Western floor cov-
erings became the rule in factory and workplace, tatami floors took on
new meaning as significant exceptions: the one tatami room in a concrete
and marble company headquarters functions as a sanctified place where
the president receives special guests to discuss special matters.

Kelly suggests that contemporary Japanese are pulled between modernization and nostalgia. The farmers he studies in Shōnai are simultaneously anachronistic country bumpkins, scions of a proud rural
tradition, and efficient, modern businessmen employed in a thoroughly
rationalized agricultural industry (1986). These kikkai-binbō farmers,
like their city cousins, are caught up in the logic of frenzied consumption
as they purchase state-of-the-art technology for their farms and homes.
And yet they also take pride in their rural roots and find meaning in
the notion that they are living a more traditional, authentic Japanese
life than their kinsmen who emigrated to the city.

Kelly points out that this nostalgic longing is less for the actual Japanese past than for a sentimentalized notion of premodern Japanese
life, a fetishized past that is frozen, embalmed, and safely cut off from
the present. Rural Japanese are less interested in living as their ancestors
did than in picking and choosing aspects of their past to blend into a
comfortable contemporary middle-class life-style.

The problem is that such a life-style requires more income than most
farms can produce, with the result that most farm families must supplement their agriculture earnings with outside jobs. Some rural communities attempt to stimulate their faltering economies by appealing to
tradition-hungry urban tourists longing for traditional Japanese villages
(Robertson 1988). Kurokawa, for example, a village in the Shonai region, sells itself as "Japan's Nō Village" to urban tourists who come
to see yearly productions of authentic folk Nō mounted by amateur
thespians of the village (Kelly 1986). Jackson Bailey (1991) writes of
similar attempts by impoverished communities in Tōhoku to market
their failed industrial settings as genuine mining, logging, and fishing
villages. Ella Wiswell, returning to the village of Suye fifty years after
she and her late husband, John Embree, completed their year of field-

work, discovered that many of the younger villagers were less interested in reminiscing with her about the old days than in using her visit to launch a campaign to market their town as "Japan's anthropological village" (Wiswell and Smith 1988). At a loss for suitable tourist attractions, the tourism committee was planning an exhibit featuring the chair in which John Embree sat while writing his notes for *Suye Mura: A Japanese Village* (1974 [1939]).

In each case the commodity being marketed and consumed is authenticity: authentic artifacts and authentic traditions of an authentic Japanese past. The cultural politics of authenticity can be intense as towns compete for the title of Japan's (or their region's) most authentic paper-making, pottery, puppet-making, or mining village. These politics are played out nationally and internationally in the mass media, as in the old "Discover Japan" and "Exotic Japan" ad campaigns of the Japanese National Railway (Ivy 1988); in department stores, which sponsor exhibitions of traditional Japanese arts and crafts (Creighton); and in the activities of Bunkachō, the Agency for Cultural Affairs, which names artisans "living national treasures."

Some of the traditions that Japanese value most are in fact of relatively recent vintage. Some are simulacra, re-creations of a past that never happened and of things that never existed. Bestor (1989) has written of the sense of tradition and history infusing the life of a Tokyo community that did not exist before the war. Lacking a shared past and inherited traditions, the citizens of the community create them. Their authenticity as a community is centered on the political, economic, and emotional significance of the lavish *mikoshi* (the tutelary Shinto shrine) they bought in 1984, which they carry proudly once a year through the streets.

Western scholars have played a key role in helping foreigners and Japanese decide what is authentically and importantly Japanese about Japan. A generation of Japan specialists who got a start as translators during the war have introduced Japanese culture and arts to the West. Like Ernest Fenellosa and Lafcadio Hearn before them, many of these scholars bemoan Japan's westernization and mourn what they experience as the loss of traditional charms. Suye Mura's claims to authenticity rest almost entirely on a foreign ethnographer's declaration fifty years ago that it was a typical Japanese village. The Minaguchiya became one of Japan's best-known *ryokan* (inns) following the publication of Oliver Statler's *Japanese Inn* (1961). The reputations of Japanese artists such as Hiroshige and Hokusai have been boosted significantly by their popularity with influential Western critics and collectors of wood-block prints.

The power of the West's gaze can lead, at times, less to a rediscovery of tradition than to self-exoticization. This process can take two forms: in one, characteristic of the Meiji and Occupation eras, Japanese make themselves as Western as possible. An extreme example of this process would be the eyelid operations some Japanese women undergo in an attempt to emulate Western standards of beauty. This sort of self-exoticizing has its roots in the Meirokusha study group founded by Fukuzawa Yukichi in 1873. Through their influential *Meiji Six Magazine,* the Meirokusha urged modernization on their countrymen. To them, modernization meant westernization. They advocated individual rights, democratic government, egalitarianism, and universal education and favored Western dress, a Western diet, and Western household furnishings. Some went so far as to question whether the Japanese should give up their feudal and illogical language in favor of the more rational and modern English and whether systematic miscegenation with Westerners might not be the only way to overcome the inferiority of the Japanese gene pool.

An unfortunate but perhaps inevitable side effect of Meiji Japan's reverence and hunger for the West was a sense of inferiority brought about by seeing themselves through orientalizing Western eyes. In addition to adopting Western dress and customs, Japanese adopted Western values, tastes, and prejudices, including an ethnocentric, colonial contempt for the non-West. Seeing themselves suddenly as the unnatural, antipodal Other, Japanese exposed to the West experienced self-consciousness in their Japaneseness. As Clark's chapter points out, such accepted practices as mixed-sex public bathing came to be seen as indecorous and premodern during this era. Sophisticated urban Japanese were especially likely to evaluate themselves and one another according to Western opinion. In 1876, for example, Ōkubo Toshimichi wrote of his new Western-style house, "Even foreigners to whom I have shown the house have praised it, so I am quite pleased" (Jansen 1965, 68).

The opposite form of self-exoticization is the self-orientalizing that occurs when Japanese consciously or unconsciously make themselves into, or see themselves as, the objects of Western desire and imagination. The novelist Ōe Kenzaburō has complained that the West's fascination with his countryman Mishima Yukio is misplaced and even offensive. Ōe suggests that Mishima's samurai bravado not only does not represent an authentic Japanese sensibility but is an occidentally inspired burlesque of what it means to be Japanese. At the 1990 Wheatland Foundation Conference, Ōe accused Mishima of "shaping his life to live up to the image of Japan created by Europeans."

According to this logic, Mishima is to Japanese literature what Benihana is to Japanese cuisine: no more authentically Japanese than are the knife- and peppermill-twirling Japanese chefs who dish out beef, samurai-style, to enchanted Western diners. This is a process of self-exoticization, both for the Japanese producers (like Mishima and the steak-house chefs) and for Japanese consumers who read Mishima or dine at Japanese steak houses on the Ginza or in Waikiki. The point is not that Mishima is not a great novelist or that Benihana does not serve delicious food, but that both (and, for that matter, Ōe as well) have been heavily influenced by their awareness of the West as their potential critics and consumers.

Has Japan's recent dramatic shift from the periphery to the core of the world economy freed Japanese from the power of the exoticizing Western gaze? Japanese now have the economic power to meet the West on an equal footing, but old feelings of being laughed at, underestimated, and patronized leave a legacy of self-consciousness, bitterness, and cultural inferiority. Several of the chapters in this volume explore the interrelationships of wealth, culture, ideology, and national identity. Brannen, examining the cultural politics of Tokyo Disneyland, calls for a modification of the concept of cultural hegemony to account for contestations between two relatively equal powers like Japan and the United States. Narrating the struggles of avant-garde Japanese fashion designers to be taken seriously in Paris, New York, and Tokyo, Kondo argues that this contemporary international cultural competition is heavily colored by a history of racism and colonialism. Jeffrey Tobin suggests that although Tokyo clearly has surpassed Paris as an economic capital, the cultural capital of French cuisine continues to dominate and intimidate Japanese chefs as well as diners. Savigliano makes an important distinction between domesticating the West and domesticating westernization. She suggests that while Japanese have been able to successfully import, incorporate, and transform Latin music and dance, they have not been able to free themselves from their desire for the passion of the West or from seeing themselves, and being seen by foreigners, as exotic Others when they dance the tango.

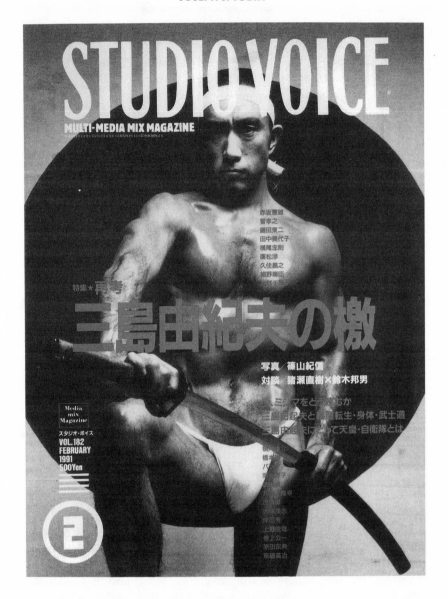

Mishima was by no means the first Japanese to attempt to establish a cultural identity by valorizing Japanese tradition and nationalism. The search for a primordial, authentic Japanese past to oppose to the modern, foreign-imbued present is an old story in Japan. Long before Big

Macs, Christian Dior, and Chivas Regal came to the Ginza, the Japanese were busily engaged in a debate about what makes them unique and in examining their feelings toward and dealings with foreign influences in their society.

Before it began to borrow from the West, Japan was already borrowing from China. *Kangaku,* the Japanese study of China, is of interest to us because it anticipates later reactions to the West. Although historically the Japanese have had little to say about the cultural influences of the aboriginal Ainu (their indigenous foreigners) or the Koreans (their unacknowledged and detested cultural source), the Chinese influence could not be ignored. For centuries the Japanese have been struggling with what they experienced as a tension between their Japanese souls and authentic traditions (wa) and their borrowed Chinese words, things, and religious and political ideologies (*kan*). Confucian filial piety, Buddhism, the tea ceremony, silk, poetry, painting, drama, architecture, agriculture, sericulture, pottery, medicine—all of this and much more came to Japan from China.

In *The Fracture of Meaning* (1986) Pollack argues that Chinese cultural and material influence in Japan has long been an especially problematic issue because the Japanese lack a language in which to write about or even talk about this threat that is not contaminated by foreign script and scripture. Pollack points out the irony, not lost on the Japanese, that even their most nationalistic writings, including the twelve-hundred-year-old *Kojiki* (Record of Ancient Matters), were written in *kanji*—characters borrowed from the Chinese.

Although the power and threat of the West have long since eclipsed China's, *wa-kan* (the Japanese-Chinese dialectic) continues to be observed in many subtle and not-so-subtle ways in contemporary daily life. Japanese-Chinese dishes such as *rāmen* (noodle soup), *gyōza* (pot stickers), and *chāhan* (fried rice) are always served in brightly colored bowls and eaten with flat spoons and round ceramic chopsticks whereas earthtone bowls and straight-edged wooden chopsticks are used for serving *soba* (Japanese buckwheat noodles), *donburi* (rice casseroles), and other traditional Japanese foods that have been purged of their historical connection to China. Less innocently, the turbulent history of Japanese-Chinese relations periodically explodes into public consciousness in events such as the textbook issue of the mid-1980s, when Chinese (as well as Koreans and Filipinos) objected strenuously to the Japanese rewriting of high school textbooks by changing the phrase "invasion of

33

China" to "incursion into China" and by dropping mention of the 1938 Rape of Nanjing. Brannen finds the question of Chinese influence in Japanese culture popping up in contemporary Japan in a surprising context: Tokyo Disneyland's "Meet the World" exhibit. In this Japanese version of "It's a Small World" a film is shown in which two Japanese children are chagrined to learn that much of their culture originally came from China, before being reassured that over the centuries the Japanese have domesticated these borrowed Chinese elements to make them uniquely their own.

Pollack suggests that millennia of Japanese poets, scholars, and linguists have struggled to find an authentic Japanese voice and life-style beneath and within Chinese influence. Nativist scholars argued that the Japanese could recover their Japaneseness only by identifying and privileging pre-Chinese Japanese discursive practices and life-styles. These authentically Japanese ways of thinking, speaking, and living, like *mono no aware* (sensitivity to things), could be salvaged in folk songs and folktales and in the labor and religious practices of the Japanese mountain peasantry.

To some Japanese nativists, their people's best hope of liberating themselves from Western cultural domination and rediscovering their Japanese souls lies in the process of *jikkan*—"retrospection through actual sensation." Thus the smell of incense at a shrine or the tactile and kinesthetic sensations of sitting on tatami (*suwaru*) rather than sitting on a chair (*koshikakeru*) can produce a reconnection with the eternal, authentic Japanese culture and soul. For example, now that Western-style toilets have been installed throughout Japan, the experience of using a Japanese-style outhouse can be charged with cultural significance, a seemingly authentic reminder of a dimly known past. As Tanizaki Jun'ichirō writes in *In Praise of Shadows:* "The Japanese toilet truly is a place of spiritual repose. It always stands apart from the main building, at the end of a corridor, in a grove fragrant with leaves and moss. No words can describe that sensation as one sits in the dim light, basking in the faint glow reflected from the shoji, lost in meditation or gazing out at the garden" (1977, 3–4). Clark introduces us to Japanese who practice jikkan as they try to make their children more Japanese by periodically taking them to the public bath, where they can experience "skinship" and body bonding (*hadaka no tsukiai*). Smith associates the recent rise in the popularity of shōchū with a thirst for the past, which some sophisticated urbanites attempt to satiate by tossing down a drink that burns the throat with the heat of the timeless, unsullied Japanese countryside.

The nativists' dream of jikkan often does not work well for contemporary Japanese. I suspect that most younger Japanese feel less themselves in traditional settings, such as a public bath, a folk village, a temple, or a Nō concert, than in westernized settings such as Disneyland, an underground mall, or a movie theater. Many of the contemporary events that feel the most Japanese are domesticated imports from the West—the annual high school baseball tournament, for example (Whiting 1989). For a week each summer, television sets are tuned to watch young Japanese ballplayers display the core Japanese virtues of teamwork, perseverance, ritual, and emotionality. In striking contrast to American baseball players, these Japanese teenagers bow to the umpire, are led in cheers by schoolmates wearing samurai-style headbands, favor bunting and other forms of sacrifice over the long ball, and, when the game is done, tearfully sing their school songs and collect handfuls of the stadium's hallowed dirt as omiyage to take home to their towns across Japan.

Throughout the postwar period, Japanese interest in Western things has remained strong, though there have been dramatic shifts in which material culture is most desired. The intensity of the struggle to keep up with just whose style one is to emulate is captured by the idiomatic expression *ron-pari,* meaning "cross-eyed," a description of an unfortunate soul who has one eye on London *(ron)* and the other on Paris *(pari)* (Stanlaw 1988).

A significant development has been the recent decline in the importance of American cultural capital and an accompanying rise in the importance of European, especially Italian, design. This shift can be seen in the consumption histories of a variety of imported products. In the 1960s, for example, the car preferred by Japanese gangsters was quintessentially American: the Cadillac convertible. In the 1970s, American cars remained popular among this group of consumers, the top choice having become the Lincoln Continental. A huge white convertible full of white-suited Japanese toughs squeezing its way down a narrow street was once a common sight. By the 1980s, the gangsters' suits had become a bit more subdued, and the Lincoln had been replaced by the

Mercedes-Benz. Most recently, in accord with the Italian boom of the 1990s, Lamborghinis and Maseratis have become popular with trend-conscious Japanese gangsters.

The urban elite's consumption patterns of Western goods are just as trendy. Conservative Englishmen's clothing, popular from the early days of Meiji modernization until the mid-1970s, was replaced by the more sophisticated cuts of French designers in the late 1970s. By the late 1980s, financial and political crises in Japan, like those involving Ivan Boesky and Charles Keating in the United States, led some politicians and businessmen back to suits tailored in London, which suggest greater fiscal and moral conservatism. Today, the taste is Italian: fifteen-hundred-dollar suits by Giorgio Armani are increasingly common attire for upscale Tokyo businessmen.

Japanese tastes in foreign perfume, whiskey, and gourmet foods are similarly subject to sudden shifts. As Nitta describes, Japanese now prefer to purchase Chivas Regal over Johnny Walker Black at duty-free shops in Honolulu and other foreign cities. France continues to enjoy a high cultural cachet in Japan: exploring the "neo-Japonesque" move-ment in fashion, Kondo discusses the interface of Japanese designers with haute couture. Jeffrey Tobin tells the strange but not atypical contemporary saga of the quixotic attempts of a French-trained Japanese chef to serve an authentic French-Japanese Mediterranean cuisine to diners in his restaurant in Honolulu.

Plastic food, sweatshirts with mangled English slogans, group hon-eymoon tours—there is a thin line between studying Japanese material culture and ridiculing it. I am not saying that there is nothing funny about an electronic toilet seat.[5] I am saying that the humor and ridic-ulousness we find in the consumer behavior and material culture of contemporary Japan suggest a continued orientalizing condescension even as, or especially as, we find ourselves being eclipsed economically by the Japanese.

In the arenas of money and things, Japan has become for us the most important Other. Once the inscrutable antipode, our would-be colony, our fierce enemy, and our eager apprentice, Japan has now become our ally, competitor, and secret sharer. We too easily project onto Japanese consumers our embarrassment, shame, and uneasiness about the allo-cation and meaning of goods in our own society. We see in Japanese consumer behavior both where we have been and where we fear we are

headed. We see in Japanese weddings, with their plastic, reusable cakes and matching his-and-her honeymoon aloha wear, a parody of our customs and domestic paraphernalia. But to read Japanese consumption as meaningless, ridiculous, or parodic is to engage in a smug orientalist discourse. Are our wedding customs less ridiculous, more authentic, more genuine? Are any culture's?

In this book we have tried to avoid projecting onto consumption and daily life in contemporary Japan our own culture's past, present, or future or our culture-bound narratives of modernization and post-

modernism. We also have tried to avoid seeing the Japanese appropriation and use of Western words, objects, and practices as imitative, unimaginative, or peculiar. The chapters that follow aim to describe, explain, and deexoticize the contemporary Japanese use of Western things and practices. From home to department stores, nightclubs, and vacations in Hawai'i, the book traces the ongoing process of domesticating the once-exotic West and thereby redefining what it means to be Japanese.

NOTES

1. Although the great majority of recent Western academic writing on Japan has focused on the productive sector, there have been some excellent books published in English on Japanese consumption and leisure. See, for example, David Plath's *The After Hours: Modern Japan and the Search for Enjoyment* (1964); Ian Buruma's *Behind the Mask:*

INTRODUCTION

On Sexual Demons, Sacred Mothers, Transvestites, Gangsters, Drifters, and Other Japanese Cultural Heroes (1984); and Richard Powers and Hidetoshi Kato's *Handbook of Japanese Popular Culture* (1989).

2. For essays on Japanese modernization, see Jansen's *Changing Japanese Attitudes toward Modernization* (1965). For a critical discussion of this modernization literature, see Koschmann (1989), De Bary (1989), and Najita (1989).

3. As Stephen Melville (1989) puts it, "Both 'Japan' and 'woman' are sites in which that which has been imagined now seeks to imagine itself" (285).

4. Norma Field (1989) summarizes the central meaning of *Somehow, Crystal* as "Japanese identity is nothing more than the ability to purchase Western commodities," p. 177.

5. Referring to ironic and humorous dimensions of the transformation of Japan earlier in this century, the critic Kobayashi Hideo suggested that, following Marx, if the modernization of the West was a tragedy, the modernization of Japan is a comedy (Harootunian 1989, 69).

REFERENCES

Appadurai, A. 1986. *The social life of things.* Cambridge: Cambridge University Press.

Arima, T. 1961. *The failure of freedom: An intellectual portrait of Taishō Japan.* Ph.D. diss., Harvard University.

Bailey, J. 1991. *Ordinary people, extraordinary lives: Political and economic change in a Tohoku village.* Honolulu: University of Hawaii Press.

Barthes, R. 1982. *Empire of signs.* Translated by Richard Howard. New York: Hill and Wang.

Baudrillard, J. 1981. *For a critique of the political economy of the sign.* Translated by Charles Levin. St. Louis: Telos.

Bellah, R. 1965. The search for meaning. In M. Jansen (ed.), *Changing Japanese attitudes toward modernization.* Princeton: Princeton University Press.

Bernstein, G. 1983. *Haruko's world.* Stanford: Stanford University Press.

Bestor, T. 1989. *Neighborhood Tokyo.* Stanford:Stanford University Press.

Bourdieu, P. 1984. *Distinction: A social critique of the judgement of taste.* Cambridge: Harvard University Press.

Buruma, I. 1984. *Behind the mask: On sexual demons, sacred mothers, transvestites, gangsters, drifters, and other Japanese cultural heroes.* New York: Pantheon Books.

Creighton, Millie R. 1991. Maintaining cultural boundaries in retailing: How Japanese department stores domesticate "things foreign." *Modern Asian Studies* 25(4): 675–709.

De Bary, B. 1989. Karatani Kojin's *Origins of modern Japanese literature.* In M. Miyoshi and H. Harootunian (eds.), *Postmodernism and Japan.* Durham: Duke University Press.

Edwards, W. 1989. *Modern Japan through its weddings.* Stanford: Stanford University Press.

Embree, J. 1974 [1939]. *Suye Mura: A Japanese village.* Chicago: University of Chicago Press.

Field, N. 1989. Somehow: The postmodern as atmosphere. In M. Miyoshi and H. Harootunian (eds.), *Postmodernism and Japan.* Durham: Duke University Press.

Harootunian, H. 1988. *Things seen and unseen.* Chicago: University of Chicago Press.

———. 1989. Visible discourses/invisible ideology. In M. Miyoshi and H. Harootunian (eds.), *Postmodernism and Japan.* Durham: Duke University Press.

Imamura, A. 1987. *Urban Japanese housewives: At home and in the community.* Honolulu: University of Hawaii Press.

Ivy, M. 1988. Tradition and difference in the Japanese mass media. *Public Culture Bulletin* 1(1):21–29.

——. 1989. Critical texts, mass artifacts: The consumption of knowledge in postmodern Japan. In M. Miyoshi and H. Harootunian (eds.), *Postmodernism and Japan.* Durham: Duke University Press.

Jameson, F. 1984. Postmodernism, or the cultural logic of late capitalism. *New Left Review* 146:53–92.

Jansen, M. 1965. Changing Japanese attitudes toward modernization. In M. Jansen (ed.), *Changing Japanese attitudes toward modernization.* Princeton: Princeton University Press.

Kato, H. n.d. America as seen by Japanese travelers. Manuscript submitted to the Mutual Image project of the U.S.–Japan Joint Committee on Educational Cultural Exchange.

Kelly, W. 1986. Rationalization and nostalgia: Cultural dynamics of new middle-class Japan. *American Ethnologist* 13(4):603–618.

Kondo, D. 1990. Orientalism, gender, and a critique of essentialist identity. *Cultural Critique* 5:5–29.

Koschmann, V. 1989. Maruyama Masao and the incomplete project of modernity. In M. Miyoshi and H. Harootunian (eds.), *Postmodernism and Japan.* Durham: Duke University Press.

Lefebvre, H. 1947. *Critique de la vie quotidienne.* Paris: L'Arche.

Mandel, E. 1978. *Late capitalism.* London: Verso.

Maruyama M. 1965. Patterns of individualism and the case of Japan: A conceptual scheme. In M. Jansen (ed.), *Changing Japanese attitudes toward modernization.* Princeton: Princeton University Press.

Mauss, M. 1967. *The gift.* New York: Norton.

Mayo, M. 1959. The Iwakura Mission to the United States and Europe, 1871–1873. *Columbia University East Asian Institute Studies,* no. 5. New York.

Melville, S. 1989. Picturing Japan: Reflections on the workshop. In M. Miyoshi and H. Harootunian (eds.), *Postmodernism and Japan.* Durham: Duke University Press.

Miyoshi, M., and H. Harootunian. 1989. Introduction. In M. Miyoshi and H. Harootunian (eds.), *Postmodernism and Japan.* Durham: Duke University Press.

Najita, T. 1989. On culture and technology in postmodern Japan. In M. Miyoshi and H. Harootunian (eds.), *Postmodernism and Japan.* Durham: Duke University Press.

Nitta, F. 1988. *Kokusai kekkon:* Trends in international marriage in Japan. *International Journal of Intercultural Relations* 12:205–232.

Passin, H. 1977. *Japanese and the Japanese.* Tokyo: Kinseido.

Plath, D. 1964. *The after hours: Modern Japan and the search for enjoyment.* Berkeley: University of California Press.

Pollack, D. 1986. *Fracture of meaning: Japan's synthesis of China from the eighth through the eighteenth centuries.* Princeton: Princeton University Press.

Powers, R., and H. Kato. 1989. *Handbook of Japanese popular culture.* New York: Greenwood Press.

Robertson, J. 1988. *Furusato* Japan: The culture and politics of nostalgia. *International Journal of Politics, Culture and Society* 1(4):494–518.

Rohlen, T. 1974. *For harmony and strength: Japanese white-collar organization in anthropological perspective.* Berkeley: University of California Press.

Sakai, N. 1989. Modernity and its critique: The problem of universalism and particularism. In M. Miyoshi and H. Harootunian (eds.), *Postmodernism and Japan*. Durham: Duke University Press.

Salamon, S. 1975. "Male chauvinism" as a manifestation of love in marriage. In D. Plath (ed.), *Adult episodes in Japan*. Leiden: E. J. Brill.

Seidensticker, E. 1983. *Low city, high city: Tokyo from Edo to the earthquake*. New York: Alfred A. Knopf.

———. 1990. *Tokyo rising: The city since the great earthquake*. New York: Alfred A. Knopf.

Singleton, J. 1989. Japanese folkcraft pottery apprenticeship: Cultural patterns of an educational institution. In M. Coy (ed.), *Apprenticeship: From theory to method and back again*. Albany: State University of New York Press.

Stanlaw, J. 1988. Englanese: English loanwords and the Japanese language. *The World and I* 7(8):522–533.

Statler, O. 1961. *Japanese inn*. New York: Random House.

Tanizaki J. 1977. *In praise of shadows*. Rutland, Vt.: Charles E. Tuttle.

Vogel, E. 1963. *Japan's new middle class*. Berkeley: University of California Press.

Vogel, S. 1978. Professional housewife: The career of urban middle-class Japanese women. *Japan Interpreter* 12(1):16–43.

Wallerstein, I. 1979. *The capitalist world economy*. Cambridge: Cambridge University Press.

Whiting, R. 1989. *You gotta have wa*. New York: Macmillan.

Wiswell, E., and R. Smith. 1988. Suye Mura fifty years later. *American Ethnologist* 15:369–381.

Yoshimoto M. 1989. The postmodern and mass images in Japan. *Public Culture* 1(2):8–25.

• • • • •

2

THE DEPĀTO: MERCHANDISING THE WEST WHILE SELLING JAPANESENESS

MILLIE R. CREIGHTON

The Japanese have two words for the modern department stores that abound in large urban areas. The older word, *hyakkaten,* which is seldom used in daily speech, can usually be found engraved in ideographs in a building cornerstone, and it is part of a store's official title. Literally "a store with one hundred items," this word was coined during the late Meiji era (1868–1912), when clothing stores began to expand their product lines and railroads began to build commissaries at major train crossings. The more recent and more commonly used word is *depāto* (from the English "department store"), which can be written in either roman letters or the *katakana* syllabary used for words borrowed from a foreign language (see Stanlaw, this volume).

These words reflect the dual nature of Japanese department stores. Words written in ideographs can impart an aura of antiquity and tradition. Frequently, as in the case of the word *hyakkaten,* they suggest

My research on Japanese department stores, conducted from 1985 to 1987, was supported by a Fulbright-Hays Department of Education grant. All quotations and references appearing without citation are from my field notes and interviews. Translations are my own unless otherwise indicated.

indigenous origin. In contrast, foreign borrowed words often give a feeling of modernity and foreignness. Many Japanese department stores actually originated in Japan several hundred years ago as dry goods stores that later patterned themselves after foreign department stores. Even the trendiest and most avant-garde of these stores practice patterns of merchandising and retain forms of prepaid credit, customer service, and special relationships with suppliers characteristic of merchandising during the Tokugawa era (1600–1868). To many Japanese these large urban stores may seem like a direct import from the West, but like the word *depāto,* they have undergone a transformation in the process of becoming Japanese.

Throughout the Tokugawa era, Japan was closed by decree to foreign influences. During the Meiji era, however, Japan reopened to the Western world; concurrently, depāto emerged as large-scale merchandisers in Japan. The Meiji depāto were soon perceived by Japanese customers as glamorous places to shop because of their Western, and hence exotic, aura. The early stores became display palaces for Western imports, which the Japanese were eager to see and buy. Depāto also sold Japanese goods but often followed practices that people of the time considered foreign, such as having customers leave their shoes on while in the store (Seidensticker 1990, 30).

A representative of the Japan Department Store Association told me that throughout their history depāto have played on the Japanese interest in foreign places, cultures, and objects and that to a great extent these were introduced to Japan through department stores. I suggest that in addition to this role of cultural importer depāto have also been involved in the creation of domestic cultural meanings. They have made foreign customs, ideas, and merchandise familiar by giving them meanings consistent with Japanese cultural practice.

In *Japanese Society* (1970), Nakane Chie contends that life in Japan is conceptualized and lived hierarchically. Indeed, hierarchy permeates the Japanese system of distribution and retailing. Department stores, partly because of their size, their cosmopolitan image, and the prestigious histories of their forerunners, are generally viewed as outranking wholesalers and suppliers, as well as other categories of retailers, such as specialty shops, discount stores, and *sūpā* (supermarkets), which sell food, clothing, and household goods. Their high rank in the retailing world means that contemporary department stores offer their customers not just goods and services but also status, prestige, and respectability. Prices at depāto tend to be high, but these stores are expected to offer higher-quality goods, free wrapping of all purchases, delivery, maintenance, and a standard of customer service featuring ritualized expressions of politeness.

Japanese social behavior is characterized by acute attention to proper form. Even mundane aspects of life are wrapped in a cocoon of ritualized etiquette (see Ben-Ari, Moeran, and Valentine 1990). The belief that there are appropriate forms of conduct for every occasion extends to the world of material goods—a world in which department stores act as arbiters of the nation's taste and etiquette. It is the department store's business to know everyone's proper place in society and to know the corresponding social conventions. If, for example, a gift-giving occasion is approaching, department stores must have consultants available to instruct consumers concerning to whom they are in debt, to what extent, and what gifts are expected as a result of that indebtedness.

As the acknowledged experts on Western goods and customs, department stores are particularly influential in prescribing the appropriate practices surrounding foreign holidays, traditions, and merchandise. To imbue Western imports with meanings relevant to the Japanese context, depāto have found it necessary to define the proper behaviors and etiquette surrounding them. Manufacturers or wholesalers attempting to introduce foreign goods to the Japanese market have often conducted their promotional campaigns in conjunction with department stores to take advantage of these stores' marketing expertise, upscale image, and large volume of customers.

The practice of giving engagement rings is an example of a Western custom introduced to Japan and extensively promoted by depāto. In Japan the primary emphasis surrounding marriage and prenuptial gift exchange has traditionally been on forging a relationship between households rather than between the individuals getting married. The idea of a groom giving his betrothed a ring to seal their engagement was cleverly reinterpreted to fit existing prenuptial customs. Marriage negotiations customarily are sealed and an engagement made public after the bride's household has accepted a series of gifts, referred to as *yuinōhin,* from the groom's household (Embree 1974 [1939]; Beardsley, Hall, and Ward 1959). Yuinōhin traditionally consisted of a large monetary payment accompanied by items symbolizing a long and lucky life together, such as dried fish, seaweed, and green tea. For either party to end marriage negotiations after yuinōhin had been given and received would constitute a serious social breach. Depāto promotions for engagement rings defined the gift not so much as a romantic gesture of affection but as a new item to be included among the yuinōhin passing from the groom's household to the bride's.

Department stores also established precedents regarding the price for such gifts. According to promotional literature circulated by depāto, proper etiquette prescribes that the engagement ring cost two and a half times the man's monthly salary. Although this sounds like a large expense, the stores were able to capitalize on another cultural practice: parents are expected to supplement an adult child's income at least until he or she is married. The expenses involved in a wedding and in setting up a household are typically borne by the two families rather than by the couple. These expectations made the high cost of an engagement ring feasible.

The role of department stores as arbiters of fashion and custom is particularly important for the gift-giving occasions that punctuate Japanese social interactions. Gift giving acknowledges the embeddedness of individuals in groups, the importance of social hierarchy, and the centrality of *giri* (duty and obligation). The two major gift-giving seasons are *oseibo,* occurring in December, and *ochūgen,* in July or August. During these two periods gifts are given to those in established relationships based on principles of hierarchy, duty, and group membership. The oseibo gifts are offered to assist the transition to the New Year, and ochūgen gifts to mark mid-year. In addition to these traditional seasons, in which gift-giving is largely impersonal, department stores in Japan, like greeting card companies in the United States, have been instrumental in popularizing such holidays as Christmas, Valentine's Day, and birthdays as times for exchanging gifts that signify intimacy and affection. This created a new niche for imported Western holidays that contrasted, but did not compete with, Japanese gift-giving occasions emphasizing social obligations and relationships between groups.

Gift-giving occasions have become so numerous that a typical household now gives about three hundred gifts a year. Although a family may buy items for its own use at a discount store or at a sūpā, respect for the recipient of a gift dictates that it be purchased from a prestigious store. As a representative of the Japan Department Store Association put it, "Good wrapping from a department store with a good name is more important than a good present!"

Depāto often alter foreign goods and customs when they introduce these to Japan. The Seibu Department Store, for example, established a special "Sears Corner." Although in America Sears has the image of catering to the common person, Seibu gave the Sears Corner an aura of elegance and exoticism. To the Japanese consumer, Sears was presented as the vanguard of chic and flair, like the boutiques of the famous foreign designers—Fiorucci, Dior, Calvin Klein—that Seibu has assembled for its shoppers seeking brand names. Seibu markets Sears goods in some interesting ways; for example, by selling American lawnmowers to Buddhist temples so that they can vacuum fallen leaves.

Department stores have long been a key site for the introduction of foreign foods to Japan. Basement food floors offer a variety of free samples intended to widen people's tastes. When Japan first opened to the West, depāto marketed foreign foods by offering instruction in cooking, the use of cutlery, and table setting. Sometimes this education included suggestions for converting particularly exotic foods into something more palatable to the Japanese. For example, historically the Japanese have shunned dairy products. Although the consumption of milk, butter, and cheese has risen dramatically, sour cream is still repugnant to many Japanese. Russian *pelemini* (a stuffed pasta typically served with sour cream) was domesticated by substituting yakitori sauce for the sour cream. The pelemini-yakitori combination is now a standard dish in Russian restaurants in Japan.

Recently, Western fast foods have been marketed with a Japanese twist. The first Japanese McDonald's opened in 1971 in a Tokyo branch of Mitsukoshi Department Store with the advertising slogan, "If you keep eating hamburgers, you will become blond!" (Moritsugu 1986).

Western food items have become popular gifts. Fancily wrapped gift sets of beer, coffee, soup, and salad oil now take their place alongside elegant gift sets of sake, green tea, seaweed, and noodles. One reason for the popularity of food items is that they are consumable—a quality especially appreciated by those living in small apartments with limited space in which to store the several hundred gifts received each year. Another reason for their popularity is that in Japan foods are strongly suggestive of the areas that produce them. For centuries Japanese domestic travelers have brought back regional delicacies as symbolically significant souvenirs (see Nitta, this volume). Since the early days of Western contact, the Japanese have viewed foreign food as a means of physically interacting with a far-off land by ingesting something of its natural environment.

Originally desired as symbols of westernness, food items that have been successfully domesticated are bought and sold in depāto at prices sometimes shocking to Western visitors. The cantaloupe is a striking example. Too expensive to purchase for personal consumption, cantaloupe in Japan are primarily packaged and sold as gifts—the packaging being more important than the flavor in establishing value and price. Each gift-packaged cantaloupe has a beautifully formed T-shaped stem. Each comes covered in gold foil and rests in its own cushioned box lined with purple velvet or red satin. The price per melon is typically ten thousand yen (about seventy-five dollars). Its primary value as a gift is that everyone knows that a cantaloupe, when elegantly boxed and wrapped in the paper of a major depāto, is an expensive purchase.

Famous brands of imported alcohol also claim a large share of the gift-giving market. The allure of foreignness imparts glamour and value to whiskey (see Smith, this volume). As with cantaloupe, the price paid for a bottle of alcohol bought as a gift must be consistent with the status of the recipient and the cultural demands of the situation. Thus, decreasing the price of an imported whiskey will not necessarily enhance sales. Fields (1983) explains how the importers of Johnny Walker Black, by reducing the shelf price, ended up reducing its sales. The popularity of Johnny Walker Black in the 1970s and 1980s was due partly to its attraction as an import, partly to its distinctive brand name, and largely to the fact that everyone knew that it sold for exactly ten thousand yen. If one was obliged to give a ten-thousand-yen gift, Johnny Walker Black was a logical choice. When it no longer cost ten thousand yen, it lost much of its validity as a gift item.

In addition to gifts, the other mainstay of the department store industry is clothing. From early in the Meiji era, depāto facilitated the transition from kimono to Western dress. In the aftermath of a department store fire in which several women died—supposedly because they were too modest to allow their kimono flaps to spread apart while attempting to glide down escape ropes—department stores promoted the adoption of Western undergarments as a means of protecting both women's honor and their lives (Seidensticker 1990; Creighton 1991). In

the transition to Western forms of dress, depāto also played an educational role, by hiring people to teach customers how to don Western
garments. One sees vestiges of this even today. On the seventh floor of
one major department store, for example, there is a Western clothing
section designated for elderly women who have never worn anything
but kimono.

These days, kimono are reserved for holidays, and *yōfuku*, or Western clothing, dominates daily wear. Department stores emphasize
famous-designer brand names in Western clothes. Some social analysts
suggest that the immense popularity of brand name clothing among
Japanese results from their lack of faith in their ability to judge Western
style. Department stores offer an array of boutiques boasting prestigious
brand names: Via Spiga, Céline, Delvaux, Dana Paris, Chloë, Bill Blass,
Calvin Klein, Fendi, and Chanel (voted "the clothes I most want to
own" in a poll of Japanese female office workers).

Designer boutiques provide the depāto with the sophisticated, cosmopolitan image for which Japanese customers clamor. This merchandise is therefore displayed to attract them as they enter the store:
Moschino, with a style straight from Milan; Yves Saint Laurent, with a
panache and elegance straight from Paris; Geoffrey Beene, with a flair
straight from New York. The goods themselves, however, are often
straight from Tokyo. Japanese customers wonder why the prices of
famous designer brands have not declined with the rise of the yen. Part
of the answer is that few of these goods are imported any longer from
North America or Europe. Most are now produced in Japan or by
Japanese subsidiaries in Southeast Asia under license agreements with
the designers and original manufacturers.

Japanese fashion designers are clearly gaining in prestige in Japan as
well as abroad (see Kondo, this volume). But for now at least, an
association with the West continues to add value and glamour to a
design. Western brand names are often invented to enhance sales of
fashionable clothing lines designed in Japan. "Madame Nicole," for
example, is the name of a line of Japanese designer clothing featured
in depāto boutique sections.

In 1985 Isetan Department Store made a bid to increase its share of
the youth market by capitalizing on a foreign name familiar to all Japanese: Cinderella. A second-floor fashion center was built specifically
to attract teenage and preteen girls. This "municipality of sweet dreams"
was christened "Cinderella City." Isetan's strategy is to build sales re-

lationships with young customers that will continue as these girls move into adulthood. As an Isetan manager explained, young customers can establish "residency status" in Cinderella City: "We issue our young customers Cinderella Cards. These are not credit cards. They are membership cards for the Cinderella Club. If you join, you get a 5 percent discount on items in that area. You also are mailed information about special sales and so forth. Everything is planned to promote sales among young customers."

Japanese culture does not encourage outward expressions of romance, so in contemporary Japan Western symbols are typically used to express love (see Stanlaw, this volume). It makes sense, therefore, for a store to turn to the heroine of a Western fairytale to appeal to the romantic dreams of its younger clients. Ironically, this commercialization of the Cinderella story in Japan came just at the time when the Western world was criticizing the ideological message of Cinderella. Western feminist criticism of Cinderella argues that this and other such tales create passivity and dependency in girls by suggesting that life's problems can be solved by finding the perfect man (Dowling 1981). In the Japanese version of the story, it is Cinderella's luck rather than virtue that is the key to the happy ending. As one Japanese analyst commented, "To the Japanese, Cinderella seems very lucky. She suddenly became a princess. You can't get much luckier than that!" Though Isetan cannot offer a prince, Cinderella City promises to make young girls lucky by providing membership in an organization offering fashion tips, special events, and discounted clothing.

THAT'S "EDUTAINMENT"

In the process of domesticating the West, depāto have become educators and also advocates of education. As one store employee stated, "The introduction of foreign goods to Japan largely was made possible by the department stores' efforts to educate the public." The depāto's commitment to education stems from a simple marketing principle—to sell unfamiliar goods one must first sell the knowledge required to use those goods.

From early on, department stores have provided Western culture and goods as part of their mission of "edutainment" (education and entertainment). The study of Western goods and practices is consistent with *benkyō* ethics—the high social value given to education as a path to self-improvement—but also presents the possibility for playful immersion in fantasy (see Savigliano, this volume). The entertaining side of consuming the West is coupled with an educational dimension in many sections of the depāto.

Depāto offer a variety of courses designed to provide customers with knowledge of Western habits and pastimes. Popular courses include Western cooking, theater, languages, sports (skiing, tennis, and golf are the most popular), and handicrafts (knitting, crocheting, quilting). Education is valued in Japan as a route to economic success but also because of the belief that people can find a reason for living *(ikigai)* through the earnest practice of a hobby.

Although many of the courses offered by depāto introduce and popularize Western culture, they are organized around an old Japanese retailing practice known as *tomo no kai* (a gathering of friends), which involves a form of prepaid merchandise credit. It was common practice in the Tokugawa era for regular customers to accumulate credit with a merchant by making monthly advance payments. At the end of the year the customers could make purchases up to the accrued amount augmented by an additional percentage earned as a sort of interest on their loyalty and investment.

The tomo no kai classes offered by Mitsukoshi operate along similar lines. Membership in the Mitsukoshi shopping club includes enrollment in a course on Western theater. Members pay 5,000 yen monthly and each month receive tickets to a play performed at the Mitsukoshi Theatre, near the store. Before the performance a theater critic or professor lectures on the play or on some aspect of Western culture; afterward, the class members are involved in a discussion. By year's end each member has spent 60,000 yen (around $450) on the course. The store presents each member with 70,000 yen in store shopping certificates in December, just in time to purchase year-end (oseibo) gifts.

Recently, Seibu took the edutainment concept a step further by introducing the first community college to Japan. Seibu built its Seibu Community College on the eighth floor of its sports pavilion, which adjoins the flagship store in Tokyo's Ikebukoro district. The words *community college* appear in the promotional literature in both roman letters and katakana script. Seibu Community College involves classroom instruction, but it is not an accredited educational institution leading to an Associate of

Arts degree or providing occupational training. Instead, Seibu's courses cater to the personal and recreational interests of customers.

Most classes appeal to the Japanese interest in the West. An example is a cooking class held on Seibu's luxury yacht, the 73.4-ton *Cynara*. As Seibu's promotional literature makes clear, the *Cynara,* which was built in England in 1927, was once used by Winston Churchill. The yacht is rented out on an hourly basis, but through the Community College, those who cannot afford to rent it for personal use can enroll in a natural foods course held on board and sponsored by Walk Co., a Seibu subsidiary.

When I last visited, in 1987, the college offered over 430 classes. Customers pay a basic enrollment fee and additional tuition for each course they take. The extensive edutainment offerings of Seibu Community College reflect the ardor with which self-development and entertainment are pursued in modern Japan. The existence of such a program in a department store exemplifies how Japan's large-scale retailers domesticate a Western concept such as the community college and popularize it by adapting it to Japanese tastes and social values.

EXHIBITING THE WEST

Retailers and customers agree that the depāto exists not just to sell goods but also, as a 1986 Mistukoshi publication puts it, "to promote the revival of learning and culture" (18). Department stores are central to the circulation of art in Japan. Many depāto have full-fledged, legally designated art museums (*bijutsukan*); all have exhibition halls and art galleries. More foreign art circulates through department store museums and galleries than through private and public museums (Creighton 1989). The director of Isetan's Museum of Art told me that there are numerous exhibits of foreign art at department stores because "for the Japanese, looking at foreign art is still a relatively new phenomenon. Even now, Japanese have an intense interest in viewing foreign culture." He claimed that depāto museums and galleries "fulfill the important educational function of introducing children to art," adding that field trips to art museums are rare in Japanese public education.

Exhibits of such famous artists as Van Gogh, Picasso, Renoir, and Miro usually run for six to eight weeks and can take years to plan and millions of dollars to produce (O'Donnell 1982). Entrance fees cannot

51

nearly cover the enormous costs involved. Contributions from corporations and foundations sometimes help, but the greatest share of the costs is borne by the department stores.

Clearly, depāto mount exhibitions of foreign art to attract customers. But these exhibits also serve another purpose, one that can be traced back to the traditions of the great mercantile houses that spawned these Western-looking institutions. The merchant ethic of the Tokugawa era condoned the pursuit of profit only when coupled with a sense of duty and social responsibility. Department stores in contemporary Japan present their art museums and galleries as evidence of their contribution to the greater social good. As a Seibu publication puts it: "The Seibu Saison Group aims not only to generate profit, but to balance material and mental well-being through a lively engagement in art and cultural activities" (1985, 30). Similarly, the director of Isetan's art museum explained that "we consider our art museum a service to our customers. In Shinjuku and Ikebukuro there are no public museums, but Seibu has a museum at Ikebukuro and Isetan one at Shinjuku. There are still few public museums in Japan compared to Europe or the United States, so it is up to depāto to fill this role."

Not all stores feel compelled to present intellectual topics and renowned artists. Unlike Seibu and Isetan, the Tōbu Department Store has no legally designated art museum. A member of Tōbu's special events staff calls the store's exhibits "amusement oriented." In 1986 an eerie poster with a black cat and a broken china doll advertised their innovative mystery exhibit. A young staff member told me proudly that "it's the first mystery exhibit done in Japan and Tōbu is the first to do it!" The exhibit featured such Western authors as Agatha Christie and P. D. James. It followed the smashing success of the previous year's horror exhibit, which featured campy Western films. A staff member suggested that exhibits of this type are consistent with Tōbu's image, which is not particularly intellectual.

Depāto claim that their exhibits help repay the obligations they incur by making a profit. Hosting exhibits transforms the stores into cultural sites, not just showplaces of consumerism. Exhibits featuring foreign art and culture, including popular culture, reinforce the public's conception of these stores as cosmopolitan brokers, mediators, and explicators of foreign goods, concepts, and practices.

SELF-EXOTICISM AND THE MARKETING OF JAPANESENESS

As discussed, depāto have long offered customers excursions into the exotic. In the post–World War II era, however, the national goal was "catching up to the West." During this period goods were scarce, and small retailers had difficulty acquiring Western consumer items, so department stores, with wealth, size, and status on their side, played a major role in distributing Western commodities.

Japan has now entered a new age, permeated by customs and goods of Western origin. Far from the impoverishment of the postwar era, the country is affluent. Far from struggling to obtain material goods in an era of paucity, most Japanese now struggle with a very different problem—how to make space for their possessions in their cramped dwellings. This new age, characterized by a highly educated, affluent, and urban populace living a modern or postmodern Western life-style, is being swept by nostalgia for indigenous folk festivals, village craft traditions, and the roots of Japanese identity. As increasing affluence has made the West attainable, increasing westernization has transformed Japaneseness into the exotic (Ivy 1988). As art critic Kurita Isamu puts it, "No period has ever seen Japan so open to the outside than today, in terms of goods, information, and way of life. . . . The very international-ness of the life-style makes the traditional Japanese arts appear quite alien and exotic. We look at our tradition the way a foreigner does, and we are beginning to love it. . . . The fact that Japanese are seeing charm and depth in their tradition reveals just how alien it has indeed become" (1983, 131). As material goods and customs associated with the once-exotic West have become a routine part of life, the customs, goods, and habits believed to symbolize the timeless Japanese past have been embraced as the new exotica.

Japan is in the age of *mono igai no mono,* or "things other than things." Among the most important of the things other than things that department stores sell are nostalgia and self-exoticism. As part of a *matsuri būmu* (festival boom), regional events symbolizing pre-westernized Japan, such as the *himatsuri* (fire festival) of Soma, Fukushima, have been staged recently in metropolitan department stores as "authentic regional traditional events." Other regional re-creations have included a Miyagi culture fair, a Kyoto crafts day, and a sake-tasting fair offering twenty varieties of sake from Niigata.

In addition to displaying the works of Western artists, department stores promote Japan's artistic heritage. During the Hyogo products fair sponsored by Keiō Department Store, a folk version of Kabuki, which dates back more than three hundred years, was brought to Tokyo and performed twice daily in the store. *Tsugaru* puppet plays that originated a century ago in Aomori Prefecture have been re-created at Isetan. Both Mitsukoshi and Takashimaya host annual exhibits of traditional Japanese crafts (*Nihon no dentōten*). Such sponsorship is not new for department stores. Seidensticker (1990) notes that in the 1940s Mitsukoshi hosted the Kabuki after the major theaters were destroyed by bombings. What is new is the fervor with which contemporary Japanese customers consume their own arts as exotic artifacts.

Depāto, long brokers of Western goods and customs, now also play the reverse role of reeducating a westernized consuming public in their own cultural heritage, real or imagined. Stores that once hired consultants to familiarize the Japanese with Western apparel now hire teachers to demonstrate how to put on kimono. This instruction is needed because, despite the renaissance of interest in Japanese tradition, most young women are unschooled in the intricacies of dressing, walking, and sitting in kimono, and often their mothers do not know enough to help them.

On the food floors, where depāto continue to introduce (and sometimes invent) Western foods, employees dressed in *hanten* (happy coats) and *hachimaki* (headbands) clap and chant the virtues of their noodles, pickles, and bean cakes using the same boisterous sales techniques favored by street vendors of three or four centuries ago. Marketing displays much like those once used to promote turkey at Christmas and chocolates on Valentine's Day explain which foods are appropriate to serve friends, relatives, and ancestors during traditional seasonal celebrations such as the autumn and vernal equinoxes. Instruction is offered in the preparation of Japanese delicacies served to guests during the first few days of the New Year and during the tea ceremony.

The revival of interest in Japanese tradition is also reflected in depāto art exhibits and course offerings. Along with classes in English conversation, golf, and French cooking, department stores now serve the growing popular interest in Japanese pottery making, *minyō* (folk songs), *shodō* (calligraphy), *kadō* (flower arranging), *sadō* (the tea ceremony), and musical instruments, such as the *koto* and the *shamisen*. Depāto today are pivotal players in exhibiting artworks in traditional Japanese genres. Brian Moeran (1987) points out that having one's work exhibited and sold in department store galleries is an important part of making it in the Japanese art world and an essential step en route to being designated a "living national treasure."

Superficially the depāto mirrors its Western counterpart. Building facades and the layout of sales areas at Isetan and Mitsukoshi closely resemble Macy's and Harrods, which is not surprising since Japanese department stores pattern themselves on Western models. From the beginning this Western image has given depāto an aura of glamour, prestige, and exoticism. Yet depāto remain very much a Japanese institution.

As the progeny of both a Western and Japanese heritage, depāto market the goods and arts of the West and East side by side. This dual role reflects a deep truth about Japanese culture. The juxtaposition of Japanese (*wa*) and Western (*yō*) has long been essential to the Japanese sense of self. Japanese identity is defined in large part oppositionally. As Roy Miller asserts, "Any facet of Japanese life or culture is thrown into sharp relief when it is brought into direct confrontation with a similar or parallel foreign phenomenon" (1977, 77). From the first contact with Portuguese and Dutch missionaries and traders, Western goods and practices have helped define Japaneseness by delineating what Japan is not. In contemporary Japan, traditional Japanese goods and practices are essential to the search for identity precisely because they provide a material contrast to Japan's modern Western veneer. In their marketing of foreign imports, depāto are key agents in the domestication of the West; in their selling of Japanese goods, they are key agents in the (re)invention of tradition (Hobsbawm and Ranger 1983).

The symbols and images of the West packaged by depāto for domestic consumption do not necessarily reflect the reality of any part of the Western world. More often they are blurred refractions, decontextualized fragments of various Western traditions and practices that have been culled and then altered to fit the Japanese cultural context and the expectations of Japanese consumers. Similarly, the symbols and images of Japan displayed and sold in contemporary depāto are not necessarily rooted in history despite being imbued with a "patina of antiquity" (Bestor 1989, 264). The depāto's "staged authenticity" (MacCannell 1973) of indigenous arts, crafts, foods, and clothing provides recognizable symbols of a shared cultural identity. Like imported Western elements, these icons of tradition have been recast to fit the realities of contemporary Japanese life and tastes.

In her analysis of American marketing, Judith Williamson (1978, 13) suggests that advertisements "are selling us something else besides consumer goods; in providing us with a structure in which we, and those goods, are interchangeable, they are selling us ourselves." Depāto similarly offer their customers the opportunity to "buy themselves." In their parallel offerings of Western and Japanese goods and services they provide the contrast through which Japanese define their cultural identity. Through this dialectic of "us" and "other" depāto help their modern clientele affirm Japaneseness in a culturally eclectic age.

REFERENCES

Beardsley, Richard K., John W. Hall, and Robert E. Ward. 1959. *Village Japan*. Chicago: University of Chicago Press.

Ben-Ari, Eyal, Brian Moeran, and James Valentine (eds.). 1990. *Unwrapping Japan: Society and culture in anthropological perspective*. Honolulu: University of Hawaii Press.

Bestor, Theodore. 1989. *Neighborhood Tokyo*. Stanford: Stanford University Press.

Creighton, Millie R. 1989. Japan's department stores: Selling "internationalization." *Japan Society Newsletter* 37 (4):2–7.

———. 1991. Maintaining cultural boundaries in retailing: How Japanese department stores domesticate "things foreign." *Modern Asian Studies* 25(4:675–709).

Dowling, Colette. 1981. *The Cinderella complex: Woman's hidden fear of independence*. New York: Summit.

Embree, John. 1974 [1939]. *Suye Mura: A Japanese village*. Chicago: University of Chicago Press.

Fields, George. 1983. *From bonsai to Levi's*. New York: New American Library.

Hobsbawm, Eric, and Terence Ranger (eds.). 1983. *The invention of tradition*. Cambridge: Cambridge University Press.

Ivy, Marilyn. 1988. Tradition and difference in the Japanese mass media. *Public Culture Bulletin* 1(1):21–29.

Kurita Isamu. 1983. Revival of the Japanese tradition. *Journal of Popular Culture* 17(1):130–134.

MacCannell, D. 1973. Staged authenticity: Arrangements of social space in a tourist setting. *American Journal of Sociology* 79(3):589–603.

Miller, Roy Andrew. 1977. *The Japanese language in contemporary Japan: Some sociolinguistic observations*. Washington, D.C.: American Institute for Public Policy Research.

Mitsukoshi Department Store. 1986. Press release of May 11. Tokyo: Mitsukoshi Ltd.

Moeran, Brian. 1987. The art world of contemporary Japanese ceramics. *Journal of Japanese Studies* 13(1):27–50.

Moritsugu Ken. 1986. Understanding double-deck psyche of Japan a must for foreign firms. *Japan Times,* January 30.

Nakane Chie. 1970. *Japanese society.* Los Angeles: University of California Press.

O'Donnell, Peter. 1982. Take a lesson (and more) from retailers in Japan. *Stores* (January):49–54.

Pul-eeze! Will somebody help me? 1987. *Time,* February 2, 48–56.

Robertson, Jennifer. 1987. A dialectic of native and newcomer: The Kodaira citizens' festival in suburban Tokyo. *Anthropological Quarterly* 60(3):124–136.

———. 1988. *Furusato* Japan: The culture and politics of nostalgia. *International Journal of Politics, Culture and Society* 1(4):494–518.

Seibu Saison Group. 1985. *Seibu saison group 1985.* Tokyo: Seibu Saison Group.

Seidensticker, Edward. 1983. *Low city, high city: Tokyo from Edo to the earthquake.* New York: Knopf.

———. 1990. *Tokyo rising: The city since the great earthquake.* New York: Knopf.

Shoji Kaori. 1990. The glitz and glamour of the *depaato. Business Tokyo* (July):32–37.

Williamson, Judith. 1978. *Decoding advertisements: Ideology and meaning in advertising.* London: Boyars.

· · · · ·

3

"FOR BEAUTIFUL HUMAN LIFE": THE USE OF ENGLISH IN JAPAN

JAMES STANLAW

A stylish young *OL* (office lady) wanting a *pāma* (permanent wave) stands outside a fashionable shop reading the neon sign flashing in the window:

> ARE YOU SATISFIED WITH YOUR HAIR?
> IF YOU ARE LOOKING FOR SUPER BEAUTICIAN
> TRY "KENZO" BEAUTY SALON.
> WE KNOW YOU WILL BE HAPPY!!

Two teenagers in Hokkaido run up to the *coin snack* (vending machine) and peruse the selections. The machine displays a picture of two young Americans, one dressed as a motorcycle cop, the other wearing a leather aviator's jacket, each looking off into the sunset and holding a small can bearing the words *"Georgia Kafe Ore"* (Georgia café au lait). After the teenagers make their purchase, the machine flashes:

> THANK YOU!
> Anytime you want to take a rest
> please remember we're always
> here and waiting for your coming.

In a coffee shop in Tokyo I hear a song by Matsutoya Yumi—Yuming to her fans—a major proponent of the *new music* movement of the 1970s and 1980s and still one of the most popular singers and songwriters in Japan. I am struck again by her images and rhymes and by the clever mix of English and Japanese phrases in the chorus: "*Itsu datte* / I love you more than you / You love me, *sukoshi dake,* / *Kata omoi* more than you." Roughly translated: "It's always the case / that I love you more than you love me ./ You really only love me a little bit ./ Whenever we're together I feel this must be unrequited love. And I feel this way more than you do."

Japanese has probably been borrowing English words ever since the errant pilot Will Adams—immortalized in James Clavell's novel *Shogun*—washed ashore four hundred years ago. During the Meiji Restoration, English became the chosen foreign language for those who wanted to modernize Japan. It became fashionable to spice a Japanese conversation with English, as the following dialogue between university students circa 1870 shows: "Wagahai no UOCCHI dewa mada TEN MINYUTTSU gurai. WEBSTER no daijiten jitsuni kore wa YUSUFURU ja. Chotto sono BUKKU o misete kurenka? . . . Jitsu-ni Nihonjin no ANPANKUCHARU niwa osore iru" (By my WATCH there are still TEN MINUTES. This WEBSTER's Comprehensive Dictionary is really USEFUL. Can I take a look at that BOOK for a moment? . . . I'm sick of these Japanese being SO UNPUNCTUAL). By the 1880s, many prestigious public and private universities had introduced *Eigaku* (English studies) programs. Native English speakers were imported to organize new departments and to teach the thousands of curious new students.

The use of English in the Meiji period was not limited to the educated or political elite. Furthermore, different kinds of Englishes were spoken in different strata of society. In port cities, dockworkers, shopkeepers, and entertainers developed a pidgin mixture of English and Japanese—the so-called Yokohama dialect—to communicate with newly arrived sailors and businessmen (Stanlaw 1987b). This interlanguage is notable for its many colorful terms: *cheese eye* (from the Japanese *chiisai*) was the word for "small." A Western dog was a *kameya,* from the English "Come here!" A sailor was called a *dam your eye sto*—the "sto" was a corruption of the Japanese *hito* (person); the first part of the term came from the salty nineteenth-century mariner's phrase "Damn your eyes!"

Influential Meiji leaders such as Mori Arinori and Fukuzawa Yukichi publicly supported efforts to promote the use of English in place of Japanese. Mori, the first minister of education in the new Japan, coined the phrase *"Kokugo haishi eigo saiyōron"* (Abolish Japanese, adopt English). He argued: "Under the circumstances, our meager language, which can never be of any use outside of our islands, is doomed to yield to the domination of the English tongue, especially when the power of steam and electricity shall have pervaded the land. Our intelligent race ...cannot depend upon a weak and uncertain medium of communication" (1873, lvii). Mori sought advice for his proposal from W. Dwight Whitney, the foremost American linguist of the day. Whitney opposed the notion of replacing Japanese with English, but he did urge Meiji leaders to reform the writing system so that Western words and concepts could be more readily absorbed into Japanese.

Around the turn of the century the middle classes joined the upper classes in the study of English. Using British and American texts, they were taught sometimes by native speakers and sometimes by Japanese who had lived abroad (Ikeda 1968). During this time, an increasing number of Japanese—especially those who would become influential writers—were going abroad to study foreign languages firsthand.

In the years before World War II many English words were imported as new products were brought into the country. Examples of words entering popular parlance at this time include *rajio* (radio), *kā* (car), and *infurē (shon)* (inflation).

Knowledge of English began to have practical consequences for business as well as for personal prestige. Teaching English in the schools produced few fluent speakers, but the exposure made Japanese less intimidated when an English word popped up in a conversation or magazine article.

World War II was a low point in the encounter between the English and Japanese languages (Sonoda 1975). The government tried to ban the use of English and even constructed "native" Sino-Japanese words to replace the thousands of common English loanwords already in circulation. For example, *anaunsā* (announcer) was replaced by *hōsō-in* (broadcast person). *Rekōdo* (phonograph record) was succeeded by the awkward *onban* (euphonic board). The rumba became the *gumba* (military horse), and the tones of the musical scale (do through ti) were renamed for a sequence from the *katakana* syllabary, one of the phonetic writing systems used in Japan (Havens 1978, 149).

The Occupation brought English back in new forms and styles. In addition to GI vernacular, technical terms associated with Western social programs and economic and political reform entered the language. As one informant described the resulting admixture, "It sometimes sounded as though we learned our English in a brothel outside Harvard."

The Occupation also produced a new pidgin—known as Bamboo English—which had two distinct dialects. The first was used by American soldiers with shopkeepers and employees at United States military bases. The second was used for "what verbal communication [was] necessary between non-Japanese-speaking foreigners and . . . their local lady friends of every variety and description." (Miller 1967, 263). Two of the most colorful and enduring Bamboo English terms are *Mama-san* (proprietress of a bar) and *moose* (girlfriend, from the Japanese *musume,* daughter). Bamboo English turned out to be a brief linguistic encounter. Once the Occupation and the Korean War were over, this pidgin died out.

Today, English loanwords are found in every field; loanword dictionaries and almanacs number in the hundreds. Even traditional Japanese poetic forms, such as *haiku* and *tanka,* employ English devices. For example, every poem in Tawara Machi's humorous collection *Sarada Kinembi* (Salad Memorial Day) contains some English. Examples include *botoru kippu* (a bottle of whiskey kept at a bar), *bāgen* (a one-day-only sale), *romansu-kā* (a railroad car with "romantic" side-by-side seats), and *hambāgā shoppu* (a hamburger joint, as, for example, *Makudonarudo*).

In addition to the direct importation of English terms a vast number of quasi-English loanwords are produced in Japan for domestic consumption. *Pirō furendo* (pillow friend), for example, is a sex partner with whom you are not necessarily in love. *Onna-petto* (from the Japanese word for "woman" and the English "pet") refers to an object of sexual fantasy.

The average Japanese speaker uses three thousand to five thousand loanwords, which constitutes as much as 10 percent of daily vocabulary items (Kokuritsu Kokugo Kenkyūjō 1970–1974). The majority—94.1 percent—of these borrowed words comes from English (Morito 1978). Loanwords vary according to speaker and audience. As shown in table 3.1, for example, the loanwords most frequently found in a general newspaper survey are quite different from those found in women's magazines.

Raymond Firth (1973) suggests that it is useful to distinguish between

Table 3.1
The Top Twenty Loanwords in Japanese in Rank Order

A. Newspapers		B. Women's Magazines	
1. *biiru*	beer	*kappu*	cup
2. *terebi*	television	*batā*	butter
3. *kiiro*	kilogram	*sekkusu*	sex
4. *nyūsu*	news	*taipu*	type
5. *karā*	color	*terebi*	television
6. *supōtsu*	sports	*bitamin*	vitamin
7. *basu*	bus	*pēji*	page
8. *rajio*	radio	*dezain*	design
9. *gasu*	gas	*pantsu*	pants
10. *hoteru*	hotel	*sūpu*	soup
11. *mēkā*	maker	*amerika*	America
12. *resutoran*	restaurant	*dorama*	drama
13. *kēsu*	case	*mama*	mother
14. *chiimu*	team	*sōsu*	sauce
15. *puro*	professional	*burausu*	blouse
16. *sābisu*	service	*ōbun*	oven
17. *reberu*	level	*sutecchi*	stitch
18. *membā*	member	*bōnasu*	bonus
19. *rūto*	route	*kādo*	card
20. *pēji*	page	*pointo*	point

Sources: Morito 1978, 597–613; Inoue 1985, 29.

the collective (public) and individual (private) origins and meanings of symbols. Public symbols are associated with acts of communication, while private symbols are associated with expression (Leach 1976). English loanwords are involved in both of these processes in Japan.

A good example of the public aspects of loanwords are the *CM*s (commercial messages or advertising slogans) for Coca Cola used in Japan. The slogan "Sawayaka, teisutii, I FEEL COKE!" appears in commercials in three forms to appeal to three different audiences. The video portion of one version of the commercial shows young people on skateboards, bicycles, and motorcycles. Everyone is dressed in a casual style, and each person is holding a Coke can. The background song says:

Itsumo machi ni I FEEL COKE!　　Always, the town feels I FEEL COKE
Kanji no mama kono toki yo!　　Feel what you want, be who you are
Sawayaka, teisutii I FEEL COKE!　　Refreshing, tasty, I FEEL COKE!

The song is designed to appeal to the *shinjinrui,* the "new generation" of Japanese teenagers and young adults. Look at all the fun things you can do while drinking Coke, and see how cool you look!

A second commercial is targeted for older people who are uninitiated into the wonders of this drink.

Itsuka kimi ni I FEEL COKE!　　Someday you'll know as I do
Wakaru hazu sa, itsuka datte!　　the feeling of I FEEL COKE!
Sawayaka, teisutii, I FEEL COKE!　　Refreshing, tasty, I FEEL COKE!

This time we see traditional scenes: people pulling up fishing nets, grandmothers sitting on the steps of traditional country houses, summer festivals, a smiling kimono-clad girl holding a can of Coke. Her smile beckons grandma to try it and discover the feeling of "I feel Coke."

The third commercial is designed for everyday working adults. It features housewives in aprons doing the laundry, firemen, a woman talking on a pay phone, mothers with babies meeting on the street.

Itsuka aeba I FEEL COKE!　　At times, when we meet, I FEEL COKE!
Wakaru hazu sa, itsuka datte　　You should know the feeling as I do
Sawayaka, teisutii, I FEEL COKE!　　Refreshing, tasty, I FEEL COKE!

The final shot is of a Coke machine in front of a Japanese-style house at dusk, just as the family prepares for dinner.

An example of loanwords used as private symbols is found in color naming. The Japanese have appropriated the English color vocabulary into everyday speech (Stanlaw 1987a; Hinds 1974). These borrowed terms, when added to native color terms, allow Japanese speakers to be innovative and even playful in describing colors.

I asked one informant, for example, to name the hues of a number of ambiguously colored objects. In the face of uncertainty—that is, when the object was not obviously a simple *akai* (red) or *ao* (blue)—she often responded using English terms. When basic English terms did not suffice, she refined her answer by creating English-based compound terms—for example, *rōzu pāpuru* (rose purple), *hotto burū* (hot blue), and *howaito gurē* (white gray). When I inquired whether these were common words

for her, she said, "I guess I just made some of them up but I have used *peiru pāpuru* [pale purple] often many times before. My friend has a dress that is almost that color."

Many others responded in similar ways during my interviews. This suggests that Japanese people often use English loanwords to create new vocabulary items in their everyday speech, or simply to play with their language. Other investigators (Sibata 1975) support this contention. Most important, these new linguistic forms are understood and accepted quite readily by others.

A mixture of public and private displays of English can be seen in the group names and song lyrics of the amateur musicians who gather in Tokyo's Yoyogi Park to give rock concerts on Sundays. Most of these groups have English names, and their signs, costumes, and posters are full of English phrases and loanword creations. The van of one group, the Tomcats, was spray painted with various graffitilike chants ("*We Are Big Bad Cat*"), complaints ("*No Money*"), and nascent philosophies of life ("*Mad Route*"). Often these weekend concerts are used as opportunities for a little self-promotion. A sign made from a sheet hanging on the Tokyo Rocan Roller van invited everyone to their upcoming performance on amateur night at an *E.S.P.*—an "EXCITING SUMMER-PARTY"—at Kōrakuen Stadium.

English is used liberally and colorfully in the lyrics of many contemporary Japanese songs (Stanlaw 1989). Matsutoya "Yuming" Yumi, for example, uses English images and metaphors in her pop hit "*Dandiraion*" (Dandelion):

Kimi wa DANDIRAION	You are a DANDELION.
kizutsuita hi-bi wa	Those days when your heart
kare ni de-au tame no	was hurt were necessary LESSONS
sō yo unmei ga	that fate arranged
yōi shite kureta	for you
taisetsu-na RESSUN	in order to meet him.
ima suteki na REDII ni naru	Now you've become a lovely LADY

The English loanword *dandiraion* conjures up an image of something simultaneously ordinary and significant. Informants have told me that if Yuming had used the Japanese word for dandelion, *tampopo*, the song would have sounded like a folk song about a country girl in love with a country boy. (Itami Juzo's "noodle Western" entitled *Tampopo* does have a rather rustic flavor.) Yuming told me she used the word *dandiraion* because she likes the impression it gives of an English hill-

side. She said she wanted to throw in "a little fragrance of Western culture to give the song some elegance."

There are several possible relationships between how symbols are created and how they are used. Yuming assembled private symbols—images of "dandelions," "lessons" of love—and institutionalized them permanently on records. She was trying to make an individual artistic statement and relied to a great degree on the sympathetic cooperation of her listeners to accomplish her task. The Coca Cola advertisers coined the term "I feel Coke," but theirs was no private response to personal sensations, nor were they depending on any poetic empathy on the part of the public. Like Yuming's song, the commercial became institution-alized and permanent, but the words and symbols were communal and, hence, more public than private. The amateur rock and rollers create English phrases that have personal meaning to them and that they hope will catch the attention of their listeners. But groups like the Tomcats have little or no expectation that the English terms written on their van will become institutionalized. The woman who discussed color termi-nology with me created personal terms to express private feelings.

LOANWORDS AND COMMODIFICATION

In consumer societies product names readily enter everyday vocab-ulary. In English, for example, Xerox can refer to any brand of pho-tocopy. Many of the trade names of imported Western products have become generic labels in Japan. *Shāpu* (mechanical pencil) was taken from the name of the American company that produced it, Eversharp. *Hotchikisu* (stapler) came from the name of its American inventor. Similarly, the Japanese word for automobile horn—*kurakushon*—came from a manufacturer, Klaxon (Arakawa 1977). Some foreign brand names become so popular that they displace previously adopted loan-words. In the 1980s, for example, the term *ray ban* became a popular synonym for *sungurasu* (sunglasses), especially when entertainers like Yuming sang about them.

The most notorious recent case of commodification is found in Tanaka Yasuo's novel *Nantonaku Kurisutaru* (Somehow, Crystal). This 1981 book became an instant best-seller, rocketing Tanaka, a university stu-dent at the time, into media stardom. Tanaka explained that he invented the term *kurisutaru* (crystal) to describe the nihilistic attitudes of his materialistic soul mates. Members of the crystal generation define their identity by what they wear and acquire. A lengthy glossary to *Nantonaku Kurisutaru* contains 442 entries explicating the loanwords and foreign products mentioned in the text. This glossary can be read as a guide to how to be hip. State-of-the-art loanwords such as *sunobbari* (snobbery), *kāresu* (caress), and *rando sāfā* (land surfer; a surfer who does not go into the water) are explained for readers who have not kept up with the latest linguistic trends. Chic brand names such as Fila, Calvin Klein, and Lee also are elucidated for the uninitiated.

Tanaka suggests that an item labeled with an English loanword is transformed into something special, as, for example, in Tanaka's definition of *rein būtsu* (rain boots): "They are just *nagagutsu* (boots; literally, "long shoes"). *Nagagutsu!* However, when they are called *rein būtsu* even a rainy day makes us feel real up, and when there is a puddle we try to jump into it with a splash, on purpose. It [the term] makes us feel just like kindergartners" (1981, 151)

THE PROBLEM OF ENGLISH LOANWORDS

Issues of language are often among the most volatile a society faces. The use of English in Japan these days is not as divisive a problem as it is in, say, Canada or parts of Africa. But it is tied to the crucial issues of self-definition, national identity, and Japan's place in the modern world. Are people who use many loanwords modern, cosmopolitan, and scientific—or pretentious? Are people who use very little English old-fashioned and down-to-earth—or affected and pretentious in a different way? Could Japanese be spoken today without loanwords? If not, what does this suggest about the integrity of the Japanese language and culture? The problem of English in Japan has a number of interrelated aspects.

The problem of pollution. On May 27, 1963, the newspaper *Asahi Shimbun* published the following letter: "I can remember coming across the following words in your paper: *low-teen, morale, instant, start, hospitality, trouble,* to mention but a few. Could these not have been expressed equally comprehensively in Japanese?" The paper replied: "Words we feel to be strange to the average reader and words which in our estimate are still unfamiliar to the public are usually withheld; the newspaper should try to reach as wide a range of readers as possible by using a vocabulary easy to grasp. Of late the use of foreign words has grown by leaps and bounds. . . . For all intents and purposes we appear to be a foreign-loving people. Anything in *katakana* looks sweet and fresh. We bow to it and value it too much."

Many purists bemoan the use of loanwords. Though there is no Japanese equivalent to the Académie Française—the Kokuritsu Kokugo Kenkyūjō (National Language Research Institute) notwithstanding—some government employees denounce English loanwords and attempt to proscribe their use. Ironically, however, government memos often contain an above-average number of borrowed words. As the *Asahi Shimbun* commented in an editorial a few years ago (August 24, 1984):

> I did not realize English words had been added to the "officialese" used in government offices. . . . In these reports *kokoro* [heart] becomes English "mind," *henka* [change] becomes "shift," *koyaku* [promise] becomes "commitment," *choten* becomes "peak," *soko* becomes "bottom," and *akichi* [vacant lot] becomes "open space." There is a certain charm to affectation when it goes only as far as this, but it becomes tiresome to read such terms as "crowding out effect," "portfolio shift," "impact loan," "the scale of merit of family finances," and "reschedule request." After a time one cannot continue reading under the pretense that one understands all these words. . . . Why do they use so many English words? Do they want people to feel that their work really must be the compositions of "bureaucrats" at the "center" of an "economic superpower"? Do they feel that in order to create a "high level" of "academic" and "international" mood, they must have the help of English words that people find difficult to understand?

Westerners also have lamented the presence of English in Japanese. Basil Chamberlain, an eminent interpreter of Meiji Japan to theWest, expressed curiosity at "English as she is Japped" (1904, 137). No less an authority than Ivan Morris cried that "unless something is done to curb the pollution of the vocabulary by English and pseudo-English words, the Japanese language will soon become as ugly and unpotable as the Sumida and those other great rivers whose fresh waters have been irretrievably contaminated by poisonous foreign matter" (1970, 454).

Roy Andrew Miller argues that the Japanese define themselves largely in terms of their language (1982; 1986). Those who are Japanese—and only those who are Japanese—can speak Japanese. Miller overstates his case (Unger 1988), but there is no doubt that many Japanese feel a close tie between their language and culture. The problem is one of identity: If speaking Japanese is so important to being Japanese and to maintaining Japanese culture, what can be done about the mass importation of English?

The problem of intelligibility.   Another complaint against the presence of English in modern Japanese is that much of it is unintelligible. Older people in particular ask, "How are you supposed to understand something the first time you hear it?"

Advertising is often accused of being the great culprit in the growing pollution and unintelligibility of Japanese. Many product names—perhaps as many as half—come from English. In commercials the use of English is almost compulsory (Horiuchi 1963; Haarman 1984, 1989).

When I raised these points with executives of one of Japan's largest advertising agencies, they told me that their campaigns use words that most people recognize and respond to. Although the intent of using loanwords written in katakana or *rōmaji* (roman letters) is certainly to create eye-catching copy, obscure terms are scrupulously avoided.

In his research on Japanese advertising, Harald Haarman found that "although a majority of viewers can recognize catch phrases in English from TV commercials, their meaning is completely clear only to a minority" (1989, 145). Haarman based his findings on a questionnaire given to about eight hundred college students who were asked to supply meanings for nine common slogans such as "For beautiful human life" (for Shiseido cosmetics), "My life, my gas" (for Tokyo Gas Company), and "Do you know me?" (for American Express). Less than half of their responses were judged correct.

The problem with this research is the assumption that there are "true meanings" for these English phrases somewhere out there waiting to be understood. But how many Americans can give the true meaning of "It's the heartbeat of America"? Where exactly is Marlboro Country? There are no real meanings of loanwords waiting to be discovered or known only to fluent English speakers. Rather, as we saw in the case of the woman creating her own English color terms, meaning is constructed and negotiated by speakers in a particular context for particular purposes.

Loanwords or foreign language terms?   It is impossible to determine the precise moment that a word makes the transition from foreign term to domesticated vocabulary item. Americans are only vaguely aware that the word *restaurant* came to English from the French sometime in the distant past. *Rendezvous* and *lingerie* are a bit more exotic, and *ménage à trois* still sounds foreign to most of us.

Because of the extensive study of English in Japan, it is hard to distinguish loanwords that have entered daily speech from English terms that are widely understood but still considered foreign. English numbers, color terms, and body parts are learned by most Japanese in school, though these terms were not imported into the language in, say, the same haphazard way that *konpyūtā* (computer) or *fasshon* (fashion) were.

The problem of orthography.   The katakana that Japanese use for writing foreign words facilitates importation and nativization. When English borrows a foreign word, the pronunciation may be at odds with spelling (for example, *coup de grâce*), creating confusion and slowing nativization. In Japanese, by contrast, writing a word in katakana instantly domesticates it by forcing the borrowed term to conform to the Japanese phonological system.

Some argue that any word that is customarily written in rōmaji (the Western alphabet) rather than in katakana should be considered a *gairaigo* (a loanword that has not yet become a naturalized term). But this argument assumes that the most important medium of communication is writing (Yotsukura 1971). Clearly this is not always the case.

Japanese can be nonchalant about which orthography to use at a given time. For example, last year's number one hit song by the rock band Princess Princess was sometimes written as "Diamonds" (in roman letters) and sometimes nativized using katakana as ダイアモンド (*da-i-a-mo-n-do*). Is one a loanword and the other not? The young Japanese fans do not seem bothered by the distinction.

Roman letters are sometimes used for visual impact, as is often the case for sweatshirts, T-shirts, and gym bags, where an English word or phrase is almost compulsory. One sweatshirt I saw, for instance, had six words written horizontally, with the middle letters in large bold print. Vertically, these letters spelled HOLIC, a catch phrase like "Hysteric Glamor," which was popular a few summers ago.

Japanese words or names are sometimes written in roman letters to create an artistic effect or visual pun. In an article in a popular music magazine, the radical rock group Otokogumi (men's club) wrote its name in an idiosyncratic way using four *kanji* (ideographs):   男闘呼組 These characters (literally, men, fight, call, group) usually do not occur

Table 3.2
Phonological Adaptation of English Words in Japanese

---

1. The English /er/ and /ar/ become Japanese /ā/:

butter	batā	バター	car	kā	カー
waiter	wētā	ウエイター	tower	tawā	タワー

2. The English /t/ changes to /tsu/ or /to/:

smart	sumāto	スマート	fruit	furūtsu	フルーツ
first	fāsuto	ファースト	cutlet	katsuretsu	カツレツ

3. The final English /d/ becomes /do/:

third	sādo	サード	bird	bādo	バード
red	reddo	レッド	hot	hotto	ホット

4. All English /l/ sounds go to /r/:

ball	bōru	ボール	lady	redii	レデイー
golf	gorufu	ゴルフ	leather	rezā	レザー

5. The consonant /v/ becomes /b/ plus vowel:

service	sābisu	サービス	over	ōbā	オーバー
curve	kābu	カーブ	give	gibu	ギブ

6. English consonants are separated by a vowel:

smog	sumoggu	スモッグ	negligee	negurije	ネグリジエ
Boston	bosuton	ボストン	McDonald's	makudonarudo	マクドナルド

7. The English /th/ becomes /su/, /shi/, /sa/, /za/, or /zu/:

youth	yūsu	ユース	bathe	bēzu	ベーズ
nothing	nasshingu	ナッシング	the	za	ザ

8. No word ends in a final consonant (except for /n/):

beer	biiru	ビール	toilet	toire	トイレ
rocket	roketto	ロケット	restaurant	resutoran	レストラン

9. The final /l/ becomes /ru/:

pearl	pāru	パール	bell	beru	ベル
Nobel	nōberu	ノーベル	volleyball	barēbōru	バレーボール

10. Word final /g/ and /ŋ/ become /gu/:

song	songu	ソング	building	birudingu	ビルディング
morning	mōningu	モーニング	running	ranningu	ランニング

in the same compound. By using them in this way, Otokogumi sought to present itself as a group of young men called together to struggle for recognition of their music and acceptance of their life-style. To help readers pronounce this unusual compound, the name was written above the kanji in roman letters. Thus, Japanese today are experimenting with visual aspects of their language and writing systems, just as they did with Chinese a thousand years ago.

The false metaphor of borrowing.   Traditionally, linguists have viewed language contact in terms of senders and receivers, contributors and recipients, creators and copycats, borrowers and takers. Linguistic contact is analyzed from the vantage point of the donor language. Borrowed terms are categorized as loanwords (borrowed form and meaning); loan blends (borrowed meaning, partly borrowed form); loan shifts (borrowed meaning, native form); and loan translations (borrowed meaning, translated form). Applied to the Japanese case, we can call this the "English loanword" approach.

An alternative way to look at language contact is to avoid the terms *loanword* and *borrowing* and to tell the story from the Japanese perspective. Instead of examining how English expressions used in Japan conform to or deviate from some British or American standard, I suggest we focus instead on how English words and phrases are constructed and given meaning in Japan. This alternative might be termed the"English-inspired vocabulary item" approach to looking at language contact in Japan. Here it is argued that loanwords are not really loanwords at all, as nothing is actually borrowed and nothing, certainly, is given back. *Borrowing* thus is a misleading and unhelpful term.

An English word may stimulate the local formation of a new phonological unit in Japanese, but this is hardly the same thing as being borrowed or imported from abroad. Most of the English words used in Japanese are homegrown for domestic consumption. There is often, but by no means always, significant overlap in pronunciation, referent, or connotation between the new Japanese term and its English source.

Rajio is a true loanword, whose form and meaning were imported more or less unchanged into Japanese. In the 1920s, when European wireless sets were brought into Japan, the name for the imported item came with them. But during this same period, the Japanese were creating their own new words based loosely on English, such as *moga* (a modern girl or Japanese flapper).

Even in the classic loanword case of borrowed form and meaning, Japanese borrows in unusual ways. The term *kūrā* (cooler) refers to an air conditioner, not to a meat locker or drink carrier. Often, imported terms are used to label Japanese items, habits, or concepts, as in the case of the English word *service* (*sābisu*), which is used to refer to the Japanese custom of giving regular customers small gifts or extra value for their money.

Loan blends describe situations where borrowed meanings are encoded with forms mixing both native and foreign elements. This is the case for many words in Japan. A great number of imported nouns can be paired with the Japanese verb *suru* (to do) to construct instant hybrid compounds such as *tenisu-suru* (to play tennis) or *doraibu-suru* (to drive a car). English forms are sometimes appropriated for Japanese meanings as, for example, in the term *nau-na hito,* meaning a Japanese person who is "with it," "cool," perhaps westernized.

It is clear from these and other examples that the varied uses of English in Japan cannot be reduced to a simple case of borrowing.

Meanings for borrowed terms are more often created in Japan than brought in from outside. Borrowed forms are utilized for Japanese aims and purposes, often ignoring the meaning in the donor language. *Loanword* implies stasis and absoluteness—a fixed structure and meaning imperfectly corresponding to a correct form in the donor language. "English-inspired vocabulary item" (though cumbersome) has the advantage of stressing the dynamic, negotiated dimensions of language change.

Terms such as *loanword, Japanized English,* and *Japlish* reify a belief in the existence of pure languages that are in constant danger of pollution and contamination. The loanword metaphor also carries the unfortunate suggestion of a dominance, or essential preeminence of one language or cultural system over another. Americans, after all, use very few Japanese terms. Is the Japanese language inferior? Why do Japanese borrow so many of our words? When they do, why don't they ever get them quite right? This sort of patronizing, ethnocentric point of view can be seen in the glee with which Americans collect favorite examples of Japanese malaprops. *Gems of Japanized English,* a book popular with Americans living in Japan, catalogues Japanese usages with scatological or sexual innuendos: a T-shirt saying "Green Bay Peckers," a sign reading "Baby Shitter," a vernacular newspaper clipping reporting that "a wedding was consummated in the garden of the American consul's home" (Kenrick 1988).

Internationalization. English has become the de facto world language (Greenbaum 1985; Kachru 1986). In the fields of science, commerce, and diplomacy, no Japanese can hope to rise far without it. Some Japanese scholars (Ishiwata 1982; Kindaichi 1988) have wondered how Japan's increasing economic strength will affect language contact. Some predict that with increasing Japanese confidence and muscle, the need and desire to import English words will lessen. Though it is unlikely that many current English terms will ever be purged from Japanese use, some dream that new ones might at least be kept at bay. And perhaps in the future, native Japanese terms will be exported as successfully as automobiles.

But it seems to me that to think this way, using terms such as *internationalization* and *imports* and *exports* to discuss language contact, is to miss entirely the point, which is that the use of English in Japan is an internal matter. Since the English used in Japan bears little resemblance to the English spoken in other countries (Stanlaw 1988), we should not expect it to help much in cross-cultural communication. Japanese English is used in Japan for Japanese purposes. As one informant told me, "It doesn't matter very much that Americans don't know what some of our English words mean. What matters, after all, is that *we* know, right?"

REFERENCES

Arakawa Sōbē. 1977. *Kadokawa gairaigo jiten* (Kadokawa loanword dictionary), 2d ed. Tokyo: Kadokawa Shoten.
Chamberlain, Basil Hall. [1904] 1972. *Japanese things*. Rutland, Vt.: Charles E. Tuttle.
Firth, Raymond. 1973. *Symbols: Public and private*. Ithaca: Cornell University Press.
Fukuzawa Yukichi. [1899] 1972. *The autobiography of Yukichi Fukuzawa*. New York: Schocken.
Greenbaum, Sidney (ed.). 1985. *The English language today*. Oxford: Pergamon Press.
Haarmann, Harald. 1984. The role of ethnocultural stereotypes and foreign languages in Japanese commercials. *International Journal of the Sociology of Language* 50:101–121.
———. 1989. *Symbolic values of foreign language use*. Berlin: Mouton de Gruyter.
Hall, Ivan Parker. 1973. *Mori Arinori*. Cambridge: Harvard University Press.
Haugen, Einer. 1972. *The ecology of language*. Stanford: Stanford University Press.
Havens, Thomas. 1978. *Valley of darkness: The Japanese people in World War II*. New York: W. W. Norton.
Hinds, John. 1974. Make mine BURAKKU. *Language Research* 10 (2):92–108.
Horiuchi, Amy. 1963. Department store ads and Japanized English. *Studies in Descriptive and Applied Linguistics* 2:49–67.
Ikeda Tetsuro. 1968. Eigo kyōkasho (English textbooks). In *Nihon no Eigaku hyakunen,* vol. 1: *Meiji* (One hundred years of English studies in Japan, vol. 1: The Meiji period), Nihon no Eigaku Hyakunen Henshubu (eds). Tokyo: Kenkyū sha.
Inoue Kyoko. 1985. English loanwords in contemporary Japanese: A longitudinal study of women's magazines. B.A. thesis, Sophia University.
Ishiwata Toshi. 1982. *Gairaigo to Eigo no tanima* (The valley of English and loanwords). Tokyo: Akiyama Sōsho.
Kachru, Braj. 1986. *The alchemy of English*. Oxford: Pergamon Press.
Kenrick, Miranda. 1988. *Gems of Japanized English*. Tokyo: Yen.
Kindaichi Haruhiko. 1988. *Nihongo,* rev. ed. Tokyo: Iwanami Shoten.
Kokuritsu Kokugo Kenkyūjō (National Language Research Institute). 1970–1974. *Denki-keisanki ni yoru shimbun no goi chōsa* (A computer study of the vocabulary of modern newspapers), 4 vols. Tokyo: Shuppan.
Leach, Edmund. 1976. *Culture and communication*. Cambridge: Cambridge University Press.
Miller, Roy Andrew. 1967. *The Japanese language*. Chicago: University of Chicago Press.
———. 1982. *Japan's modern myth: The language and beyond*. New York: Weatherhill.
———. 1986. *Nihongo: In defence of Japanese*. London: Athlone.
Mori Arinori. 1873. *Education in Japan: A series of letters addressed by prominent Americans to Arinori Mori*. New York: Appleton.

Morito Y. 1978. Japanese English: The use of English by the Japanese today. In *The teaching of English in Japan*, I. Koike et al. (eds.), 597–613. Tokyo: Eichosa.

Morris, Ivan. 1970. Mind your language! *Japan Quarterly* 17:454–456.

Sibata Takeshi. 1975. On some problems in Japanese sociolinguistics: Some reflections and prospects. In *Language in Japanese society*, F. Peng (ed.), 159–174. Tokyo: University of Tokyo Press.

Sonoda Kōji. 1975. A descriptive study of English influence on modern Japanese. Ph.D. diss., New York University.

Stanlaw, James. 1982. English in Japanese communicative strategies. In *The other tongue*, B. Kachru (ed.), 168–197. Oxford: Pergamon Press.

———. 1987a. Color, culture, and contact: English loanwords and problems of color nomenclature in modern Japanese. Ph.D. diss., University of Illinois, Champaign-Urbana.

———. 1987b. Japanese and English: Borrowing and contact. *World Englishes* 6 (2):93–109.

———. 1988. Englanese: English loanwords and the Japanese language. *World and I* 7(8):522–533.

———. 1989. Not East not West, not old not new: Trends and genres in Japanese popular music. *World & I* 8 (11):622–633.

Tanaka Yasuo. 1981. *Nantonaku Kurisutaru* (Somehow, Crystal). Tokyo: Kodansha.

Tawara Machi. 1987. *Sarada kinembo* (Salad memorial day). Tokyo: Kawade Shobo.

Ungar, J. Marshall. 1988. Review of Roy Andrew Miller, *Nihongo: In defence of Japanese*. *Journal of Asian Studies* 47:891–893.

Yotsukura Sayo. 1971. Review of Roy Andrew Miller, "The Japanese Language." *Linguistics* 76:103–132.

• • • • •

4

TRACTORS, TELEVISION, AND TELEPHONES: REACH OUT AND TOUCH SOMEONE IN RURAL JAPAN

WILLIAM W. KELLY

What is needed to understand the transforming power of media technology, from print to electronics, on cultures generally is a subtle understanding of the interplay between ideas, symbolic modalities with their varied potentialities, and the ability of the media to create new social relationships and contexts (as well as to alter old ones). Of that subtle understanding there is as yet little in the anthropology of complex cultures, at least in any systematic form.
—Ulf Hannerz, "The World in Creolization"

Perhaps the most famous telephone conversation in Japanese literature occurred in *The Makioka Sisters,* Tanizaki Jun'ichirō's evocative novel of merchant family life in the 1930s. It consists simply of the brief, awkward, and muffled response of Makioka Yukiko to the innocuous invitation of one of her suitors, Mr. Hashidera, to accompany him on a walk: "The maid who answered the telephone said that Yukiko was at home, and then there was no Yukiko. He waited and waited. When she finally came to the telephone he asked if she was free that evening. 'Well,' she said, and it was impossible to tell whether she meant yes or no. As he pressed her for a clearer answer, she finally said, in a voice he could barely hear, that there were reasons why she could not see

him. She said not another word. He left the telephone in great anger"
(Tanizaki 1966, 413).

The most memorable moment of telephone talk in my years of fieldwork in a rural region of Japan was the embarrassed predicament of
Tokuzō, the fifty-five-year-old *jiichan,* or grandpa, of a three-generation
household with whom I have occasionally lived. The telephone rang in
the family room (*chanoma*) where the two of us sat talking. As was his
habit, Tokuzō ignored it, waiting for someone else to answer it. By the
sixth ring and after some uncomfortable glances, he reluctantly picked
it up with a gruff grunt. The female caller, I later surmised, asked for
Keiko, his daughter-in-law, and identified herself as Keiko's sister.

There were several terms of reference and address for Keiko within
the household, including "our bride" (*orai no yome*), "Mom" (*kāchan*),
and, only rarely, her given name. Tokuzō, however, avoided addressing
his daughter-in-law (and, for that matter, his wife and his oldest son)
by any term, relying instead on mute hand gestures and head nods. This
telephone call thus put him in an extremely uncomfortable situation.
Except for the interloping ethnographer, who only later would be expected to answer the phone, no one else was within sight. After futilely
searching for anyone to whom he might silently hand the phone, he
finally called out, "Uh-uh-uh, Daiei!" the name of the department store
where Keiko worked (which had no relation to the caller or substance
of the call!). He was saved only when his six-year-old granddaughter
eventually appeared and took over.

This power of the telephone to daunt older men and younger women
(and uncertain foreigners) always comes to mind when I see the advertising slogans in Japanese magazines for electronic hardware and computer software that is "high-touch" high tech, which I take to be a
Japanese version of "user-friendly." The telephone, of course, is but
one of the many new production and consumption technologies that
have spread rapidly and pervasively throughout urban and rural Japan.
Of perhaps greater import to residents of the region I know best, Shōnai
in Yamagata Prefecture, have been the tractor and the television. These
advances form the three Ts of technology that I shall discuss.

Such a triad of technology is admittedly contrived, although it does
follow the time-honored East Asian penchant for mnenomic formulas,
so crassly appropriated by postwar Japanese advertising. These have
included the three Ss of the late 1950s and early 1960s: *senpūki, sen-*

takuki, and *suihanki* (fan, washing machine, and electric rice cooker); the three Cs of the late 1960s: *kā, kūrā,* and *karā terebi* (car, air conditioner, and color TV); and the three Js of the late 1970s: *jūeru, jetto,* and *jūtaku* (jewels, jetting, and a house). Nonetheless, tractors, televisions, and telephones do provoke some significant questions about technology and social change, three of which I introduce in the following section. These issues are hardy perennials and thus unlikely to be tamed by academic discourse, especially in this brief discussion. Still, the conjunction of these three issues of technology with three items of technology forces one to think about the nature of that "*zone* of cultural debate" that Arjun Appadurai and Carol Breckenridge have labeled "public culture" (1988, 6), the subject on which I shall conclude.

Considerations of technology and human life frequently revolve around three issues: a debate, an irony, and an ideology. The debate concerns the effects of technology on social relations and personal development: that is, are they good or bad? Do they bring potential growth or probable enslavement? Can technology create a global village, or will it reinforce a divided world? In extending human powers, does it enhance radical potentials or entrench the status quo? Such questions lie behind debates about mass communication technologies, as between Marshall McLuhan's 1966 *Understanding Media* and Brian Winston's 1986 *Misunderstanding Media* (which might also be entitled "Misunderstanding McLuhan"). Not surprisingly, these debates about new technologies in modern life tend to parallel those about social institutions in mass society. Some view public schooling, for example, as an escalator or solvent, empowering and enfranchising the dispossessed; others feel that it reproduces an elite and sanctions inequality.

As McLuhan's "cool media" become computer mania, Micaela di Leonardo (1985) sees the debate recast as a clash of two discourses: "second self" versus "labor's bane." On the one hand, she argues, Sherry Turkle's study (1984) of the computer as second self focuses on its power to shape sensibility, consciousness, and self-definition; computer culture becomes interactive in a profound sense. A different line of analysis is inspired by, among others, Harry Braverman's work on automation and "deskilling" (1974); these are labor-centered, critical accounts of the hazards and coercion of computerized workplaces. Di Leonardo's point is that second-self and labor's-bane evaluations talk past each another. It is a difference, I suppose, between a concern with how computer-age machines can be used by people to *think* about people and a concern with how such machines can be used by people to *control* people. In Japan, this contrast is illustrated by the gulf between robotics engineer Mori Masahiro's claims that robots have Buddha-nature (Schodt 1988, 206–212) and Jon Woronoff's fulminations (1981) about the deskilled and displaced "wasted workers."

An irony pervading both perspectives, however, is that technology is often both intrusive and disaggregating. Depending on one's point of view, the computerized work station and the home leisure center may either foster autonomy or enforce isolation. In either case, these technologies of individuation, by their very penetration, have a homogenizing effect. *Kōjinka* (privatization), which is the common denominator behind "my car" (*mai kā*), "office automation" (*OA*), and the ill-named "family computer" (*famicon*), is attained only at the price of *hyōjunka* (standardization).

The ideology, of course, is that of modernization and rationalization. In the case of Japan, technological innovation and adaptation are hardly new: metallurgy techniques and civil engineers from the Korean peninsula were critical in the Yamato clan's transition from kinship to kingship in the sixth and seventh centuries; the European Jesuit "soldiers of Christ" in the sixteenth century were valued more for their weapons than for their words; and the steam engines and "live machines" imported by Meiji modernizers fulfilled their fondest dreams of *wakon yōsai,* "Japanese spirit, Western learning," perhaps the origin of the expression "Japanese high touch, Western high tech."

Yet in both politics and semiotics, most post–World War II technologies have been associated with a self-consciously rational expertise, a style legitimated by its own formal characteristics of professional roles, bureaucratic institutions, and systematized procedures. In this sense, modern technologies are not all powerful but unstable and self-limiting, both because they yield diminishing returns and because this conception of the modern is incompatible with other, equally salient meanings (for example, modern participatory citizenship, *minshūshugi*).

Shōnai emerged in the twentieth century as one of Japan's few major rice-producing regions. By the 1980s, farm work directly engaged only a small portion of its population; but rice farming remains central to the identity of the region and to the activities of most public agencies and the local business community. Two changes in Shōnai agriculture have been particularly striking: a rationalization of work routines and relations and a solidification of smallholder or proprietor consciousness. By the first, I mean the increasing detachment of farm work from the household—in Shōnai, farming has become the sole province of the young adult male—and its embeddedness in a nexus of institutional expertise that links the agricultural cooperative, the land-improvement district, the extension service, and so on. By the second, I mean the contemporary farmer has become both manager and laborer, committed to continuing his control over and contribution to the farm-work process. These changes appear to entail divergent routines and consciousness; the former is more new middle class, the latter more old middle class. In fact, I believe that the first development has enabled the second to persist, while the latter has mitigated some of the acute tensions caused by the rationalization of routines. At the root of both changes has been the tractor.

These changes in Shōnai farm work are rather unanticipated results of two twentieth-century Green Revolutions on the plain, two periods of radical reform in technology and social organization that transformed rice growing and the paddy landscape. In the earlier period, 1895–1920, large landlords introduced the horse-drawn plow to replace the back-breaking spading that rice fields required. Under the banner of "the improvement of agricultural affairs" (nōji kairyō) they attempted to standardize tenancy procedures, to raise rice quality and yields, and to enhance the profitability of their operations. Instead, their reforms stimulated forms of counterorganization that shifted leverage to smallholder owner-tenants. In the second revolution of 1965–1980, state ministries vigorously promoted a "rationalization of agriculture" (nōgyō gōrika) through mechanization, led by the tractor. The ministries thus meant to encourage an exodus of labor from farming to industry and a consolidation of farms in the hands of a few large-scale, full-time operators. Again, intentions have been thwarted. Most households have instead held on to their paddies and used tractors and other new machinery, as well as generous price supports, to allow their young adult males to continue small-scale farming, while other members find jobs outside the farm (Kelly 1986).

During both rice revolutions, cultural oppositions were constructed to pit the rational and the modern against the customary and the feudal. In their respective periods, the plow and the tractor were tangible signs of the former. Yet the social outcomes of the rational and the modern were unexpected, because neither the large landlords nor the state ministries could control how and for whom the technologies were to be used. At both times, the new technology was appropriated by smallholders, who were thereby able to redefine and reassert their livelihood.

That is, concerns within households differed from considerations within policy-making circles. From the mid-1960s through the early 1970s, parents throughout the Shōnai countryside feared that metropolitan jobs would attract their children, leaving no successor to the family farm. Many parents were willing to purchase a full line of rice machinery for their sons, with the expectation that rising yields would finance repayment. Many sons were willing to remain in hopes that mechanized farming would offer a modern occupation and that machines would allow them to farm independently, autonomous of their fathers, whose expertise was rendered obsolete and whose authority they might thus usurp. These two rice revolutions have been struggles for and about the meanings of the rational and the customary and have produced an occupation whose procedures and social relations may be the most rational on the plain.

In postwar Shōnai, younger males have used tractors and other machinery to assert a new work image and to appropriate significant household authority vis-à-vis their siblings who have moved to the cities, their wives, who no longer want or need to help with the rice farming, and their parents, whose skills are outdated and whose contributions are only occasional. The new mechanization has separated the young male but not isolated him. Rather, his nexus of work relations has been reconfigured to link him, as a specialist producer, with financial, agronomic, policy, and engineering professionals. (This is an all-male field, despite some feminine high touches. The stock advertisement for rice machines shows a cute young woman riding a tractor or walking behind a transplanter, one hand lightly on the controls and the other waving gaily to the reader-buyer. As another example, control panels on the latest tractors and combines feature a dulcet, high-pitched "nightingale voice" that reminds the operator of low fuel, brake and throttle position, and the like.)

At the same time, these young men are well aware that mechanization is responsible for their heavy financial debts. As they admit, they are the highly vulnerable "machine poor" (*kikai binbō*). Their identity as modern farmers has an underside: the off-season reality of low-wage labor for taxi companies, paving contractors, textbook distributors, and print shops, to cite only a few examples. Though not happy about their predicament, they are seldom mystified about the choices they made from the alternatives they were offered.

If the production technology of the tractor brought scientific agriculture to the fields, the consumption technology of television brought mass culture to the family room. Television broadcasting began in Japan in 1953, the year the Korean War ended, and quickly became a principal vehicle for translating economic prosperity into consumption imperatives and then transmitting these imperatives to households nationally. Television, together with the washing machine, was the leading commodity in the consumer "electrification boom" (*denka būmu*) that began in 1953. In 1956, there were three hundred thousand television sets in the country; four years later, there were 3.6 million sets, a twelvefold increase, representing their use in over 40 percent of the nation's households. In particular, the live broadcasts of the Crown Prince's marriage in April 1959 were used to generate an enormous demand for this medium. By the time of the 1964 Tokyo Olympics—another marketing bonanza for manufacturers—televisions were found in over three-quarters of all households.

The extremes of sophistication and idiocy may be greater in Japanese television broadcasting than in that of any other industrial society. Certainly the same epithets used to describe American television have been applied to the Japanese *terebi*—boob tube, consumer tastemaker, electronic babysitter, political sedative, and so on (see, among many others, Kitamura and Nakano 1983). My observation, however, is about reception, not deception—about the spatial reorientation that television has prompted in the central family room of many Shōnai households, 95 percent of which had at least one set by 1971.

Nearly every study of rural Japan comments on the fixed seating arrangements of the family room—the customary positions of family members and guests around the open rectangular hearth, or more recently, the electric foot-warming table (*kotatsu*). This arrangement is oriented toward the ceremonial alcove (*tokonoma*) and the household ancestor shrine (*butsudan*) beside it. The seat with its back to the alcove, and thus framed by it, was the seat of prestige and authority, the *kamiza* of the household head. Specific patterns varied with class and area. Frequently, to the right of the household head was the guest seat and then that of live-in workers and non-successor children. To his left were his parents, his oldest son or another designated successor, his wife, and so on.

Even the most recently rebuilt houses retain this alcove, but now it is often used as a convenient location for the television set. What this means, of course, is that everyone has a good viewing angle except the household head. From my experience, he frequently moves to the side, shifting the focus of attention from the centripetal kotatsu toward the television set in the alcove. The seating order is permanently disrupted, just as the voice of the TV "caster" (*kyasutā*) challenges the voice of the jiichan as the authority of the chanoma. The intrusion of television into the chanoma has thus contributed directly to a broader reconfiguration of familial authority, which is further reinforced by the tractor in the barn.[1]

In the Shōnai villages I am familiar with, the installation of household telephones has had greater significance for women than for men, and for older women in particular—the *obāsan* generations over fifty years of age. They drive less frequently than other adults and are now the most housebound members of society, providing day care for their grandchildren while the young parents work and their husbands, the grandfathers, busy themselves with miscellaneous tasks and public service. The telephone frequently becomes both a substitute for and a supplement to other channels of communication and sociability. It has become an indispensable tool of "kinwork," which is as much a female responsibility in Japanese households as in di Leonardo's Italian-American families (1984).

In ways familiar to most of us and dear to the profits of the phone company, the telephone allows long-distance contact with children who have grown up and moved away. This is, of course, a highly charged issue in a region such as Shōnai, where parents are equally proud and wistful of their children's educational success. The *sankin kōtai* of the old provincial elite (the early-modern shogunate's requirement that domain lords leave their families in the capital city and alternate their own residences between Edo and their home domain) has become the *kyōiku esukarētā*, the "education escalator" of the new meritocracy. In Shōnai the dilemma of education is that the most successful are the most inclined to leave. One household which I often visit has two children—both daughters, both graduates of four-year universities in Tokyo. One is single and works in Tokyo; the other is married to a doctor and lives in nearby Akita Prefecture. The mother is in constant telephone contact with both. She and her husband frequently worry out loud about growing old without the companionship and support of their children. The telephone, they recognize, is a welcome solace though a poor substitute; for at least one of the daughters, it is also a handy justification for her absence and independence.

The telephone is also an important instrument in "village work," as well as in kinwork, and has provided some relief from the protocols of everyday hospitality. In another Shōnai settlement where I recently lived, the twenty-six households were involved in fifteen different organizations, to count only the most local ones. The telephone was a useful shortcut for conducting business, without the obligatory socializing (and for men, drinking) that follows most club and association meetings. (It must be added, however, that the telephone could also be an irritating reminder of meetings and agendas.)

Beyond the dense organizational connections, the constant comings and goings among neighbors (to pass time and to pass along information) proceed with tokens of neighborliness—a few apples, a bag of crackers or cookies or chips—the junk food that fills the racks of every general store in Japan. A caller at the door (more precisely, a visitor in the *genkan,* or entrance hall) thus prompts another of life's prosaic anxieties: who should be encouraged to come up from the entrance hall to the family room or guest room; when and how should one extend the invitation; and when and how should the guest resist this courtesy? This is not the stuff of major confrontations, but throughout the day it requires immediate, subtle calculations by the adult women of the household. These domestic gatekeepers (genkan guards?) must manage the flow of interhousehold information, maintain a semblance of sociability, and accomplish numerous domestic chores. More so than the men, they have become increasingly adept at using the telephone to substitute for at least some of this obligatory visiting.

Sons separated from households, household heads unseated, women reforming patterns of socializing—these tantalizing ethnographic fragments can be connected to the larger concerns of this volume with a concluding trio of issues. First, the notion that there is something called "technology" apart from the social relations of production and consumption is obviously as misleading to an anthropological inquiry as was the notion of a "natural environment" apart from the people who live in and enliven it. Efforts to measure the potential of any single technology to ennoble or enslave are better left to those involved with flow charts and simulation games—the new alchemists of social planning. Technology is neither determinative of nor neutral to the social patterns of its use or the cultural terms by which it is used. "Mechanization" (*kikaika*), "mass communications" (*masu comi*), and "lifeways improvement" (*seikatsu kaizen*) have all been potent slogans of a new-middle-class vision of postwar Japan, and the three Ts have been local and concrete expressions of those slogans and the societal model that gives them coherence. But a judgment of the ways in which such technologies have facilitated active compliance, passive accommodation, or determined resistance to that model requires a theory that reconciles the meanings that people have given those technologies with the power structures that shape and constrain those meanings.

Moreover, for such a theory to be relevant to contemporary state societies, one must recognize that technology is at once an object and a means of debate in what Appadurai and Breckenridge have called the "contested terrain" of public culture (1988, 7). I take their formulation as trying to specify the increasingly complex cross talk among the permeable cultural spheres of modern life. Public culture is a "zone" of posters and commercials (Ivy 1988), programs and speeches, cookbooks (Appadurai 1988) and textbooks, political marches and popular festivities (Kelly 1990b). In Japan, it is the transmissions across and interrogations between the national culture of the state, a mass culture of the media, a metropolitan culture of greater Tokyo, and the regional cultures of places like Shōnai. Public culture is a zone but also a process—that of continual transpositions across such cultural registers.

This may provide a better way of talking about technology than our more-familiar language of the "social consequences of new technology" or the "unintended effects of technological change." That is, it is a notion not of the social translation but of the cultural transposition of technology that draws our attention to the distinct, though articulated, constellations of interests in the several "cultures" in which a technology may be imbedded. The efficiency of tractors, the etiquette of telephone talk, and the popularity (or vulgarity) of television programs may be common idioms of debate in national, mass, regional, and domestic forums. Still, we must distinguish—and relate—the tractor as an instrument of state agricultural policy, as the subject of intense advertising

campaigns by major manufacturers, and as the object of struggles between adult men and their parents and wives. Public culture is not just
the *zone* in which the tractor moves from one arena of interests to
another but the *process* by which these interests engage one another
and mutually, though differentially, infiltrate one another's expression
(Kelly 1990b).

Finally, in part because political mobilization in prewar Japan has
given way to economic mobilization in postwar Japan, technology—
high technology—has been an especially important theme of contemporary public culture. High tech is new tech, the latest tech; it
is the horizon of the obtainable, no longer purely visionary but not
yet the ordinary. To people in Shōnai, the three Ts were the high tech
of the early to mid 1970s. Tractors, televisions, and telephones were
literally the vehicles by which the seeds of scientific production
were implanted and the sights and sounds of the city transmitted.
If these machines are still not friendly, they are at least familiar; not
human extensions, but social necessities. For Shōnai of the late 1980s
and early 1990s, high tech has come to mean computers in the workplace;
the biogenetic engineering that, it is claimed, will provide laboratory
jobs and a last hope for regional agriculture; and the airplane, in the
controversial form of the Shōnai Regional Airport, which opened in
1991.

"Modernization" (*kindaika*) and "mainstream consciousness" (*chūr-
yū ishiki*) were the rubrics for promoting the old high tech through state
policy and mass media. Underlying this new high tech is yet another
slogan of the state, Japan as the "information society" (*jōhō shakai*).
This carries an explicit promise to disperse employment opportunities
and to regionalize development as a nationwide network of postman-
ufacturing "technopolises." In this vision of a twenty-first-century Japan,
whether technology will be the vehicle for social change and regional
distinctiveness or the instrument of political stability and metropolitan
hegemony has already begun to divide both public debate and everyday
conversation.

NOTE

1. David Plath (1990) has perceptively observed that the family automobile, in becoming
   an extension and even replacement for the family living room, has put the father back
   in the driver's seat.

REFERENCES

Appadurai, Arjun. 1988. How to make a national cuisine: Cookbooks in contemporary India. *Comparative Studies in Society and History* 30(1):3–24.

Appadurai, Arjun, and Carol A. Breckenridge. 1988. Why public culture? *Public Culture Bulletin* 1(1):5–9.

Braverman, Harry. 1974. *Labor and monopoly capital*. New York: Monthly Review Press.

di Leonardo, Micaela. 1984. *The varieties of ethnic experience: Kinship, class, and gender among California Italian-Americans*. Ithaca: Cornell University Press.

———. 1985. Clericals, computers, and culture: Two discourses in search of a subject. Unpublished MS.

Ivy, Marilyn. 1988. Tradition and difference in the Japanese mass media. *Public Culture Bulletin* 1(1):21–29.

Kelly, William W. 1986. Rationalization and nostalgia: Cultural dynamics of new middle-class Japan. *American Ethnologist* 13(4):603–618.

———. 1990a. Japanese no-noh: The crosstalk of public culture in a rural festivity. *Public Culture* 2(2):65–81.

———. 1990b. Regional Japan: The price of prosperity and the benefits of dependency. *Daedalus* 119(3):207–227.

Kitamura Hideo and Nakano Osamu (eds.). 1983. *Nihon no terebi bunka*. Tokyo: Yuhikaku.

McLuhan, Marshall. 1966. *Understanding media: The extensions of man*. New York: New American Library.

Morris-Suzuki, Tessa. 1988. *Beyond computopia: Information, automation and democracy in Japan*. London: Kegan Paul International.

Peacock, James L. 1986. *The anthropological lens: Harsh light, soft focus*. New York: Cambridge University Press.

Plath, David. 1990. My-car-isma: Motorizing the Shōwa self. *Daedalus* 119(3):229–244.

Schodt, Frederick. 1988. *Inside the robot kingdom: Japan, mechatronics, and the coming robotopia*. New York: Kodansha International/USA.

Tanizaki Jun'ichirō. 1966. *The Makioka sisters*. Translated by Edward G. Seidensticker. New York: Grosset and Dunlap.

Turkle, Sherry. 1984. *The second self: Computers and the human spirit*. New York: Simon and Schuster.

Winston, Brian. 1986. *Misunderstanding media*. Cambridge: Harvard University Press.

Woronoff, Jon. 1981. *Japan's wasted workers*. Tokyo: Lotus Press.

· · · · ·

5

THE JAPANESE BATH:
EXTRAORDINARILY ORDINARY

SCOTT CLARK

Returning to his home in a modern Tokyo suburb from a hard day's work, a Japanese businessman is soon soaking in a tub of hot water. He will spend the next thirty to forty minutes relaxing in a bathtub constructed of a modern plastic with bathwater flowing from steel, copper, and plastic tubing. Located next to the tub, the water heater is fueled from a gas line and can be programmed to heat the water to a particular temperature at a specified time. A fitting connected to the heater provides the option of a shower. Bath salts produced in a modern chemical plant improve the tactility and fragrance of the bathwater. The man washes sitting on a short stool and using a small basin (both of which are plastic) or a small hand shower. He scrubs with soap—first imported in the late sixteenth century. His washcloth, of a synthetic fiber, stimulates his skin with a slight scratchy sensation. He has a choice of shampoos and rinses for his hair. After drying himself with a thick terry-cloth towel, he shaves with a battery-powered, immersible razor. Florescent bulbs provide bright light.

In all, the setting is very contemporary; even the walls and floors of the bathroom are made of a high-tech polymer. This mix of modern fixtures and objects—he might even refer to them as Western style—are all part of what is to him a traditional, quintessential Japanese practice: *furo,* the Japanese bath. Daily bathing has been a constant feature of the culture for centuries. But the technology has changed over the years, initiating changes in how, when, where, and why Japanese bathe.

One significant change is the metamorphosis of bathing from an unself-conscious everyday activity into a marker of (cultural) self-identity. Highly affected by the forces of westernization, modernization, and currently internationalization, Japanese have transformed what was once considered a mundane though important and pleasurable practice into an expression of Japaneseness and tradition. The bath and bathing are today both a familiar daily practice and an act of exoticism, the transformation of the ordinary into the extraordinary in a reflexive discourse on being Japanese.

Japanese bathing etiquette is much the same in the home bath, at the public bath (*sentō*),[1] and at the hot springs (*onsen*). People usually bathe in the late afternoon or evening after the day's work or travels. The bather disrobes in a dressing room. In houses, this room also contains a small vanity and, usually, a washing machine. The bathroom is dedicated to bathing; the toilet is in a separate room. All washing and rinsing is done outside the tub, and a drain in the floor carries the water away. Unless the individual is very dirty, a quick rinsing is normally sufficient preparation for getting into the tub. Commonly, thorough scrubbing with soap and a washcloth follows soaking in the hot water, especially in cold weather. Entering the tub, the bather submerges up to the neck. To the unaccustomed, the water feels uncomfortably hot.

The bather soaks in the hot water until the body becomes very warm. After getting out of the tub, a careful scrub with soap lathered into a small towel and perhaps a shampoo complete the bath. Many people prefer to soak once again after washing.

Until recently, one dried with the same towel used for washing. It was repeatedly wrung out and wiped over the body. Today, bath towels similar to those found in the United States are commonly used for the final drying. The bather then leaves the bathroom and puts on clean clothing.

The entire process often takes more than thirty minutes, and an hour is not uncommon.

THE EVOLUTION OF THE PUBLIC BATH

The history of Japanese bathing is long and complex. But the origins of the custom are of less interest to us here than is the popular belief that the Japanese bath can be traced back to the Tokugawa period (1600–1868), a time of modernization and proliferation of sentō in the rapidly growing cities.

By around 1700, sentō could be found in most neighborhoods of Edo (old Tokyo). The typical building was a two-storied wooden structure. Baths were located on the first floor, and a place for relaxing, drinking tea, and gossiping with friends on the second. Upon entering the sentō, the customer paid a fee (controlled by the government) for the bath. The entrance opened into a large area with baskets and lockers in which to place one's clothes. This dressing area had a wooden floor, usually covered with a mat of reeds, which separated it from the washing area located toward the rear of the establishment. The bare wooden floors of the washing area provided drainage for water. The bather used a small wooden basin to dip water for washing from a large tub, rinsed off any dirt, and then entered the bath. One washed with a small towel and a bag filled with rice bran, the functional equivalent of soap. Although soap was introduced to Japan from the West just prior to the Tokugawa period, its initial use was primarily for medical purposes (Ochiai 1984). In most instances, men and women shared the same dressing, washing, and bathing areas.

Contrary to film depictions of these bathhouses as large pools in which people soaked, the most common type during the Tokugawa period was a kind of steam bath. Scarcity of water and fuel, along with governmental restrictions on fire (a great danger in the growing wooden cities), restricted the amount of water that could be heated.

Steam baths in the Edo sentō possessed distinctive style. The entrance had a low-hanging lintel that required bathers to bend over or even crawl to enter. A step and a sill rising from the floor to the bottom of the lintel were located a few feet inside the entrance. The bather had to step over the sill, which formed the front edge of the shallow tub, and into the bath, which contained only a few inches of water. By heating the water directly from beneath the tub or by regularly adding hot water, steam filled and was effectively trapped by the low lintel. The design also largely excluded outside light, preventing observation of the cleanliness of the water, which, according to some historical accounts, was sometimes quite murky.

The abolition of the class system at the beginning of the Meiji in 1868 led to the demolition of the large houses of many samurai families. Consequently, many formerly upper-class townspeople became sentō customers. This increase in business, along with an influx of people into Tokyo, required that more bathing facilities be built, the lumber from the demolished houses providing economical building materials and fuel. Sentō in Tokyo increased threefold during the first years of Meiji (Ōba 1986), primarily of the traditional Tokugawa style.

In 1878, one Tsurusawa Monzaemon conceived a new style of bathhouse that eliminated the steam bath. This bathhouse had a large wooden tub deep enough to sit in, with water up to the chin, similar to tubs already in use at hot springs. The tub was located in the wooden-floored washing area. Tsurusawa raised the ceiling of the washing area and constructed a window at the top that let light in and could be opened to emit steam. This new style of sentō, with its well-lit interior and deep soaking tub, rapidly became popular. Recognizing that the new style also permitted closer examination of sanitary conditions, the government in 1885 banned the construction of the older, darker bathhouses.

Government regulations also required that all sentō provide separate bathing facilities for women and men. During the Tokugawa era the government had periodically issued edicts banning mixed bathing (Zenkoku Kōshūyokujōgyō Kankyōeisei Dōgyōkumiai Rengōkai 1973), but it was not until the Meiji opening of Japan and a rising sensitivity to foreign opinion that the laws became effective.

Here is an early instance of Japanese concern with the foreign in relation to bathing. Mixed bathing had for so long been a part of everyday life that people largely ignored previous edicts. Then foreigners began to write about the "uncivilized" and "licentious" nature of the Japanese, with mixed bathing offered most often as evidence. In 1861, for example, after a visit to Japan, the Bishop of Victoria (Hong Kong), George Smith, wrote:

> The public bathing-houses are an institution of Japan.... Towards the latter part of the afternoon or at an early hour of the evening, all ages and both sexes are intermingled in one shameless throng of bathers without signs of modesty or of any apparent sense of moral decorum. Some persons palliate this custom of promiscuous bathing in public by assuming the innocent simplicity of primitive habits, and dwelling on the wide difference of every country in the conventionalities of moral right and wrong. The obvious reply to this charitable theory is that the Japanese are one of the most licentious races in the world. (Smith 1861, 103–104)

Meiji Japan's exposure to foreign beliefs and ideology and its growing desire to become (and to be perceived by the rest of the world as) a modern society created a social climate in which the segregation of the sexes in bathhouses could be accomplished.

Nonetheless, the separation of the sexes while bathing was selective. Onsen to this day may be mixed-sex, as are some smaller baths in the countryside. But most sentō responded to the "modern" imperative and quickly provided separate bathing facilities for men and women.

In step with other developments throughout Japan, the sentō quickly incorporated modern architectural features. By 1921, concrete and tile were being used in the bathing area. After the great earthquake of 1923, the use of concrete and other fire-resistant materials became prevalent and in some municipalities was even required. The dark and thus conceptually "dirty" steam room had been abandoned for a cleaner, brighter, open bathtub. Hard-to-clean wooden floors gave way to tiled ones. Plumbing was improved, and large faucets were installed. Mirrors were hung all around the bathing area. The rear wall of the bathhouse was usually decorated with a large mural, portraying Japanese scenic spots, most often Fuji. Painted murals persist today but may depict popular cartoon figures, Hawaiian beaches, or figures of fish, mermaids, or flowers. Today, most sentō offer at least one shower, and many have shower attachments at each faucet. The bathing and dressing areas are separated by sliding glass doors, effectively confining most of the moisture to the bathing area.

The dressing area retains a more traditional (Japanese) flavor with wooden walls, matted floors, split-bamboo baskets, and wooden lockers. Traditional carvings and paintings often grace the walls and the ceiling. The lighting tends to be subdued, and the atmosphere more peaceful than the inner bathing area.

The glass doors between the bathing and dressing areas mark an interesting cultural and architectural separation of the modern and the traditional. One Japanese informant described the difference between the areas in terms of an opposition between Western style *(yōfū)* and Japanese style *(wafū)*. Others describe the difference as one of modern *(kindaiteki)* versus traditional *(dentōteki)* moods.

The many modern items found in the dressing area do not prevent Japanese from describing this space as having a traditional feel. Large mirrors, hair dryers, plastic clothing baskets, lockers made from laminates or metal, floors covered with parquetry or carpet, color television, and air conditioning are all virtually obligatory. Coin dispensers for toiletries, underwear, and cold drinks are often placed near the entrance.

Electric massage chairs, scales, and sometimes fitness equipment are conveniently made available to customers.

To my informants who described the gadget-laden, heavily synthetic dressing area as traditionally Japanese, the juxtaposition of new and old materials and technologies is not incongruent. Smith (1990) has persuasively argued that Japanese cultural traditions are nearly always a combination of old and new. Traditions are traditional not because they are old but because the people, for conscious and unconscious reasons, perceive them as traditional. As McFee (1975) has shown, the introduction of new elements into a culture does not necessarily displace the old. People are not "culture containers" with limited capacities. Thus, in the case of the Japanese sentō, Western customs and technology have been incorporated without threatening tradition.

PUBLIC VERSUS PRIVATE BATHING

Not everyone bathes at public facilities; small baths for home use have existed for centuries in Japan. These were normally portable units that could be set up outside or in an earthen-floored room of the house. In rural villages, several neighboring households often shared a bath. Some were small steam baths, again reflecting the scarcity of fuel and water. By the beginning of the modern era, the most common private baths were small, deep tubs that allowed only one individual to soak at a time. Constructed of wood or cast iron, these home baths either had built-in heaters or were heated directly by a wood fire below.

For urban populations, the luxury of a bath in the home was reserved primarily for the wealthy or powerful, until recently. The economic affluence of the 1960s led to the development and adoption of small bathtubs suitable for use in even the tiniest urban apartments. The bathtub must be deep enough for submersion to the neck. Large tubs are preferred to small ones, but for economic reasons tubs in most houses are large enough for only one adult and, perhaps, a young child.

In homes, the tub is filled once each day, and all bathers soak in the same water. Those who wish or need to conserve water may use the same water for two or more consecutive days. Usually, however, the remaining bathwater is used for washing clothes the next morning. In sentō, fresh hot water is continually running into the tub.

Inevitably, as home tubs became more common, the number of people visiting sentō decreased. To reattract customers, sentō proprietors introduced innovations that could not be enjoyed at home, such as jets and bubbling mechanisms for water massage in the tub, bathtubs that generated small, supposedly invigorating electric shocks, exercise equipment, and a variety of bath additives, including radon for (alleged) health benefits. The number of sentō peaked at just over 21,200 in 1972 and then continually declined to approximately 13,250 in 1985 in spite of innovations (Statistics Bureau 1987).

Sentō have been valued by Japanese as an important locus of social interaction since at least the Tokugawa era. In 1810, for example, the satirist Shikitei Sanba illustrated the social scene of the time by characterizing the customers, conversation, and interaction of an Edo bathhouse (Leutner 1985). Today, public commentary about sentō focuses primarily on the theme of vanishing tradition and the attendant loss of cultural values. Although no one attributes the perceived loss of Japanese core values entirely to the decline of sentō, the decline is seen as symptomatic of more comprehensive changes in Japanese society. To many Japanese, the decline of the sentō represents the vanishing of a more public, communal, traditionally Japanese way of life.

In contemporary Japan, many children have never been to a sentō. A popular theme on television variety shows is to show clips of children visiting a public bath for the first time. The children's ignorance of appropriate sentō behavior becomes the subject of both humorous and serious social commentary.

Many Japanese ascribe dire social consequences to the fact that a generation of children is being raised with little or no public bathing experience. Letters to the editor, decrying the absence of consideration for others that they suggest is typical of today's young people, attribute this feeling to substandard childhood training and discipline. Many writers go on to argue that traditionally one of the first and primary places for training in public social interaction was the sentō. There a child learned how to greet others and interact in a proper fashion. The demise of this institution is, for these people, both a symptom of and cause for the perceived degradation of Japanese customs and traditions.

Thus on the men's side in sentō today, one frequently encounters fathers introducing their young sons and daughters to the experience of bathing with a large group of people. For these families who have baths in their homes, the expressed intent is to have their children experience a vanishing form of Japanese social interaction.

An illustration from Ofuroyasan *(The Public Bath), a children's book by
Shigeo Nishimura. (Reproduced by permission of the author and the
publisher, Fukuinkan Shoten.)*

Whether or not social bathing is in fact a vanishing tradition is de-
batable. There are "sentō connoisseurs" who, with friends or family,
patronize a different neighborhood sentō each week in the tradition of
the temple pilgrimage. Another popular new trend is the health center,
a cross between a health club and a public bath. In addition to a choice
of baths, health centers offer food and drink, exercise equipment, work-
out rooms, and massage. These centers have become so popular that
when combined with remaining sentō the number of public bathing
facilities is greater than ever before.

In addition to their hygienic functions, sentō serve as important communication and social centers. Contemporary sentō and health centers
tend to attract customers from all over town, unlike the public baths in
earlier times whose customers were almost all neighborhood "regulars."
Because of the increase in homes with baths and the resultant decline
in sentō, public bathing facilities today serve a diverse group of customers.

The clientele of a sentō during an afternoon and evening in 1988, in a district of Tokyo's old downtown, illustrates the range of purposes for which people visit a contemporary sentō. At 4:00 P.M. the sentō opens to a group of five elderly customers—three women and two men—who have arrived to get the first baths of the day, when there are fewer people and the bathwater is fresh. Four of them have baths in their homes or apartments but prefer to bathe where more water and space are available. Although these individuals rarely interact anywhere else, they commonly meet a few minutes before the sentō opens each day to exchange greetings and news.

During the next hour several elderly couples as well as three young mothers with their small children arrive. These mothers do not have baths at home and prefer to bathe before their husbands (who will go to the sentō later) return home from work. One of the elderly couples had lived in a nearby neighborhood until deciding to sell their house to developers. Although the couple now lives in a distant suburb, they regularly visit the neighborhood to shop and to see friends. During each visit they come to the sentō for nostalgic reasons: they enjoy the atmosphere and always engage in conversation with other customers who pass on local news. For them, the bath at home is a lonely activity.

Between 5:00 and 7:00 P.M., the sentō's customers are primarily construction workers, carpenters, and others whose work makes them particularly dirty. They prefer to bathe at the sentō even though many have baths at home. Also during this time period several small groups of middle-school children who live in low-rent housing without baths come for a bath. These workers and children are regulars who know the *bandaisan* (the person collecting the fee and watching over things generally) by name and usually keep their personal bathing supplies at the sentō. Because they know many of the other customers through daily visits, the conversation is lively and often intimate.

Between 7:00 and 9:00 P.M., many families arrive with their children. Also present are locals living in apartments without baths, others who have baths but prefer the sentō, and two fathers with their sons and daughters who want their children to experience the sentō. Women take infants to the female side of the bath, while men usually take the other young children, sons and daughters, although the children may move freely from side to side through a connecting door. Men scrub their children's backs, and some of the children in turn scrub their fathers'. Children generally enjoy the bath except for some squirming and objections while being washed. Adult acquaintances, especially women, sometimes reciprocate in a ritualistic scrubbing of backs, a symbol of friendship and communication.

Families usually spend between thirty minutes to an hour at the bath. Parents teach their children how to wash and rinse without splashing others, how to politely enter and leave the tub, and other matters of social and bathing etiquette. When the bathing area is uncrowded, children are allowed to play more freely, blowing soap bubbles off their towels or sliding around the floor on small basins. Nonetheless, parents always take care that their children not bother others.

Later, a middle-aged man brings his father, who is no longer able to walk or dress himself, for a bath. The son undresses his father, washes him, carries him into the bath, and finally redresses him, paying careful attention to his needs. People look on this act with approval. The consideration of his father at the bath is a powerful statement of filial piety and affection, an affirmation of traditional values. One sees such care of the aged or of incapacitated adults at the sentō throughout Japan.

During this same period, one is also likely to encounter groups of friends or families seeking relaxation and recreation. Groups in Tokyo and other cities plan visits to different sentō in the best traditions of tourism, complete with maps and guidebooks for local cuisine, historic sites, shrines, and temples.

After 9:00 P.M., young couples or other young adults arrive from their nearby dwellings, wearing slippers and casual dress. Many keep their bathing necessities at the sentō. Though some do have baths in their apartments, they claim it is cheaper and easier to visit the sentō than to prepare a bath for one or two at home. In addition, the bath at home is often too small for comfortable and relaxing bathing. As the evening goes on, university students who live in cheap housing and must bathe at the sentō increasingly appear. Also, a few businessmen stop for a bath on their way home from work or after-hours drinking. The sentō is a place for these men to separate their working lives from their private ones and, for some, a place to sober up before greeting their wives. The intoxicated usually wash but do not soak in the tub because of warnings that soaking in hot water may be dangerous with alcohol in the blood.

The customers in this Tokyo sentō vary from infants to the aged, the poor to the upper-middle class, and regulars to one-time visitors. They come for reasons ranging from simple daily hygiene to child training and recreation.

The proprietor of this bath estimates that from 60 to 70 percent of his customers have a home bath. If those who must bathe at the sentō feel any resentment toward those who bathe there by choice, the feeling is well hidden. Some express envy of the latter but good-naturedly share the bath with everyone and agree that they, too, would visit a sentō regularly even if they had a bath at home.

Bathing continues to affect the material culture of the domestic unit. Advertisements for new housing often highlight the bathing facilities. I saw a number of examples that illustrated only the bathroom and gave a minimal description of the rest of the living areas. Some new condominiums and apartments not only have baths in each of the units but also provide a large bath for use by groups. A trade show in Tokyo in 1988 exhibited many bathing innovations, one of which was a unit that combined a rather typical (although slightly larger-than-average) bathtub and bathing area equipped with an elaborate entertainment center consisting of a laser video, compact disc stereo, television, and AM-FM radio. All the mechanical functions, including filling, draining, and heating the bath, could be programmed into a computer to operate either automatically or by manual control from inside the tub.

More commonly, however, people look to simpler material changes in their baths, usually manifested in a mixture of the traditional and the modern. An older house may be remodeled to accommodate a larger, more comfortable furo. In a nostalgic mood, a woman in an ultra-modern house may order the installation of a wooden bathtub (often constructed from Japanese cypress, considered to be the best and most traditional of bathtub woods). Others profess a wish for such a bathtub but hesitate because of ambivalent feelings, recalling that such baths are much more difficult to clean and maintain than the modern examples. In any case, the modern wooden bathtub will be heated by gas, not by wood.

Some bathhouses and hot springs, capitalizing on this connection of traditional materials with traditional values, have recently constructed wooden and stone tubs to replace those made of concrete and tile. As materials for bathtubs, wood and stone more than any other material suggest Japaneseness.

As has been cogently documented (Kelly 1986), Japanese display ambivalence about the past, which can represent both backwardness and a better time. Few wish for the former, but many feel nostalgic about the latter. The domestic bath is another example of this phenomenon. Few would give up the convenience and social prestige ("keeping up with the Tanakas") of a domestic bath, but many long for the neighborhood cohesiveness, social mores, and sociability nostalgically associated with the sentō.

Despite a certain sense of loss associated with once-common bathing practices, Japanese are mostly pleased with the modern developments that have made bathing more convenient and sanitary. They have willingly, even eagerly, adopted modern innovations into this aspect of their everyday lives, an accommodation that has been an ongoing process for centuries.

To foreigners, for whom bathing with members of the opposite sex (or sometimes the same sex) is a highly sexualized experience, the lack of eroticism associated with a Japanese bath, whether at home, sentō, or onsen, is somewhat surprising. Although bathing with others in Japan normally occurs in an atmosphere of sexual nonchalance, the bath or, more accurately, nudity in Japan does have erotic connotations. This association is immediately apparent in movies, paintings, illustrations, photographs, comics, and television shows.

Eroticism and bathing have been explicitly related in Japan for many years, as is easily demonstrated by the number of *ukiyoe* (wood-block) prints and paintings portraying women at the bath. Another example is the large number of baths *(yunafuro)* in the early Tokugawa period attended by females who were often prostitutes. These yunafuro have a modern counterpart known as "soaplands" where a variety of erotic massage is available along with the bath. Soaplands flourished after World War II, at which time they were known as "Turkish baths." In the early 1980s, in response to vigorous objections by Turks, proprietors changed the name of these baths to the current term, soapland. Still, soaplands are an exceptional kind of bath, symbolically and legally in a category separate from sentō.

One form of mixed bathing—parents or other adults with children—is emphatically nonerotic. As mentioned, preadolescent children of either sex may bathe on either the men's or the women's side of a sentō, without embarrassment to the children or the adults. Young children, according to the Japanese, are presexual or innocent. At home, also, children regularly bathe with parents, grandparents, or older siblings of either sex. These bathing experiences are thought to create a special bond between parent and child (Lebra 1976).

Adults bathing in mixed-sex circumstances or peeking into women's baths are another matter. Advertisements, movies, and television shows provide titillating glimpses of women's baths. A weekly situation comedy set in a sentō was extremely successful and frequently featured scenes of men bursting into the women's bath (in reality a rare occurrence) and the embarrassment and resolution—usually comical—of the situation. The sexuality in these scenes, while subdued, is apparent and illustrates that bathing is at least minimally connected to sexuality.

In older sentō peeking sometimes occurs. Upon entering, the customer pays a fee to the attendant who is seated between the men's and women's dressing area, with a view into both. Men are especially noted for looking surreptitiously past the attendant into the women's dressing area. Many newer or remodeled sentō often have screens placed in such a way that peeking is not possible, and some new sentō are proud of their modern lobbies with the attendant behind a desk at the entrance, in the same manner as a hotel. These recent developments reflect changing attitudes toward the appropriateness of nudity.

After the demise of mixed-sex sentō, the only public facilities allowing such bathing are onsen. Although virtually all onsen were at one time mixed-sex, in recent decades most resorts have provided separate facilities for men and women. Indeed, many Japanese have never participated in mixed-sex bathing and express embarrassment at the possibility. Although the image has changed in the recent decade, for several years onsen were characterized as places for men to play with prostitutes or to take young women for possible sexual relations. Such was not the case previously, when families and tour groups were frequent visitors. Today, onsen are once again seen as appropriate places for families and travelers.

Mixed-sex bathing continues at some hot springs. An organization has even been created to preserve this traditional mode of bathing. Older people often participate in mixed-sex bathing, but many younger people also frequent such baths, the atmosphere of which is congenial and open. Many bathers express the opinion that the mixed-sex bath offers the most equality and friendliness. The inherent eroticism of the experience is carefully suppressed through postures and other behavior calculated to avoid overt sexuality. Offenders are avoided or asked to leave. Those who arrive at the bath hoping for an erotic experience are invariably disappointed.

Although Japanese may acknowledge and enjoy a certain amount of sexuality at the bath, they prefer to focus upon the physical and social pleasures of bathing. Caudill (1962) suggests that Japanese ignore, exclude, or isolate the sexuality that may occur in these situations to assure the continued existence of bathing and its pleasures. Nonetheless, mixed-sex bathing has certainly decreased as Japanese feelings about the appropriateness of such activities have changed. Many Japanese doubt that a future exists for mixed-sex bathing at onsen. Most who participate feel that it would be a great loss, akin to the loss of sentō, should it disappear.

Bathing in Japan is, of course, much more than its mere material manifestations. It involves notions of status, purity, cleanliness, and bonding through naked association (*hadaka no tsukiai*).

Hadaka no tsukiai is felt to be an important means of bonding between individuals within a group. The relationship of parents to children is especially enhanced by bathing together—commonly known as "skinship" (*sukinshippu*). Other groups, from businessmen or neighboring housewives to hikers and classmates, often seek to increase the strength of a relationship by engaging in hadaka no tsukiai at a sentō, health center, or onsen. The practice is so pervasive that members often give it no conscious thought and may overlook it when describing the group's activities. For many groups, if hadaka no tsukiai is neglected, members begin to feel that something important is lacking from the communal relationship.

For many contemporary Japanese, bathing, whether at home, a sentō, or an onsen, has something to do with feeling Japanese. As Japanese began to travel outside their country, they came to see their daily bath as exotic, as something distinctively Japanese. In his 1914 book, for example, Fujimoto makes an explicit comparison of Japanese bathing habits to those of others: "Bathing seems to be neither the habit of the German race nor of the Chinese. . . . The Europeans are compelled to take [a] bath in order to clean off the filth. . . . If there is no necessity to bath, they are glad to be without bathing; but on the contrary, bathing of the Japanese is far beyond the simple object of cleaning their body" (70). As indicated by this statement, in the early part of this century Fujimoto and his countrymen were already concerned with the question of what it means to be Japanese, and for them the bath was part of the answer.

The notion of equating bathing with being Japanese was expressed in a 1932 tourist magazine: "To keep the body always clean is one of the national characteristics of the Japanese" (Japan Travel Bureau 1932, 59). Fukuda Ippei (1934) described the nature of Japanese people as follows: "Either consciously or subconsciously, there runs throughout the nation a 'philosophy of the bathtubs' which is as fully alive in the minds of men of leisure as in those of common workers" (118). He further implied a certain superiority in the Japanese way of bathing: "Love of humanity irrespective of race and nationality may well be born of the state of mind which is generated within the moist and dripping walls of a Japanese public bath-house" (119).

Since the early 1980s, onsen have experienced a boom as attractive sites for vacations and business meetings. This renaissance has been spurred by mass media campaigns urging a rediscovery of Japan and the (Japanese) self via domestic tourism (Ivy 1988). Onsen offer guests this chance to feel Japanese.

The owner of a hot spring resort suggested to me that as young Japanese travel abroad and become acquainted with the wider world, their curiosity about their own culture is piqued. They seek to satisfy this curiosity by learning more about and experiencing the "real Japan." Two important elements of their cultural identity, in his opinion, are an appreciation of Japan's natural beauty and the experience of social bathing. And this, of course, along with a menu of regional traditional delicacies, is just what the onsen offers.

Newspapers and magazines strengthen the connection between bathing and identity with frequent articles on bathing and hot springs. These essays generally begin with a statement like: "It is said that of all the peoples of the world, Japanese love bathing the most." An exhibit of a model reconstruction of a Tokugawa-era bathhouse in Tokyo during 1988 was advertised with a large poster depicting scenes of contemporary bathhouses and a large red script proclaiming, "Bath-Loving Japanese" (*Ofuro Daisuki Nihonjin*).

Bathing in a particular manner may even lessen the perceived foreignness of non-Japanese.[2] One evening at a remote mountain onsen, for example, an elderly couple and I were the last guests in the bath. The gentleman stated that I apparently enjoyed bathing in such circumstances. When I replied that I did, he commented that I must genuinely understand Japan's "heart" (*Nihon no kokoro*), indicating a closeness or decreased foreignness.

This connection of the Japanese bath to Japaneseness became even clearer when, while returning from this trip to my home in Tokyo, I saw a large billboard advertising a hot spring resort with an illustration of a person soaking in a tub and the words *Kokoro no Furusato* in large script. *Kokoro,* meaning heart, spirit, or mind, is the same word as in the phrase above. *Furusato* denotes one's natal home but signifies as well the traditional and the old, the real Japan and Japanese ways. Together, the words nostalgically evoke the past and explicitly connect Japanese culture with a particular manner of bathing. This most ordinary of daily behavior has thus become extraordinary in the construction of Japanese cultural identity.

During the past few centuries, Japanese baths and bathing practices have changed dramatically in response to modernization and to exposure to foreign materials and customs. And yet the Japanese bath, in its various forms, is perceived as quintessentially Japanese. The traditional steam bath was replaced by a tub of hot water; the wooden bath became tile or plastic (or a cast-iron tub became a stainless steel one); the wooden basin and stool became plastic; the rice bran was replaced by soap; showers, shampoo, and terry-cloth towels were added; and mixed-sex bathing became less common. But the adoption of these foreign goods and practices has not transformed a traditional practice into a modern one. As Japanese have come to see themselves from the point of view of the Other, the once-ordinary bath has become a marker of the Japanese people's extraordinary Japaneseness.

NOTES

1. *Sentō* is the most commonly used word for public bathhouse, although a more accurate one, *kōshūyokujō,* appears in official documents.
2. Failure to observe proper, sometimes subtle, bathing etiquette will accentuate the foreignness.

REFERENCES

Caudill, William. 1962. Patterns of emotion in modern Japan. In Robert J. Smith and Richard K. Beardsley (eds.), *Japanese culture: Its development and characteristics.* Chicago: Aldine.

Fujimoto T. 1914. *The nightside of Japan.* Philadelphia: J. B. Lippincott.

Fukuda Ippei. 1934. *New sketches of men and life.* Tokyo: Kenkyusha Press.

Ivy, Marilyn. 1988. Tradition and difference in the Japanese mass media. *Public Culture Bulletin* 1(1):21–29.

Japan Travel Bureau. 1932. *The Tourist* 20:9.

Kelly, William W. 1986. Rationalization and nostalgia: Cultural dynamics of new middle-class Japan. *American Ethnologist* 13(4):603–618.

Lebra, Takie Sugiyama. 1976. *Japanese patterns of behavior.* Honolulu: University Press of Hawaii.

Leutner, Robert W. 1985. *Shikitei Sanba and the comic tradition in Edo fiction.* Cambridge: Council on East Asian Studies, Harvard University, and Harvard-Yenshing Institute.

McFee, Malcolm. 1975. The 150% Man: A product of blackfeet acculturation. In Ivan A. Brady and Barry L. Isaac (eds.), *A reader in culture change,* vol. 2, 13–38. New York: John Wiley.

Ochiai Shigeru. 1984. *Arau fūzokushi* (History of washing customs). Tokyo: Matsukisha.

Ōba Osamu. 1986. *Monogatari mono no kenchikushi: Furo no hanashi* (Narrative of the construction history of things: Story of the bath). Tokyo: Kashima Shuppankai.

Smith, George. 1861. *Ten weeks in Japan.* London: Longman, Green, Longman, and Roberts.

Smith, Robert J. 1990. Something old, something new: Tradition and culture in the study of Japan. *Journal of Asian Studies* 48(4):715–723.

Statistics Bureau. 1987. *Japan statistical yearbook,* 37th ed. Tokyo: Management and Coordination Agency.

Zenkoku Kōshūyokujōgyō Kankyōeisei Dōgyōkumiai Rengōkai (National Association of Public Bathhouse Environmental Hygiene Trade Associations) (eds.). 1973. *Kōshū-yokujoshi* (History of public bathhouses). Tokyo: Zenkoku Kōshūyokujōgyō Kankyōeisei Dōgyōkumiai Rengōkai.

· · · · ·

6

IMAGES OF THE WEST: HOME STYLE IN JAPANESE MAGAZINES

NANCY ROSENBERGER

The search for status in contemporary Japan is closely linked to home buying and decorating in Western style. "Prestige!" "Urbanist!" "High Society!" "Rank One-Up!" "Status of the Next Century!"—these and other English words and phrases, written in *katakana,* are sprawled across advertisements for houses, apartments, and home furnishings.[1] Although soaring land prices have slowed the building of new homes and large additions, home renovation on a smaller scale is common "to improve the quality of one's life-style" (*Keizai Kikakuchō* 1989, 72–73).

"Life-style" and "catalog" (home redecorating) magazines have burgeoned in the past ten years in Japan, introducing consumers to a variety of westernized items that promise to create an "independent life-style"—a concept that guides consumer choice in today's Japan.[2] No longer bound by obligatory relations, individuals can live as they choose, expressing their identities in the marketplace, where their consumer selections become signs of their unique tastes.

Jean Baudrillard and Pierre Bourdieu have argued that in cultures of late capitalism, consumer choices, more than income, legitimate status and define class. "Through objects, each individual and each group searches out his/her place in an order, all the while trying to jostle this order according to a personal trajectory" (Baudrillard 1981, 38). Consumer choice is a "production of signs" (83 n. 24) that distinguishes one person from another, not as individuals but as members of classes enjoying different status levels. Bourdieu (1984) describes how people with inadequate money (economic capital) simulate the tastes (cultural capital) of the higher classes they aspire to. In Japanese home decorating, Western styles are generally a mark of status; the purchase of a wooden door with arched windows or a big refrigerator is a sign that announces to the world, "I am wealthy and cosmopolitan." Those who cover old tatami with carpeting are also speaking in a code that testifies to their class aspirations, although they also may be signifying a "rhetoric of despair" that whispers their inability to move as far as they would like (Baudrillard 1981, 41).

Home magazines display a growing variety of items, in response—government sources say—to the demand for increased choice by more sophisticated consumers (*Keizai Kikakuchō* 1989, 57). A complex system links producers, media, consumers, and government in the formation of interior design tastes. This chapter emphasizes the media's role. Together, and with the government's blessing, magazines and "makers" (as housing companies are called) produce and nurture the consumers they need to sustain an expanding domestic business. They sell not only furnishings but also status through consumption.

Japanese home magazines target aspiring and wealthy classes in different ways. The aspiring classes are made up of workers on a daily treadmill who have high hopes but little likelihood of significant promotion. Magazines present the argument that by redecorating a rented apartment in Western style, a housewife in this group can improve family relationships and find self-fulfillment while augmenting her family's cultural capital and social rank. To the wealthy classes—those in which the head of the household has reached a position of power, prestige, and high salary—media and makers promise that home renovation and building will result in more opportunity for self-expression and greater privacy within families.

For both groups, Western styles and goods hold the promise of Western-style relationships. Westernization of the home indicates a move from feudal relations, associated with obligation and hierarchy, to democratic relations, characterized by choice. Freed from the restraint of hierarchical households (*ie*), contemporary Japanese consumers can create family dwellings (*sumai*) of pleasure and relaxation.

107

Some would argue that what the Japanese government is heralding as a "new stage in consumer demand" is in fact the production of individuals with needs that can be satisfied only by consumption (Baudrillard 1981, 82). Unlike their parents, such individuals find identity not through participation in a pattern of reciprocal obligation but through the goods they purchase. The emergence of such a concept of the individual stands in contrast to conceptions of the Japanese self invested in context and relationship (Rosenberger 1989). I shall return to tensions raised by this conflict in the conclusion.

Subtly opposing the Western styles pictured in magazines is the Japanese style, which these days is associated with poverty, old people, and bumpkins. Japanese poverty is hard for Westerners to grasp, because it receives little publicity and because foreigners rarely meet the poor. When I lived in Tokyo ten years ago, I knew a family of four who lived in one eighty-square-foot room, covered in worn tatami, in a barracks-like apartment building. They shared sinks, countertop burners, and nonflush squatting toilets with others in the building. They slept and ate in their room, putting out a foldable low eating table during the day and cotton-filled mats (futon) at night. They bathed in the nearby *sentō* (public bath; see Clark, this volume).

People decorating their homes for status want to set themselves apart definitively from the poor. They expect private, flush, sit-down toilets, sinks, a bath, a refrigerator, and cooking facilities. They also want more room; but for the aspiring classes, most of whom live in rented apartments, the average household space in 1989 was only 150 square feet (*Keizai Kikakuchō* 1989, 71). The aspiring want some Western-style furniture, such as a dining set and a couch, but not necessarily beds, which take up precious space during the day.

In addition to differentiating themselves from the poor, aspiring classes seek to disassociate themselves from the Japanese-style houses in which most of them grew up. The most characteristically Japanese features of interior design are tatami, *shōji,* and *fusuma.* Tatami are two-inch-thick mats, approximately three feet wide and six feet long. (Rooms are measured according to the number of tatami they hold.) Shōji, the sliding screen doors in tatami rooms, are covered by two wooden frames, one containing glass, the other translucent rice paper, often imprinted with designs of maple leaves or waves. The shoji dim the light that shines in on the tatami. Fusuma, the sliding panels that function as the doors and walls of tatami rooms, are made of thick paper with a band of subtle design across the middle. Because these panels easily lift out, whole walls can be removed to make space for large gatherings.

Tatami rooms usually have a *kotatsu,* a low square or rectangular table, encircled by pillows for sitting on the floor. In the winter these tables are a popular gathering spot as family members tuck their feet under the blanket draped over the table and into the warmth created by a traditional charcoal pit or, these days, by an electric heating unit attached to the table.

Fancy tatami rooms feature a *tokonoma,* a wood-floored alcove, displaying a scroll, flower arrangement, or household treasure. Near the tokonoma people often install a Buddhist altar (*butsudan*), a carved closet housing ancestors' pictures and tablets (Plath 1964).

Formal tatami rooms have a sparse appearance, but those in daily use often become quite cluttered. A six-mat room that is lived in and slept in, like the downstairs tatami room where my friend's parents slept, would be filled during the day with a low table, a *tansu* (a dresser that the wife brings as dowry for her clothes), and a *chadansu* (a chest for tea cups and bowls). Futon stored during the day in deep closets that border the room are spread out at night, virtually eliminating walking space.

In a traditional Japanese house, a series of concentric circles go from inside to outside, signifying private to public and pure to impure. Inner tatami rooms have a symbolic purity because no footwear is worn there. These rooms are bounded by areas of wood flooring where slippers are worn—halls, kitchen, veranda, and sometimes a guest parlor. These areas in turn are bordered by stone and dirt in the entryway and garden. A fence and gate form the perimeter of the household. Advisers on auspicious directions place the tatami rooms in the south so that good spirits and sunlight can flow in, and the impure kitchen and toilet in a dark northeasterly direction.

Even before World War II, higher-status urban homes boasted a parlor, a Western room with wood floors, hinged door, glass windows, and a couch. It was located off the front hall, on the periphery of an essentially Japanese private life.

Status seekers are determined to distance themselves from such traditional interior arrangements, but many families of the aspiring classes are living in circumstances uncomfortably reminiscent of their pasts, in tiny apartments consisting of two or three small tatami rooms and a dining-kitchen area. One significant difference is the location of the kitchen, now brought in from the margins to the center, into a space called the *DK* (dining-kitchen) or *LDK* (living-dining-kitchen), which is floored with wood, tile, or carpeting. Prefabricated housing of this style was introduced in the impoverished postwar period. Units known as *2DK* and *3DK* (two or three tatami rooms plus a dining-kitchen area) continue to be built in crowded urban areas, where they become rental units for the aspiring classes.

Magazines such as *Hōmu Cōdii,* (Home Coordy, hereafter *HC)* and *Utsukushii Heya,* (Beautiful Room, hereafter *UH)* target housewives aspiring to a higher class through the hard work of their salaried husbands.[3] These women lack the economic capital to change their life-styles significantly, but they have the education and energy to imitate higher-status life-styles in interior design. They hope to learn from these magazines how to give the appearance of class through the self-conscious creation of an "interior"—"something made, not inherited" (*UH* 1988, 174). Desiring, but not really expecting, to join the ranks of the privi-leged and powerful, they reject Japanese styles for Western ones, but their efforts are confined to inadequate imitation by their modest fi-nancial and cultural resources.

That the readers have little money to invest in home decoration is implicit in the presentations of these magazines. Prices for small items are sometimes listed, but the overall cost of a redecorating project is seldom mentioned. Redecorating requires "hardly any expense" if it is done "gradually, piece by piece, born from a vision held for many years" (*HC* 1988, 1).

Most of the readers are high school or junior college graduates who have six or more years of English as cultural capital to invest in reading the English words sprinkled throughout advertisements and articles. Readers can add to this cultural capital by studying the vocabulary of the magazines' mini-courses in interior decoration—"ottoman," "blind," "fireplace."

Rather than producing a desire that cannot be satisfied for expensive large-scale renovation, these magazines urge shaping an interior through ingenuity and grit. The lead article in a 1990 issue of *Utsukushii Heya* pits twenty housewives in a redecorating competition, with readers as judges. A woman earns status by working harder and using her wits more effectively than the next housewife. In these aspiring classes, still closely identified with the industriousness of the poor and the middling classes, comfort and style are rationalized by hard work.

These aspiring housewives mask the old-fashioned dullness of their rented 2DK and 3DK apartments by covering the quintessential markings of Japanese decor with Western goods and surfaces. The first items to disappear are the tatami, shōji, and fusuma. "Create a 'one-room open space,' " a magazine writer suggests. By taking out the sliding panels that divide tatami rooms, housewives make a larger space that seems Western, connecting the wood-floored kitchen with the tatami dining and living areas. They cover tatami with rugs or, more stylishly, with "wood carpets" that unroll to resemble hardwood floors. Shoji are removed, and curtains hung in their place. Westernness is confirmed by the addition of a couch, dining set, VCR, and stereo. In the words of one magazine,

> Wife Yuki-san, who is dreaming of playing on a couch with a cute child, wished for a Western-style living room to relax in. She was shocked when she moved in to learn that all three rooms of her 3DK were tatami. She really wanted Western style. So first she put up lace curtains and spread a "wood carpet." She covered a sofa with a floral print. She thought this would be enough to make it Western, but she still wasn't quite convinced. So as if to bury the loneliness of the [childless] room, she added an elegant flowered carpet and finally she was satisfied. (*UH* 1990, 32)

Unable to make fundamental transformations, the readers are encouraged to define themselves through redundancy—that is, by covering the already covered and by endlessly repeating the Western motif. In some homes, large lace doilies adorn the tops of pianos, dressers, and couches. Dressers and remaining fusuma are covered with pieces of material or "roll screens" (blinds). In the extreme, a floral or checkerboard pattern is used to cover the whole interior, wrapping toasters, microwaves, pillows, and cabinet doors.

Western style is also represented in these magazines by the myriad of small but significant Western items appearing in each photo. Readers gaze upon Western-style tea pots with cups and saucers, potted plants, French lithographs, cuckoo clocks, and large stuffed facsimiles of the Seven Dwarfs. Ideally, these nonfunctional accessories are handmade, a testimony to the housewife's effort and virtue. If the Western item is expensive, it is functional, with a flair—a large, bright yellow refrigerator, high-backed chairs, a purple toaster, a green microwave. The entries in the housewife competition show little understanding of actual Western styles, but the magazines challenge readers to learn to distin-

The kitchen of a middle-class housewife aspiring to higher status. (Photo from Utsukushii Heya, vol. 14, no. 72 [1990]: 30; reproduced by permission.)

guish and imitate natural, pop, urban country, casual, high-tech, sporty, Santa Fe, and New York motifs.

The magazines use other subtle devices. Folksy language makes readers feel they too can improve their lives through redecorating. "Why, with just a little use of cloth and with little things, you can make a 'country' atmosphere." The culturally atypical use of first names fosters a feeling of intimacy: "Riko-san has a bag of tricks for creating rooms. With her sparkling energy, she transforms an inadequate apartment into a relaxing home" (*UH* 1990, 12).

Almost every issue suggests that the secret to a perfect interior is storage. The key words are *seiri seiton,* organization and cleanliness. It looks easy as the reader learns of the ingenious ways Yoko has devised to store books and clothes in old futon closets, and Michiko to organize her stylish clothes in tansu drawers. Such endeavors create a "pleasurable space" and in doing so spread virtue because "though the parent doesn't force it on the child, the child learns the joy of decorating and putting things away" (*UH* 1990, 88).

These magazines link Western interior design with Western-style relationships, as understood by the Japanese. In the housewives competition, the ultimate goal is the establishment of a feeling of "our house" (*wa ga ie*), consisting of a close-knit nuclear family. Successful redecoration should draw the busy father and husband into the family circle. Hisako's redecorating satisfied "her husband's strong wish for a 'simple interior' despite her own preference for 'being surrounded by things.' . . . Three years ago she put in a 'cushion floor' and her husband painted the walls white. This clean-lined, pleasurable place attests that this is a wife with heartfelt understanding of what the concept of 'our house' is all about" (*UH* 1990, 22). Mayumi's industrious redecorating made her "no-touch" (no housework) husband into one who could not resist painting and wallpapering on Sundays. Kayako "made a space which will warm the brief time that children have with their father" (24). Sachiko made a place for her husband and herself to relax together, even with three energetic children.

Redecorating Western-style promises happier children with better grades and closer ties to parents. Mizue created a study area for her son who was preparing for the entrance exam to high school, prompting him to say, "My cramming time seems happy now" (*UH* 1990, 21). Sachiko's efforts gave her young children a space in which to run and make noise. Yukiko opened up space between the kitchen and playroom so that she can watch her toddler as he plays. Another young mother reports, "We now have an open space that the children can grow in. We can share all of each other's joys and troubles" (36).

The clearest indicator of the new style of family relationships to be achieved by Western redecorating is the absence of elderly parents and in-laws. The home magazines that target the aspiring classes avoid referring to relationships that have strongly hierarchical and obligatory elements or produce emotional hardship. They focus instead on voluntary ties based on warmth and fun. The Western-style home produces bonds that are unfettered (*kaihōteki*). As Japanese panels are taken down, so are the walls of restraint that enclose a woman's heart when she lives with elders or with a tyrannical husband. The magazines garnish their articles and advertisements with words that imply pleasure and relaxation. Through redecorating, space becomes "enjoyable" (*tano-shii*), "comfortable" (*kokochiyoi*), "agreeable" (*kaiteki*), and "relaxing" (*kutsurogi aru*). Each of these interchangeable terms suggests a space in which people can enjoy themselves in the kind of intimacy Japanese have seen for years on dubbed rebroadcasts of "Father Knows Best," "The Brady Bunch," and "The Cosby Show." Interior decorating is like "walking into an American home drama" (*UH* 1990, 90).

Home redecorating is the "first step to finding fulfillment as a housewife." Atsuko's new Western-style living room is a place where her friends can come to enjoy a cup of coffee or tea. "She has just moved into the neighborhood, but with her pleasant place to entertain, she has already developed a group of friends" (10). Another woman is shown serving coffee to a group of friends from behind her handmade coffee bar, using her personal collection of Western coffee cups. She has made it, for "the gourmet person is one-rank-up" (*HC* 1989, 116). Successful redecorators can even use their Western-style homes to earn money. In *Utsukushii Heya*, housewives, taking advantage of their newly decorated interiors, are shown teaching English to children, distributing health food, and selling handmade goods in a home boutique.

Individuality (*kosei*) is the central idea behind the magazines' promises of close family ties, freely chosen friends and work, and higher social status. Individuality is associated with expressing personal tastes (*kodawari*, literally, what one is "stuck on") and secret yearnings (*akogare*). Decorating allows a woman to express the whims of her "spirit, just as it is" (*kimama*). A message on the inside cover of *Hōmu Cōdii* (1988) reads, "I want to live by 'my own color' . . . a life that expresses a likeness of myself [*jibunrashisa*]." Purples and greens in carpets, refrigerators, or couches almost always elicit the caption "Individual."

Individuality does not necessarily suggest social isolation or asocial behavior. Expressions of individual preference are frowned upon in formal, hierarchical groups but are welcomed in intimate social situations in which emotional closeness is favored over hierarchy. The expression of strong individual tastes is not new to Japanese culture, but it is now privileged by the political economy, for it is just such individual consumer preferences and desires that the maturing domestic economy needs for its next stage of expansion. Home decorating magazines nurture the concept of consumers expressing individuality by creating unique life-styles through the purchase of goods. They mute the note of selfishness by linking the consumption of personally desired items with closer relations to family members and friends.

In the aspiring classes, the housewife is clearly the central consumer for the home. The ideas associated with interior design—Western-style comfort, individuality, and egalitarian, voluntary relationships—are associated to a great extent with women. But, ironically, by containing consumption within the home women of the aspiring classes limit the penetration of these new concepts into the larger society. Their consumption serves the needs of the political economy to expand domestic spending while allowing men to spend most of their time and energy in the hierarchical, group-oriented arena where goods are produced and sold.

For many years, Western-style has been associated not only with status and individuality but also with *gōritekisa,* rationality and functionality (see Kelly 1986 and this volume). In the postwar period, the emphasis was on improving life by supplying each home with "necessary" goods—a small refrigerator, a vacuum cleaner, a water heater, a small black-and-white television set. Although efficiency and rationality are still highly valued in contemporary Japan, "style" and "fulfillment" are increasingly the focus of consumer desire. Magazines sell renovations and goods that "improve the quality of life"—with the government's approval (*Keizai Kikakuchō* 1989, 50).

Home magazines for the aspiring classes often recommend complementing the rationality of Western furnishings and appliances by reintroducing touches of Japanese form and style. As a writer in *Hōmu Cōdii* puts it,

> Our westernization has been amazing. The kitchen, toilet, and bath have been so thoroughly westernized that they are now easy to use and keep clean. But could it not be said that westernization has run its course? As we've become more concerned with leisure, we've begun to notice that relaxing on the floor ["floor life"], much as we were used to in the past, is best. The West is functional and rational, but from now on the emphasis will be on adding Japanese feeling [*wa kankaku*]. (1989, 21)

Photos of a Western room, with wood flooring and a leather couch, extending into a tatami room with shōji carry the caption "Western rationality and Japanese luxury [*zeitakusa*]" (*HC* 1989, 24). Another article refers to the West's "boastful self-ism and casualness," which can be offset by inserting Japanese style with its quiet design and color that expresses the "heart's luxury" (*HC* 1988, 13).

The reassertion of Japanese style is important in the political economy of contemporary Japan because it introduces the ideas of luxury, relaxation, and stability in shockingly familiar terms. Home redecorators are encouraged to go back to their roots, but this time tatami, shōji, and *ofuro* represent not the impoverished, feudal past but the pleasurable, individualized life-style of the future.

For the aspiring classes, whose lives are still close to the drudgery and poverty of the immediate postwar era, this reinsertion of Japanese style must be carefully manipulated. One method is by appealing to the close family relationships associated with Japan's past. Another is by introducing items reflecting a mixed Japanese-Western style. One article, for example, suggests reintroducing the kotatsu (the low warming table) into the westernized home, because the kotatsu brings together friends and family, among whom there is no restraint. Photos show new shapes and designs for kotatsu covered with blankets of Western design and fabrics (*HC* 1988, 42). Other Japanese-Western hybrids include neon-colored chopstick holders, mink-lined futon, and feather-stuffed futon from Poland.

Reintroduced Japanese style raises status a rung higher by championing comfort and beauty over rationality, and simplicity over gaudiness. The style is associated with the core characteristics by which Japanese distinguish themselves from Westerners: quiet assuredness over noisy self-assertion, respect for ritual over self-indulgent casualness, and commitment over shallow, easily severed relationships.

The home decorating industry gives special attention to DINKS (couples with "double income and no kids"). This short phase in the Japanese family life cycle is a key time for establishing lifetime consumption habits. This is the group that will lead Japan into an era in which personal consumption promises to take on "cosmic value" (Baudrillard 1983, 149).

Although the magazine *Futari no Sumai* (A Dwelling for Two) concentrates on the wife, the husband's participation in decorating is strongly encouraged.[4] At the very least, he is pictured sitting alongside his wife in a redecorated apartment, a romantic mate in a leisured life. In some lauded cases, the husband has actually designed a whole house with a masculine touch. A rustic wood cabin is decorated with tools and equipment. Another house features a billiard table in the living room, with a tatami room in the background.

Rifōmu Jitsurei 1000 (Reform, 1000 Examples) devotes a fourth of its pages to remodeling apartments of under three hundred square feet.[5] The well-to-do owners of these urban dwellings make major alterations with the help of architects and outside contractors. Some spend as little as four thousand dollars, some as much as sixty thousand dollars. The redecorating invariably leans toward Western styles, but with a flair and luxury beyond the reach of the aspiring classes. The young urbanites described in the articles add distinction to their homes by creating, for example, a purple computer room, a kitchen with see-through counters, or a bedroom with a wood floor raised several feet for storage underneath. Spotlights set off hardwood floors and unusual furnishings: a table too high for floor sitting and too short for chair sitting; a triangular table with chrome legs. Colors are monotone; rooms are accented sparingly, with a Balinese puppet or a Persian screen. The simplicity of these tiny but convenient apartments clearly differentiates them from the redundancy characteristic of the aspiring but stagnant classes (Baudrillard 1981, 34).

THE WEALTHY CLASSES

The wealthy classes' most characteristic sign of status is the size of their dwellings, which cost two to four million dollars—exclusive of the land. Houses in central Tokyo, where land prices are astronomical, are typically seven hundred square feet or more; most also have small gardens and large gates. The style is again Western, but designers of homes for the wealthy eschew the suburban style identified with American television families and turn instead to the Italian and French—whom designers consider arbiters of style and class. Marble and gold-accented interiors are described in such foreign words as "aristocratic," "classical," and "smart."

Designers often exaggerate familiar Western styles, taking them into the realm of the superluxurious, superfunctional, and supermodern. Maker companies, architects, interior designers, and magazine writers present homes which suggest that Japanese consumers outclass and outrank not only their aspiring countrymen but the middle classes of other nations as well. After all, modern Japanese enjoy the best of both

A wealthy housewife in her ultramodern kitchen. (Photo from Rifōmu Jitsurei
1000, *February 1990, p. 74; reproduced by permission.)*

worlds: the high technology of the West combined with the high grace
of Japanese style.

High-tech terms such as "rationalization," "systemization," and "total coordination" are used to appeal to these wealthy classes. Currently,
the most highly advertised part of the home is the "system kitchen"
with matching drawers and cupboards, tile counters, and the latest gadgets. "Grade-up" equipment such as built-in ovens and ranges, dish-
washers, and side-by-side refrigerator-freezers are featured.

Along with the system kitchen comes "system storage"—built-in closets in bedrooms and hallways in which to store Western-style clothes,
shoes, and bedding. Pantries under the kitchen floor provide extra space
to keep the kitchen "pure and organized."

A multiple-cycle washer and an electric dryer, still rare for the aspiring
classes but a necessity for the wealthy, are placed in a special room just
off the kitchen. People of high status prefer convenience to the econ-
omizing mentality of middle-class housewives, who locate their washers

A modern toilet, equipped
with refreshing scents.

near the *furo* (bath) in order to use the still-warm bathwater from the night before for the morning wash.

"System baths" create a "functional, enjoyable, pretty life that is easy on the housewife" (*Sumai no Sekkei* 1990, 145).[6] One article tells of a couple who searched through countless stores and catalogs for the perfect yellow-and-black faucet and shower head from Italy to be the "points" of their black-and-white bathroom. The top-of-the-line system bath includes computerized controls that allow the housewife to preset the desired water temperature and level for individual family members, who, even in the wealthy classes, still bathe one after another in the same bathwater (see Clark, this volume).

Toilets continue to be located in separate rooms but are now brought into the high-tech world under the banner "sanitary." Toilet seats are heated, even in the homes of the aspiring classes, but the wealthy outdo them with space-age toilets featuring a control panel: push one button to spray your derriere with a built-in bidet nozzle; push another button to control the water temperature, and yet another to aim the bidet stream. Some models even release fragrances, which erase all memory of the nonflush toilets of the recent past.

"Home automation" (*HA*) is another trendy feature. From a central control panel, home owners can switch lights on and off, lock and unlock doors, and open and close shutters. HA provides home security, "tele-control" (telephone control), and "intahon" (intercoms). The security system contacts fire or police and allows a housewife or elderly family member to call a "safety pro" by pushing a button on a device worn around the neck. The telecontrol system permits the home owner to call home to turn lights on or off, heat the bath, or turn on the rice cooker—"Good if both of you are working or if you live alone in the city." The intahon connects all phones in the house and enables one to call home and listen to sounds in a room where a child or elderly parent may be alone. It includes a cordless feature "that allows busy people to talk from the toilet" (*Sumai no Sekkei* 1990, 181–185). HA does not yet run the "central cleaner," but this feature nevertheless rationalizes the life of the "lively working 'Mrs.' " who can vacuum noiselessly so as to not wake a napping baby or husband by using hoses built into each room and connected to a central motor and disposal tank (*Rifōmu* 1990, 102).

In living rooms, dining rooms, and bedrooms, the emphasis turns from superfunctionality to superluxury. Living rooms either are carpeted in wool or have wood flooring and are furnished with large coffee tables, couches, and stuffed chairs. Bedrooms are also carpeted, with large mirrors and two single beds or a double bed for the "ideal couple," now freed from sleeping with children.

Entertaining takes place in a dining room that blends into a living room, with adjoining kitchen. Though generally hidden from view, the kitchen is clean and organized so that it can be seen by guests without embarrassment. Divisions of the traditional Japanese house that pro-ceeded gradually outward from private toward public space have given way to a bifurcation into private areas, where the nuclear family sleeps, bathes, and relaxes, and public areas, for hosting friends and acquain-tances. Because guests can now be entertained in the living-dining room, the public space has increased. But the public space has decreased in another sense, as verandas and dirt-floored entrance ways to the kitchen that once provided places to chat with workmen and neighbors have disappeared.

Makers and architects are busy creating new solutions to the layout of public and private space. In one maker's model home, an "FF plan" is proposed, in which the house is divided into Family and Friends zones. From each side of the kitchen extend paired living rooms, one dimly lit, with a grand piano and heavy European table and chairs, the other brightly lit, with large colored pillows on a gray couch facing a television. "The basic theme is to spend life pleasurably, to develop, to round out 'relations' with family, friends, acquaintances, society, and nature" (*Rifōmu* 1990, 104).

Another approach is the "twin family" house where three generations live "like neighbors under one roof" (*Rifōmu* 1990, 108). The older couple lives downstairs in tatami rooms, with a big Japanese-style table "so they can invite the younger family over for dinner." The younger couple and their children live upstairs in Western style with an even larger dining table "for entertaining their friends." Friends are brought into the inner sanctum, whereas elders, who once had free access to private rooms, are kept in the house but at arm's length. Grandparents, who are deliberately not mentioned in magazines for the aspiring classes, are back in the picture here, but carefully compartmentalized. The wealthy classes thus fulfill their duties to the elderly while avoiding feudal family relationships.

In a third model home, a maker suggests that family members interact like friends in a house that encourages relations through "privacy pres- ervation." In place of a living room, the plan provides for a "gathering room," a site for mingling while living individualized lives free of mutual obligation (*Rifōmu* 1990, 100). Another article presents the same theme: "With a big family, where there is little time to meet and you often miss each other, you need a big space where you can keep an eye on each other while you work, talk lightly, and lend a hand if needed. . . . The feeling is one of a 'free flexible family.' " Here is a house that is "rational for housework and adaptable to no one being home" yet also "improves the quality of interpersonal contact" (*Rifōmu* 1990, 102).

In magazines targeting the wealthy, the housewife is almost invisible. When she is mentioned, the reference is often to her "busy life," which necessitates greater rationalization of housework. When wealthy house- wives appear, it is as professional dilettantes, as in the case of a "kitchen pro" who teaches cooking classes in her spacious kitchen. If they decorate their houses, they do so under the tutelage of a housekeeping scientist (*Modan Ribingu* 1990, 26).[7]

In home decorating magazines for the wealthy, it is the designer or architect rather than the housewife whose efforts are featured. At the end of each article, there is typically a box containing a photograph of the interior designer, a summary of his education and training (I saw no women featured), and the address and phone number of his office. Prices generally are included, broken down into electricity, plumbing, floors, and so on. The "master builder" (*kenshu*), usually the husband but occasionally the wife as substitute, speaks in a small box at the end of the article, thanking the architect or decorator to whom everything has been entrusted. Thus the wealthy classes distinguish themselves not through their creativity or effort in home decorating but through their power to employ a highly trained interior designer. As the Daiken Home Company puts it, "We're the ones who individualize your spirit" (*Sumai no Sekkei* 1990, 115).

Western styles for the wealthy are far more subtly differentiated than for the aspiring classes, who settle for a generic Western look. An article entitled "Basic Lectures in Interior Coordination" describes ten distinct Western styles including Italian modern ("sharp and individual; an inorganic space with concrete walls and world-leading furniture"), "all-deco" (circa 1905–1930), "classic" (Georgian or Louis XV), "ethnic" (hardwood furniture with batik upholstery and accessories from Thailand and Indonesia), and *shinowazuri* (a pastiche of Chinese and Western). Most interesting is "Japanesque":

> A mixture of Japanese and Western. Italian modern furniture with tatami, shoji, and fusama in one space, or the opposite, Japanese traditional furniture in a modern room. Whichever, the style of relaxing while sitting on the floor is crucial. Decorate with Japanese fans, traditional chests, lights, or even Buddhist statues. You often see this look in foreigners' houses in Japan, but now even Japanese dwellings are rethinking the value of tradition. Interiors with the added spice of Japanese style are gaining in popularity. (*Modan Ribingu* 1990, 113)

For the wealthy classes, Japanese style has become one alternative among many, a commodity to be self-consciously chosen and consumed.

The Japanese style favored by the wealthy is an exaggeration, a staged re-creation of a decor associated with the old aristocracy, as seen, for example, on visits to restored samurai villas, palaces, and castles. Most of the recently built or redecorated homes have one formal Japanese room just to the right of the entryway, featuring carved wooden transepts above fusuma doorways, a tokonoma containing a flower arrangement or a reproduction of a scroll painting, shoji windows, and a low lacquer table. One model home includes a corner reserved for the tea ceremony. Another features a black kettle hanging from a carved bamboo pole over a central fire pit, as in old farmhouses.

Embedded in the midst of a Western life-style, a Japanese feeling (*Nihonteki kansei*) is valued because it "harmonizes with the surroundings, fits all seasons, and does not change like Western styles" (*Sumai no Sekkei* 1990, 83). The "New Japan Style" contributes to a stable, calm house, expresses Japanese confidence, and represents "Japan's gift to the world" (238). The tattered tatami and torn shoji of well-lived-in Japanese rooms safely forgotten, Japanese style is praised as a haven of tranquility and beauty in a westernized world of rationality and stress.

Having described the contemporary decorating styles that distinguish the aspiring classes from the poor and the wealthy from the only aspiring, I return to the tensions raised by the contrast between the media's creation of individuality based on consumption of Western-style interiors and a Japanese self rooted in relationships and mutual obligation.

This juxtaposition of individual preference in consumer tastes, life-styles, and friendships against the demands of obligatory social relationships produces many points of tension in contemporary Japan— most obviously in the care of the elderly (see Bethel, this volume). The government professes concern for the physical and emotional needs of the elderly and encourages women to work only part-time in order to care for their parents and in-laws. Yet this same government seems to encourage the media and makers' campaigns to make Japanese life more individual, more private, and more Western. Unless a woman is very wealthy and has the space and money to build a separate apartment within her home for aging parents or in-laws, her attempt to establish a Western-style family life through home redecorating is likely to be interrupted by a long interlude of intergenerational service and coliving.

These publications also produce tension by encouraging women to fulfill themselves by staying at home to raise children, care for their husbands, and redecorate; the reality, however, is that women of the aspiring classes feel compelled by rising housing and educational costs to work full- or part-time outside the home if their families are to have any hope of improving their quality of life.

Children, too, get caught in the tension of paradoxical messages. The media shamelessly target children's consumer desires and appeal to parents to shower them with special cribs when they are young and expensive toys, sports equipment, household furnishings, and clothing as they grow older. And yet these messages supporting parental indulgence in children's leisure, individuality, and material desires are complicated by contradictory messages from parents, teachers, and the society at large that the child be relentlessly self-disciplined if he or she hopes to achieve success educationally and professionally.

Husbands are often silent in the world of home redecorating and consumption. Nonetheless, many redecorating articles present the goal of reformulating the space and feel of the home so as to transform Japanese men into attentive, romantic husbands and involved, playful fathers. These plans fly in the face of the pressures Japanese men of the wealthy and aspiring classes face; they feel compelled to commit their time and energies to their careers, especially if their family is saving to redecorate or buy a home.

The most divisive, unspoken tension of all is that between rich and poor, a tension symbolized by the difference in the size and quality of rented and owned homes, by the difference in quality and style of home goods available to the wealthy, the aspiring, and the poor, and the rapidly fading chances of today's renters to ever own a home. Surely the poor feel it ironic that more and more gadgets and appliances are available to rationalize housework for the rich, when the poor housewife is the one most in need of respite when she returns from work. The promises and glamour of these popular home magazines only serve to emphasize the disparities between classes.

NOTES

1. *Katakana* is the syllabary used for foreign words. In advertising katakana is widely employed in graphics to draw attention (see Stanlaw, this volume).
2. Such magazines increased from about 800 in 1980 to 2,253 in 1988 (*Keizai Kigakuchō* 1989, 57).
3. *Hōmu Cōdii* is a catalog magazine selling for 480 yen (about $3.50) and published seasonally by Jasco, a catalog housewares company. *Utsukushii Heya* is a monthly lifestyle magazine that sells for 1,320 yen (about $9). It is put out by Shufu to Seikatsusha,

which publishes many other magazines and books targeting women. All translations from magazines are mine.

4. *Futari no Sumai* is published seasonally by CBS–Sony Publishing, a company that does not usually target women. It sells for 980 yen (about $7) an issue.

5. *Rifōmu* is a supplement of *Futari no Heya "Plus One"* (A Room for Two Plus One), which is published by Shufunotomosha, a large publishing house targeting women. The supplement sells for 1,520 yen (about $11).

6. *Sumai no Sekkei* (Dwelling Plans) is published by the Fuji Sankei Communications Group, heavily supported by homemaker companies. It sells for 870 yen (about $6) an issue.

7. *Modan Ribingu* (Modern Living) is a catalog magazine published by Fujingahōsha. It costs 1,700 yen (about $12).

REFERENCES

Baudrillard, J. 1981. Translated by Charles Levin. *For a critique of the political economy of the sign*. St. Louis: Telos.

———. 1983. *Simulations*. New York: Semiotext(e).

Bourdieu, P. 1984. *Distinction: A social critique of the judgement of taste*. Cambridge: Harvard University Press.

Futari no Sumai (A Dwelling for Two). 1988. Autumn. Tokyo: CBS–Sony Publication.

Hōmu Cōdii (Home Coordy). 1988. No. 7. Tokyo: Home Coordy Catalogue Publishing House.

———. 1989. No. 12. Tokyo: Jasco Home Coordy Catalogue Publishing House.

Keizai Kikakuchō (Economic Planning Department). 1989. *Kokumin seikatsu hakusho* (Citizens' life white paper). Tokyo: Ōkurasho (Ministry of Finance).

Kelly, W. 1986. Rationalization and nostalgia: Cultural dynamics of new middle-class Japan. *American Ethnologist* 13(4):603–618.

Kenchiku Bunka (Architecture Culture). 1988. *Senzai fukkō Jūtaku* (Residences of the postwar reconstruction); *Kōgyōka jūtaku no hasshin* (The development of prefab houses) 43(500):95, 127.

Modan Ribingu (Modern Living). 1990. Vol. 174, no. 67. Tokyo: Fujingahōsha.

Plath, D. 1964. Where the family of God is the family: The role of the dead in Japanese households. *American Anthropologist* 66:300–317.

Rifōmu Jitsurei 1000 (Reform, 1000 Examples). 1990. Supplement to *Futari no Heya "Plus One."* Tokyo: Shufunotomosha.

Rosenberger, N. 1989. Dialectic balance in the polar balance of self. *Ethos* 17:88–113.

Sumai no Sekkei (Dwelling Plans). 1990. Vol. 30, no. 337. Fuji Sankei Communications Group.

Utsukushii Heya (Beautiful Room). 1988. Vol. 12, no. 65. Tokyo: Shufu to Seikatsusha.

———. 1990. Vol. 14, no. 72. Tokyo: Shufu to Seikatsusha.

• • • • •

7

ALIENATION AND RECONNECTION IN A HOME FOR THE ELDERLY

DIANA BETHEL

Japanese perceive institutions for the elderly as both a blessing and a curse. The demographic, socioeconomic, and cultural changes that come with modernization undermine the traditional Confucian ethic of filial piety which sanctions family care for aging Japanese. Increased longevity, urbanization and migration of young people from the country to the city, an increase of women (the traditional caretakers of the elderly) in the work force, crowded housing conditions, and regional economic hardship have made it difficult for many Japanese families to care for their older members (Maeda 1983). Yet despite this decreasing capability, expectations for family care remain strong.

The dread with which the Japanese elderly view institutionalization reflects the social stigmatization of this deviant fate combined with a fear of the old-age home as unfamiliar and even alien. These fears are well grounded, because institutions, by their nature, strip newcomers of their identities, autonomy, social roles, material possessions, and a sense of place in a familiar social universe (Goffman 1961; Tobin and Lieberman 1976). This chapter examines the lives of residents of the Aotani Institution for the Elderly, located in a rural area of central Hokkaido, and identifies the ordinary features of everyday life such as food, clothing, furniture, and spatial organization that residents use to establish a familiar domestic space in an unfamiliar institutional environment.

The Aotani Institution for the Elderly is a social welfare institution whose requirements for admission include a minimum age of sixty-five and an inability to live at home because of decreasing physical strength or mental acuity, economic hardship, or difficult social circumstances (Ministry of Welfare 1985). An applicant must be relatively healthy and able to manage daily affairs. Meals are prepared on site by cooks and served in the common dining hall. Residents who become too sick or frail or exhibit abnormal behavior are sent on to other institutions or must return to their families.

Most Aotani residents are grateful to be in the institution because it is warm in winter, boasts modern indoor plumbing, and has staff on duty twenty-four hours a day. Living in such an institution (especially a social welfare institution), however, is dissonant with cultural norms and sets up a psychological dilemma that every resident must resolve in the struggle to adapt.

The trauma of residents' institutionalization comes from being thrust into an environment that is not only impersonal and unfamiliar but also foreign. As it happens, a Christian Englishwoman and her congregation founded the first institution for the elderly in Japan, known as St. Hilda's, in 1896 (Ogasawara 1986). Before that time, the elderly poor and infirm with no family support were placed in poorhouses along with orphans, the sick, and vagrants.

The founding of St. Hilda's marked the recognition that in a modernizing Japan, social welfare institutions would be needed to address the special needs of older people. As this awareness grew, more homes for older people were established. The number was drastically reduced during World War II, when many of them in the major cities were burned or totally destroyed. Since the war, the number of institutions for the elderly has increased dramatically. In 1963 there were only 690, but by 1984 this figure had grown to 2,814 (Ministry of Welfare 1985). Each year approximately one hundred more homes are built. Clearly, a need exists for this alternative to family care, and increasing numbers of older people and their families are making use of it. This change in tradition and attitude has brought about a corresponding increase in discussion about institutions and care for the elderly. But as cultural norms lag behind social reality, resistance to the idea of institutionalization remains strong.

The architecture, schedule, food, and loss of familiar furniture and belongings when they enter the facility contribute to residents' difficulty in adjusting. The facility, with its poured concrete construction, dining hall set with tables and chairs, staff dressed in white uniforms, and rigidly structured routines, is the epitome of an unnatural, alien, Western lifestyle.

Newcomers to Aotani are stripped of familiar reminders of their preinstitutional lives through the restriction—because of space limitations—against bringing bulky items and too many belongings. They must give up all worldly possessions except for those that will fit into the small closet assigned to them. No personal furniture is allowed. Even the cherished family *butsudan* (Buddhist altar) must be disposed of or entrusted to one's children. In its place, the institution provides its own Buddhist altar in which memorial tablets of deceased family members may be placed together with those of other residents.

Residents must adjust to a new way of life determined by the schedule of the institution, which now sets the rhythms of their lives. Waking, eating, and going to bed are all precisely regulated. Without exception, all able residents must rise with the 6:00 A.M. wakeup music and be in bed by the 9:00 P.M. "lights out." Mealtimes are at 8:00 A.M., 12:00 P.M., and 5:00 P.M., and residents are always expected to be present unless they have notified the staff otherwise.

The staff at Aotani have organized meals into tightly structured rituals that are orchestrated by work groups made up of residents. Prior to each meal, those assigned to dining hall duty set the tables and bring food from the kitchen, a process that also provides an opportunity for residents to socialize.

Residents who gather outside the dining room chat as they wait for the music that signals permission to enter the dining room. A staff member sometimes attempts to shoo them away, berating them for waiting "like animals at feeding time." She says, "What will visitors think when they see you crowding around the dining hall entrance? They'll think we never feed you!" Though the residents scatter obediently, a few minutes later, without fail, they begin to drift back toward the cafeteria entrance.

Suddenly, the music begins and waiting residents pour into the dining room. They sit patiently in their assigned seats at their tables until a staff woman announces *"Itadakimasu!"* (Let's eat!) As if runners on their mark, residents take up their chopsticks and begin eating. Because only fifteen minutes are allotted for a meal, slow eaters hurry to avoid being left behind when the staff woman dismisses them with *"Gochi-*

sosama deshita!" (Thank you for the meal). In unison, residents rise from their seats, holding their emptied dishes, and proceed hurriedly to the kitchen counter to stand in line. Each dish is deposited in its designated collection pot for the cooks to wash.

The rigorous schedule is part of the tradition of institution life and is designed to make the management of approximately eighty older people go as smoothly as possible. All residents must adhere to the schedule, whether they like it or not, or face eviction from the home. The rationale for the strict daily schedule is the traditional philosophy that one must lead an orderly and disciplined life (*kisoku tadashii sei-katsu*). The staff's need to run mealtimes efficiently contributes to the residents' sense of being confined and manipulated.

The one-taste-fits-all cafeteria cuisine is a frequent source of contention between residents and food providers. The administration attempts to determine the residents' food preferences, but dissatisfactions inevitably arise. Though residents look forward to mealtimes as the high points of their day, some are picky and refuse to eat unfamiliar foods. Mrs. Sasaki explained that eating "is our only enjoyment" (*tatta hitotsu no tanoshimi*), so residents are naturally particular about what they are served. Most of the cuisine is Japanese, modified somewhat by the young dietician's westernized palate. Conflicts sometimes arise because of the desire of these elderly people for more familiar fare. This difference in food preferences between residents and staff mirrors differences in food tastes in intergenerational households among grandchildren, parents, and grandparents. Often the only solution at home is to cook two separate menus, one for the younger generations, based on meat and "new" dishes, and one for the older generation, based on fish and traditional dishes.

The dietician's job is stressful because she must listen to complaints and try to balance diverse and often-conflicting demands. Generally residents do not like food they have never eaten before or have eaten only rarely during their childhood. They have no taste for newfangled foods such as spaghetti, hamburgers, ketchup, sauces such as curry, or creamed dishes poured over rice. When curry or creamed sauces are served, some request only the plain rice served with them. Most residents, who rarely had the chance to eat eggs during their youth, avoid them now. Others avoid cold foods such as Jell-O, ice cream, or sodas because it "chills" their bodies (*karada ga hieru kara*).

Although residents have some input in making up the menus, they have to eat what is served—unless they can come up with something they like better from the local food stores. But because buying food for meals soon becomes expensive, most residents strike a happy medium by eating the basic foods offered in the cafeteria, such as rice and miso soup, and sampling the side dishes, then supplementing their meal with more appetizing traditional and familiar fare, either before or after their cafeteria meal.

The fact that the first institution for the elderly in Japan was founded by a foreigner has become obscure historical trivia, but a sense of foreignness is nevertheless associated with institutions. The Japanese term *rōjin hōmu* (institution for the elderly) reveals an ironic foreign nuance. In an attempt to distance postwar institutions from the image of the earlier *yōrō-in* (asylum for the elderly), a new name was chosen—rōjin hōmu, which combines the Japanese word for old people and the English word for home. The term was intended to impart a bright, pleasant, Western image of a modern facility to combat the dark, depressing, and shameful image of the early poorhouses and social welfare institutions for older people.

The sense of foreignness that pervades the home arises also from the notion that the need for such facilities is an inevitable side effect of attitudes imported from America after World War II. It is common knowledge, residents assert, that Americans treat their elderly very poorly. In Japan, they insist, institutions for the elderly are out of place and should not even exist, because Japanese feel a strong sense of responsibility toward family members.

NARRATIVES OF INSTITUTIONALIZATION

At the core of the Japanese code of social conduct is the Confucian ethic of filial piety, according to which children must honor and obey their parents. The Japanese ideal calls for aging parents to live with their eldest son and his family, surrounded by attentive and respectful grandchildren. Institutionalization represents a failure to achieve this ideal. The sense of social stigma associated with this failure can produce acute psychological discomfort in the institutionalized elderly.

Obasuteyama ("the mountain on which grannies are abandoned") is a Japanese legend that has been revived as a commentary on a new social problem (Fukazawa 1964; Imamura 1983; Plath 1972). The term

Obasuteyama is frequently used by residents as a nickname for homes for the elderly to call attention to the shameful treatment of aging parents by their ungrateful children. According to this legend, in days past in some places in Japan, older people who had outlived their usefulness and were a burden on the productive members of the community were taken by their children deep into the mountains and left to die of starvation and exposure. No evidence of this practice has been discovered, but the numerous references in early Japanese literature and folklore indicate that the myth has been around for a long time.

The legend of Obasuteyama takes on new relevance for the institutionalized Japanese elderly. Residents refer to the story to express their sense of shame, isolation, and abandonment in the impersonal environment of the institution. Residents feel not only that they have been denied their rightful place among family but that others view them as objects of pity or scorn.

The *seken* (the social circle of "others") is a powerful arbiter of social opinion and self-worth. It is composed of relatives, neighbors, and friends who one feels have the power and right to judge one's social behavior. An influential social sanction is the fear of *seken no me,* the "eyes of others," the ever-watchful guardians of proper social conduct and accepted social morality who can indicate their disapproval simply by "showing the whites of their eyes" (*shiroi me de miru*).

Mr. Matsumoto reports that after he and his wife moved to Aotani, they dared not tell any of their friends. Mrs. Iwasawa had planned on moving from her son's family to a small apartment nearby for a few years before moving into the institution. This way, she thought she could avoid giving the impression that her son had sent her to an old-age home and thereby relieve him of the embarrassment this would cause. Mrs. Iskikawa entered Aotani against the advice of her children and relatives. She now regrets her decision because it caused her son so much embarrassment and shame that he cannot even raise his head in front of relatives. She says they all criticize him unmercifully for sending his poor old mother to such a place. Mrs. Kagawa avoids visiting friends and relatives because she says they will think that she has come to ask for charity and will feel obliged to give her something.

This sense of consternation, shame, and loss of face in the eyes of their neighbors, friends, and relatives causes residents of Aotani to withdraw from their old social networks and to isolate themselves inside the institution, where everyone shares their humiliation.

The social stigma of being in an institution must be neutralized if residents are to accept and adjust to their new lives in the home. Residents feel compelled to create narratives that explain their situation as something other than deviant. To do so, they draw on the legend of Obasuteyama as well as on their own social analyses of postwar Japanese society.

Obasuteyama provides a vehicle for describing the painful and unacceptable experience of being institutionalized. It allows residents to objectify their emotional trauma and perceptions of stigmatization. Residents identify with the old woman who is left on Obasuteyama. The very word carries a loaded emotional charge reflecting the perception that such a fate is a shocking transgression of the ethic of filial piety. As they realize that others share similar feelings, they begin to identify their problem as a recognizable category of suffering. By shifting the focus from the individual to a generational and societal level, they gain social recognition as victims sharing a common fate—a fate given a name and social reality by the legend of Obasuteyama.

Through this shared narrative, residents begin a healing process toward restoring their feelings of self-worth and social acceptability. Identification with the Obasuteyama motif serves as a face-saving strategy of social absolution—designed to convince themselves as well as others of their moral integrity and innocence in spite of their deviation from social norms.

The motif also becomes a vehicle to express otherwise unacceptably bitter and even hostile sentiments. It allows residents to vent indirectly anger and moral indignation at being abandoned, to acknowledge publicly (among peers) their feelings of victimization, and to elicit indirectly sympathy for themselves while focusing blame on their offspring who they feel have abdicated their social and moral responsibility.

Residents also use folk analyses or postwar Japanese society to explain how they have ended up in a home for the elderly. In their sociological analyses, the root of the problem is readily identified as the moral degeneration of the Japanese character, a degeneration explicitly or implicitly associated with a loss of traditional Japanese values and the influence of the West. "Children never committed suicide when we were young," residents marvel as they shake their heads in disbelief. Mrs. Oshima proclaimed, "These days children even kill their own parents," referring to an incident in which two sons went berserk and beat their parents to death with baseball bats.

The cause of the problem, they agree, began with the abolition of the family system after the war. They are quick to explain that Japan has been contaminated by American ideas about individualism and democracy. Mrs. Kayashima explains that

> before the war, the family system was very strong. The authority of the father and mother was absolute. If they said something was white, even if you knew it was black, you had to say it was white. It wasn't the place of children to question their parents. This was all the more the case if you were a young daughter-in-law. After the war things turned topsy-turvy [*yo no naka ga hikkurigaette shimatta*]. New ideas from America, like democracy and freedom, led to the destruction of the family system. Now, newly married couples are registered separately on their own family register. They aren't included in the family register of their parents, so the ties between children and parents have grown weaker. Each person now is a separate entity [*ikko, ikko no ningen*] who has little responsibility and obligation to their parents.

Mrs. Miyake adds:

> That's why Japanese older people are abandoned, just like American old people. *"Demokurashii"* has become a creed of selfishness. Young people think they need only satisfy their own desires and ignore their social responsibilities to others. The concept of freedom has been interpreted as selfishness [*Jiyūshugi wa katteshugi toshite toraeteiru*].

Residents see themselves as the innocent victims of the foreign influences and resulting social changes that have shaken the foundations of Japanese society. They feel that since the war and Occupation period, young people have not been properly taught about commitment and social obligations because of American reforms. Mrs. Oda feels that people should strive to become virtuous, upright human beings who fulfill their obligations to others. One of the main obligations individuals incur in this life is toward their parents, who have sacrificed for many years to raise them. Reciprocally, care of parents in their old age is the duty of children. Referring to a Buddhist proverb, she says people who lack a sense of obligation and thankfulness toward others are no better than ignorant beasts. Thus, children who refuse to take care of their aging parents, and instead place them in institutions, lack moral integrity.

By mixing ad hoc social analysis with folktales, residents create a new master narrative that redirects social stigma and shifts the shame for their institutionalization from themselves to their children and to the moral decline of Japanese society. According to this narrative, the foreign concepts of democracy and freedom have undermined Japanese morality and created the need for institutions—foreign and alien to Japanese experience—to hold abandoned elderly.

RECLAIMING ALIEN TERRITORY

Upon entering the institution, much to their surprise, newcomers discover a thriving community of residents busily engaged in day-to-day routines. They gradually abandon their dark preconceptions as they begin to participate in and gain some degree of social satisfaction from interacting with peers in this bustling society. Familiar social patterns are reconstructed and enhanced by sharing familiar foods, organizing space in familiar ways, and maintaining such traditional practices as gift giving.

New residents are placed in a room with two or three other residents; this group becomes their primary social unit in the home. Roommates help to integrate the new residents by serving as guides to this new life. Given the authoritarian structure of institutional life, newcomers soon discover that their main source of support is other residents. Though caregivers may be sympathetic to their wants and needs to a degree, their ultimate responsibility is to enforce the rules that keep institutional life running smoothly. Residents thus seek out friends and acquaintances who help make life bearable and even pleasant and enjoyable. They seek out commonalities with others based on gender, age, and time of admission to the facility.

The lack of privacy demands a major adjustment from residents, even though group living in a crowded context is not an unfamiliar experience for most Japanese (Caudill and Plath 1966). In prewar homes for the elderly, eight or ten residents slept in the same room, men and women together. At Aotani, the rooms are segregated by sex, and the maximum is four people per room, allowing just enough space for each person's bedding at night.

In recent years, ideas about the rights of the individual and the value of privacy have entered the mainstream social welfare philosophy through those who have observed successful systems in Europe or the United States. Policies for new facilities for the elderly now dictate only one person per room. Where this new scheme is already in effect, however, social workers are reporting that isolation and withdrawn behavior are unfortunate by-products of increased individual privacy.

Residents attempt to remake the physical space of the institution by re-creating a social environment consistent with their preinstitutional lives. By doing so, they ward off intolerable depersonalization.

Residents' living quarters are tatami rooms, in contrast to the public areas of the facility. This context structures the kinds of interactions that develop in the room. A process of negotiation occurs as roommates carve out their own niches and reach agreement on the use of public space in the room. Enjoying food and drink facilitates a feeling of sociability and sharing. The small low folding table that is set up in each room during the day draws residents into a shared social space.

Some institutions have only Western-style rooms (*yōshitsu*) and furnishings, including a chair and small table which residents use when not sleeping or resting. These Westernlike settings, however, are less conducive to social interaction. Although not without problems, tatami-style living seems to allow more flexibility to create shared space. This Japanese feature of the Aotani facility provides a context for familiar patterns of interaction to emerge.

Gender differences are patterned in the ways men and women reconstruct their familiar social environments. For women, a primary objective is to create a warm, domestic environment in their rooms, one that draws friends and neighbors. Serving tea and food is an essential feature of creating an amiable context for social relationships. In the rural communities of earlier years, extending hospitality was considered neighborly behavior. In the institution, these same familiar patterns resurface as women construct new social networks.

The idiom of domesticity is acted out in the serving of tea and light snacks, in pickling small quantities of vegetables or beans, and, in Mrs. Maekawa's case, in making her own plum wine. Most of the women also wear the customary long-sleeved apron, the symbol of the housewife, even though they have no kitchen in which to cook.

Aotani respects and observes the important custom of providing sustenance to family ancestral spirits. The institution's Buddhist altar, the central feature of the traditional Japanese household, is located at the head of the large dining hall. In the early morning, ladies who chant sutras together place at the altar small offerings of freshly cooked rice received from the cooks. Residents who want a more intimate atmosphere in which to commune with their deceased family sometimes set up makeshift altars in their rooms. Though modest because of institutional restrictions, the altars include pictures of deceased family members decorated by flowers the residents have grown in their own garden plot on the grounds of the facility (Plath 1964).

In one room, a picture of the imperial family graces a central position of the small altar. The past emperor Hirohito was seen by most residents as an age-mate, as someone who had lived through the same history, suffering through the high points as well as the tragedies of this century along with them. He symbolized the prewar family and its espoused authority structure and virtues of social obligation.

Because mealtime at Aotani is not a pleasant occasion, the informal sphere provides an alternative for relaxation and socializing. Rooms become an environment in which residents can enjoy foods they like, at their leisure, in the company of friends. By engaging in the familiar social roles of giving and receiving, they gain the satisfaction of creating a hospitable atmosphere, of serving food graciously, and of being honored as a guest and expressing appreciation for the food.

Good hostesses make sure their tables are set with appealing appetizers and snacks to offer roommates as well as guests, one source of which is leftovers from mealtime. In the short time allotted for meals, many residents are not able to consume all the food on their plates. Because many of the older people at the home have either ill-fitting dentures or few of their own teeth, the food is sometimes too hard for them to eat. They consider it a waste to throw away leftovers of especially delicious foods and often smuggle these tidbits out of the dining room. This is against the rules, but residents manage to slip food into their pockets or into small plastic containers they sneak in and out of the cafeteria.

In the home, food has great value as currency in the reciprocal relationships of gift giving. For those of limited economic means, food from the dining hall allows them to establish their own social exchange networks among the residents. Social etiquette requires that frequent visitors occasionally bring some kind of refreshment for the people whose room they are visiting in order to maintain reciprocity. A food gift sent by family is shared with friends and neighbors in repayment for previous gifts and kindnesses.

Another source of food treats for the communal table is market day, an eagerly awaited event held three times a week by a local store that brings foods to sell to residents. The less mobile ones are thankful for this service, especially during the winter months when most residents refrain from venturing outside on the icy, snow-covered streets. Upon hearing the announcement of the store's arrival, they stream out of their rooms toward the dining hall to buy rice crackers, pickled vegetables, and other teatime treats. Some residents wait in the dining hall to assure themselves first pick of the store's selections.

Social interaction outside the room links individuals to the larger home society. Each hallway is a mini-neighborhood, and those living in adjacent and nearby rooms are neighbors. Visiting patterns reveal an active social life based on these networks. Thus, the Western architecture of the facility is transformed into a familiar, traditional Japanese neighborhood.

Neighbors try to maintain good relationships for sociability's sake as well as for mutual aid in times of emergency. The custom of gift giving helps establish and maintain these social relationships. When Mrs. Kotake came to the home, she brought a big box of grapefruit with her to share with roommates and neighbors in the tradition of *mukō sangen, ryō donari* (literally, "three across and both sides"). This custom suggests that one establish and maintain relationships with neighbors living on either side of one's house and in the three houses across the street. Mrs. Kotake initiated reciprocal relations of gift giving in her new environment to establish herself in the social networks of the home. This Japanese custom is one strategy that residents use to domesticate the home and to resist the alienation and foreignness of the institution.

In rooms that are centers of interaction, one woman usually dominates social activity. Mrs. Miyamoto, for example, commands the respect of her roommates and neighbors. She is the oldest woman in the room and takes charge of making and pouring tea for her roommates and visitors. At her invitation, roommates, friends, and neighbors drop by.

Mrs. Miyamoto and her roommates are a lively group of conversationalists, and friends enjoy their company. Their table is always set with tea, rice crackers, and other delicious tidbits to welcome friends and neighbors from other rooms. For some guests, their visit to Mrs. Miyamoto's room will be the second or third stop of their morning rounds to say hello to friends. During the prime visiting periods in the

morning—before breakfast and again before lunch—friends and neighbors gather to chat, exchange information, and snack on premeal appetizers. These times extend the brief and regimented dining period.

When guests drop by, they draw aside the curtain over the doorway
and announce their visit by saying "Excuse me!" (*Ojamashimasu* or
Gomenkudasai), as if entering a household. They are then invited into
the private, domestic space of the room. They take off their slippers in
the small entryway (*genkan*) and step up into the tatami room (shoes
are not permitted to be worn in the facility). The hostess then pours a
cup of green tea for her guests and offers them the choicest of the snacks
arrayed on the small table.

Turning institutional hallways into mini-neighborhoods allows women
to expand their domestic spheres by developing familiar visiting relationships between "room households." These social networks, based on
sharing food and hospitality, set the tone for a homelike atmosphere in
an otherwise impersonal space.

The socializing patterns of male residents in the home differ markedly
from those of female residents. Whereas most female roommates socialize over tea in their rooms, male residents rarely do. Some men may
drink tea in their rooms, but they rarely do so with their roommates.
If roommates happen to be drinking tea at the same time, each pours
his tea from his own teapots and remains in his part of the room,
interacting very little with the others. Social tea drinking for most of
these men is not an activity they would initiate.

In contrast to the female residents who socialize over tea and re-
freshments in their rooms, male residents tend to interact more in public
spaces—on the benches in the hallway, in the lounge, or on the grounds
outside the facility. Their socializing often revolves around smoking
cigarettes or drinking or activities that require little verbal interaction,
such as watching television or playing checkers or Chinese chess (*shōgi*).
The younger men generally make friends more easily and are more
talkative. This is a point of contention with some of the older men, who
resent the glib younger men's stealing the limelight.

Some men who enjoy drinking tea, but do not want to go to the
trouble of making their own, depend on females to provide the context
for socializing. They visit the rooms of female friends to drink tea and
eat pickled vegetables or sweets. In some cases, these friends are also
their girl friends. Mr. Sakashita visits Mrs. Tanaka's room quite often
to drink tea and read the newspaper (they are "going steady"). Mrs.

Tanaka's room is a favorite spot for several of Mr. Sakashita's friends, also.

Mrs. Yamamoto also entertains male visitors. She and her roommates socialize with the men while the men play *hanafuda* (a card game), in which the stakes are beans. Although the women rarely play a hand themselves, they take the supportive roles of banker (keeper of the beans) and audience. The men feel comfortable going to the room of Mrs. Yamamoto and her friends, who are tolerant of their drinking as they play cards.

According to the staff, heavy drinking is one of the major problems among the men in the institution. The staff do their best to discourage drinking, even to the point of holding a happy hour (*banshaku no jikan*) daily between 4:00 and 4:30 P.M. in the hope of controlling how much the men drink. Women are not prohibited from attending, but only men show up. This drinking period was established to curb drinking by limiting alcohol consumption to one time and place during the day and to make it a violation for residents to store or drink alcohol in their rooms.

The daily quota of alcohol is predetermined, so the caregivers pass out each man's chosen beverage, already poured. The staff women attempt to re-create the ambience of the drinking places the men like to frequent. They put up one red lantern similar to those in front of public drinking establishments, with the words "Old Folks Home" written on it. It is a symbol that the staff women hope will reproduce an atmosphere conducive to drinking and merrymaking. They play *enka* (popular ballads) and encourage the men to sing along with the new *karaoke* (musical accompaniment) tapes. By providing a substitute to rival the bars in town, they hope to restrain the men's urge to drink during unapproved periods.

In spite of staff attempts to create a fun drinking situation, complete with sing-along videos and lively conversation, something is lacking. The socializing customarily involved in the drinking ritual is absent— there is no opportunity for drinking buddies to pour drinks for one another (see Smith, this volume), no competing to pick up the tab, and no potential for drinking too much. The artificial and restrictive setting is but a pale imitation of drinking spots in the outside world.

Men are not supposed to drink beyond the confines of the institution, but once outside they are no longer within the administration's reach. On such outings they walk to town, drink their fill, then return to the home. They also like to bring liquor back with them and to relax with it in the privacy of their rooms. During the winter they can conceal small bottles in their coats as they walk past the front office and into the facility. In the warmer months, they must recruit a sympathetic accomplice who is beyond suspicion to bring in the forbidden liquor. Women friends often assist.

Among alcohol-drinking men and their networks, prohibited liquor is a prized item of social exchange and friendship. Conspiring to bring in liquor undetected gives the men a sense of competence and satisfaction in regaining control of their lives. It provides a thrill and stimulating tension in the uneventful and feminized daily life of the home. Given the restricted life-style they are forced to lead in the institution, resistance to authority is an affirmation of their autonomy and masculinity. It thus is not surprising that heavy alcohol consumption is common.

Both male and female residents use food and drink as a means to re-create the social spheres with which they are familiar and to establish continuities between their previous and present lives. The female residents are able to create a more satisfying environment for themselves and their friends that permits the expression of neighborhood patterns of social interaction, while the male residents socialize on less intimate terms in public spaces and use liquor as a social lubricant and excuse to get together. Thus, food and drink are the tools of social exchange that help create the ties binding social relationships. Through establishing satisfying and ego-enhancing social relations, residents recover a sense of their own worth and agency.

For both men and women, being institutionalized, confined, and disciplined by people almost half their age presents a profound insult and creates an overwhelming sense of powerlessness. Defying authority in devious yet innocuous ways is one means of self-assertion. Through strategies to procure food and drink, residents have created networks of conspiracy and resistance.

The importation of Western products and life-styles has immeasurably improved the quality of life for Japanese older people. Indoor plumbing, electricity, gas, and kitchen appliances are but a few examples. Yet, one import—institutions for the elderly—has been accepted with mixed feelings by those directly affected—the residents. Though generally satisfied with their daily lives in the institution, in their darker moments they blame notions of democracy and freedom, also imported from the West, for creating a need for such facilities. The perception of alienness of institutions for the aged stems from historical fact as well as from a folk analysis of morality and social change in postwar Japan. From the perspective of their years, residents view (post)modern Japanese society as a ghastly orgy of depraved consumerism and loss of humanity—and see themselves as the hapless victims of this moral degeneration—by the very fact of their institutionalization.

Yet refusing to dwell on self-pity, they resolutely reclaim the institutional environment from the threat of alienation, the stigma of deviance, and numbing depersonalization. Familiar patterns of social interaction—visiting, gift giving, and spending leisure-time—are reconstructed through the use of such traditional and commonplace aspects of material life as food, clothing, and furniture. A cohort effect makes this social reconstruction possible through the concentration of same-age peers who have experienced similar histories and share similar philosophies, cultural values, and rural working-class backgrounds.

Residents of the home represent a segment of the population that is least enthusiastic about the adoption of Western goods, ideas, borrowed words, and life-styles. Having lived through nearly a century of social change in Japanese society, they struggle to retain the traditional and familiar so as to avoid feeling like strangers in their own land.

Even as the outward trappings of foreign culture are adopted, the content reveals distinctly Japanese meanings. In the old-age home we see a Western-looking facility, but an inside look reveals a resilient continuity with a Japanese past. Residents' resistance to the alien and unfamiliar and their corresponding striving toward recovery and reconstruction of community are a microcosm of modern Japanese society.

REFERENCES

Caudill, William, and David Plath. 1966. Who sleeps with whom? Parent-child involvement in urban Japanese families. *Psychiatry* 29 (4):344–366.

Fukazawa Shichiro. 1964. *Narayamabushiko* (Ballad of Narayama). Tokyo: Shinchosha.

Goffman, Erving. 1961. *Asylums*. Garden City, N.Y.: Anchor.

Imamura Shōhei (producer). 1983. *Narayamabushiko* (Ballad of Narayama). Tokyo: Tōhei Films.

Lebra, Takie Sugiyama. 1979. The dilemma and strategies of aging among contemporary Japanese women. *Ethnology* 18:337–353.

———. 1984. *Japanese women: Constraint and fulfillment*. Honolulu: University of Hawaii Press.

Maeda Daisaku. 1983. Family care in Japan. *Gerontologist* 23(6):579–583.

Ministry of Welfare. 1985. *Rojin fukushi no tebiki* (Handbook of social welfare for the elderly). Tokyo: Ministry of Welfare, Social Affairs Division, Section for Social Welfare for the Elderly.

Ogasawara Yuji. 1986. *Ikiru: Rōjin hōmu 100 nen* (To live: One hundred years of homes for the elderly). Eds. Zenkoku shakai fukushi kyogikai (National Association of Social Welfare Organizations) and Rōjin fukushi shisetsu kyogikai (Association of Welfare Institutions for the Elderly). Tokyo: Tosho Insatsu Kabushikigaisha.

Plath, David. 1964. Where the family of God is the family: The role of the dead in Japanese households. *American Anthropologist* 66:300–317.

———. 1972. Japan: The after years. In Donald O. Cowgill and Lowell D. Holmes (eds.), *Aging and modernization*, 133–150. New York: Appleton-Century-Crofts.

Rohlen, Thomas P. 1978. The promise of Japanese spiritualism. In Erik H. Erikson (ed.), *Adulthood,* 129–147. New York: W. W. Norton.

Tobin, Joseph J. 1987. The American images of aging in Japan. *Gerontologist* 27(1):53–58.

Tobin, Sheldon, and Morton Lieberman. 1976. *Last home for the aged.* San Francisco: Jossey-Bass.

· · · · ·

8

DRINKING ETIQUETTE IN A CHANGING BEVERAGE MARKET

STEPHEN R. SMITH

The changes through which various customs and forms of etiquette of the
Japanese are now passing, from those of the feudal times to those of the
enlightened age of Meiji, and the new order of things consequent upon
the contact of the people of Japan with strangers of the Western countries,
are very great, and the question as to how far our Western ideas of etiquette
will impress the Japanese, and to what extent our customs will affect theirs, is
one of considerable interest.
—J. M. Dixon, "Japanese Etiquette" (1885)

Others have written of the orchestrated consumption of alcohol at Japanese events of sanctification (Bestor 1989, 241); of the formal exchanges
of sake cups during weddings (Edwards 1989, 17–18; Hendry 1981, 171–
172); and of ceremonial drinking during induction into criminal organizations (Ishino 1953, 696–698; Iwai 1974, 390). My subject is more
mundane: What are the customs and etiquette of everyday drinking
among friends and associates in contemporary Japan, and how have
these practices been influenced by postwar changes in the commercial
liquor market?

Although this chapter emphasizes the quotidian, I begin with an
example from the more ritualized, formal end of the continuum of
contemporary Japanese drinking practices. During my fieldwork on alcohol use and abuse in Japan I was affiliated with the alcoholism ward

of a large mental hospital in Osaka. Each autumn the entire staff went to a hot spring spa for an overnight outing, the highlight of which was a huge banquet. Following a soak in the hot spring pools, everyone dressed in the crisp indigo-and-white cotton *yukata* (robes) supplied by the inn and gathered in a vast tatami-covered dining hall. We sat on cushions on the floor—the men cross-legged, the women on their shins—in front of identical individual dining trays. Although seating was not preassigned, we arranged ourselves hierarchically, from the hospital owner and director at the head of the hall to the kitchen staff at the other end.

After the meal, the professional entertainment, and the requisite amateur performances (including a song by the mortified anthropologist), the party turned less formal. We had all been served bottles of beer or hot sake with our meal; now, as revelers left their places and began to circulate, many carried a bottle and a cup with them, stopping to pour a drink for a boss or a friend, then staying to chat. Subordinates approached the wealthy director of the hospital to pour a drink for him and to pay their respects. A driver from the motor pool, about thirty-five years old, carried a small flask (*tokkuri*) of sake and knelt before the director. Holding the bottle in his right hand, his left hand supporting his right, the driver proffered it with a hushed inquiry, "Sir?" (*sensei*). The director lifted his thimble-sized sake cup (*sakazuki*) to his lips, emptied it, then held it out with one hand to be refilled. Holding the flask with two hands, the driver poured *sake* to the rim of the cup. Mumbling a thanks, the director raised the cup in a slight toasting motion and, giving a nod of his head, took a sip. He then sat silently for a moment, holding the cup in his right hand, his hands resting on his knees. The driver, still holding the flask, spoke of his pleasure in his job and expressed gratitude for the kindness of the director; then he leaned forward, placed both hands on the mat, and said, "I humbly request that you pour [me a drink]" (*onagare chōdai itashimasu*). The director drained his drink, raised the cup over his tray, turned it over and shook it as if to remove the last drops, then held out the cup to his employee. The driver placed the flask on the tray and accepted the cup. The director picked up the flask—in one hand—and extended it to pour. The driver held his cup forward in two hands. When it was filled to the brim, the driver drew the cup back, raised it to eye level, dropped his gaze, bowed his head in a quick nod, then took the cup to his lips and drank it down in three slurps. Placing the empty cup on the tray and picking up the flask, the driver got to his feet but remained hunched over. Bowing repeatedly, he awkwardly backed away.

The formality of this particular event was heightened by the social gulf between the young driver and his older, wealthy employer. The essential elements, however, reflect a standard, idealized pattern of social drinking. As stated in an Occupation-period guide to good etiquette in Japan:

> First of all, on being served *sake,* one holds up his cup (*sakazuki*) to receive the *sake* and then takes a sip or at least puts it to his lips before putting it down. The second point to remember is never to serve oneself unless one has first picked up the *tokuri* [sic] and served the others present. More likely than not someone will relieve you of the *tokuri* so that you will not have to serve yourself. It will often happen that a guest, considered to be a senior person, will be offered the *sake* cup of the host or someone else present, in which case one is expected to accept the cup, to hold it while it is being filled, and to drink the *sake* from this cup. The cup need not be returned immediately but it should not be kept after the *sake* has been drunk. The cup is then returned to the person who presented it, and you in turn are expected to pick up the *tokuri* and serve him. Later you may wish to present your cup to the host or some honored guest or someone to whom you wish to pay respect, and it is perfectly all right to do this. (World Fellowship Committee 1955, 59–60)

The drinking behavior described in the banquet anecdote is in keeping with the etiquette outlined in the postwar manual. In fact, it is consistent with a description written almost one hundred years before:

> At Japanese dinners it is not usual to provide a wine-cup for each guest, but several wine cups go the round, and are dipped, each time they are drained, in a bowl of tepid water. The receiving and returning of wine-cups is looked upon as a sign of good fellowship. If offered a wine-cup, the guest will take it in both hands, and turning toward a waitress, ask for some *sake.* After drinking some *sake* he will dip the cup in the water-bowl, and hand it back politely to the person who presented it. (Dixon 1885, 9–10)

The water bowl for rinsing cups was absent at the banquet I have described, but the director's act of shaking the last drop from the cup symbolically cleansed it in a manner similar to washing. In truth, over a ten-year period of observing drinking behavior in Japan, I have often been told about the rinsing bowl, but I have never seen one in use.

Likewise, although I have heard about the practice of having fewer cups than drinkers—thus necessitating the circulation of cups—I have never experienced it in Japan.[1] This is not to say that these customs are not practiced, but clearly they are no longer standard.

Yet in spite of some formal changes, the central rules governing polite social drinking have remained the same for at least a century. The primary injunction is that one pour for others, not for oneself, a practice known as *oshaku*. When a cup or the pouring of a drink is offered, one should accept, raise the cup to be filled, and drain the liquor. The first drinker should then reciprocate, handing back the cup and pouring for the person who previously poured. This prescribed response is called *henpai,* literally, "the return cup."

The rules of etiquette requiring alternate pouring are classic expressions of Maussian "gift" exchange (Mauss 1967). People are obliged to offer gifts to one another, whether they be seniors who wish to show their benevolence or to avoid the appearance of selfishness; or juniors who want to give thanks or to avoid alienating a benefactor through lack of gratitude. A proffered gift carries heavy social pressure that it not be refused; and the acceptance of a gift requires a repayment.

This simple, yet profound, formula of gift circulation and obligation—giving, receiving, repaying—is the foundation of social exchange theory. Each act that necessitates a response unites people and strengthens social structure. And while a repayment will often balance the original gift—fulfilling and terminating the exchange relationship—the repayment may be treated as a new act of giving, initiating yet another reciprocation. For social theorists such as Claude Lévi-Strauss (1949), this pattern of exchange (specifically, the exchange of women by men, because the incest taboo prevents men from marrying their own kinswomen) is the very glue of human society. Although the exchange of drinks in a Japanese bar may not be an example of such profound magnitude, the principles and consequences are essentially the same. Like an imbiber's incest taboo, restrictions on pouring one's own drinks force individuals into mutual dependence and unite them in elementary exchange. Furthermore, the ritual exchange of drinks serves to bond not only equals but also the socially disparate, as seen in the banquet example. This flexibility is especially important in Japan, a vertical society (Nakane 1970) where, in even the most egalitarian relationships, social context and role constantly generate hierarchy.

In Japan there is an extensive etiquette of gift exchange (Befu 1968,

1974) and a high awareness of the manipulability of gift and service giving to extract repayment (Befu 1980; Lebra 1974). Drinking in Japan is a particularly salient context for exchange. The Japanese have a positive attitude toward drinking (Kono et al. 1977) and a great tolerance for drunken behavior; they hold the belief that, at least theoretically, anything said or done when drunk should be forgiven and forgotten because the alcohol, not the drinker, caused the mischief. Thus in Japan, the exchange of drinks affirms the bond between individuals—even people of different rank—while the alcohol defines a context in which relaxed standards of decorum are not only tolerated but expected, permitting a freer flow of information and expression of affect than is acceptable in normal social intercourse.

CHANGING TASTES

The idealized etiquette of cup and drink exchange described above developed as part of the ritual of drinking sake, the archetypical Japanese beverage, evoking homeland and mythic natal village.[2] But sake sales are on the wane and have been since their peak in 1975 (Kokuzeichō 1981, 119). The decline is all the more striking in the face of the steady increase of alcohol consumption in Japan since World War II. Between 1950 and 1980, the volume of alcoholic beverages consumed increased more than tenfold, while the per capita consumption of alcohol by Japanese fifteen years of age and older more than quadrupled, from 1.7 liters to 7.4 liters (Minai 1986, 39).

Although sake consumption has diminished—both in absolute volume and as a percentage of all alcoholic beverages—beer has more than taken its place. By volume, beer production exceeded that of sake in 1947 (Nukada 1981, 109) and has increased its lead ever since. From 1950 to 1980, the volume of beer consumed increased 2,818 percent (Minai 1986, 40). About two-thirds of all alcoholic beverages sold in Japan are a form of beer; that is three times the volume of sake (Kokuzeichō 1981, 118).

Whiskey was of little commercial significance in prewar Japan. Consumption of whiskey then skyrocketed in the postwar era, by almost 5,500 percent between 1950 and 1980 (Minai 1986, 40). Major increases first occurred during the 1960s, in response to the economic boom that gave workers more disposable income (26); sales surged again in the

1970s following the 1971 liberalization of alcohol import regulations that not only lowered the price of imported whiskey but spurred production and promotion by domestic producers (45–46 n. 20). Although the percentage of total beverage volume is still small (5.2 percent) the high alcohol content of whiskey (43 percent) makes it the source of almost a quarter (23.4 percent) of the absolute alcohol that is drunk (Kokuzeichō 1981, 118).

Perhaps the least known of Japanese liquors in the West is *shōchū*, a distilled white liquor or Japanese vodka with an alcohol content of about 25 percent. It is made from rice, sweet potatoes, millet, buckwheat, or whatever. "Whatever" was any ingredient available for making liquor in the destitute period of reconstruction immediately following World War II, and shōchū was almost the only alcohol to be had. In spite of an honorable history, particularly in southwestern prefectures like Kagoshima, shōchū was tainted by its association with poverty. Even though consumption grew steadily (Kokuzeichō 1981, 119), shōchū was considered the drink of day laborers and derelicts—until the early 1980s, when it suddenly became popular among the young.

Finally, it should be mentioned that grape wines are not unknown in Japan but have had little significance until recently. They are said to have been introduced in Japan by priests in the sixteenth century, though they were poorly received; domestic production of wines did not begin until the late nineteenth century (Minai 1986, 44 n. 11), presumably reflecting demand by the new resident foreigners following the reopening of Japan. Only in the 1980s, as wines took on a faddish appeal among upwardly mobile young adults, has there been any noteworthy consumption.

Japanese taste in alcohol is dominated by a limited spectrum of beverages. Over 97 percent of the alcohol consumed in 1981 was in the form of beer (66.1 percent), sake (22.2 percent), whiskey (5.2 percent), and shōchū (3.6 percent) (Kokuzeichō 1981, 118). But there has been a striking increase in the types and brands of the "big four," as well as an elaboration of the ways in which these beverages may be consumed.

CHANGING OPTIONS

Since the war, there has been a miraculous transformation in the Japanese economy, a change that has created disposable personal income on a scale that was inconceivable thirty years ago. And where extra cash appears in a capitalist context, entrepreneurs and commercial interests are never far behind.

As attested to by omnipresent advertising, producers of alcohol obviously believe that they can enlarge their market share by appealing to old consumer tastes in new ways and by creating tastes that did not exist previously. Producers advertise to draw attention to the advantages of their brands as well as to create new appetites. Some advertising campaigns work better than others. Managers at Sapporo Beer proudly told me of the 10 percent per month increase in sales of canned beer following their campaign to promote beer in cans as masculine. On the other hand, product lines may fail through misperception of demand or misdirected advertising. Sapporo Beer also tried marketing a low-alcohol beer and then a no-alcohol beer for drivers. Company officials reported that the campaign was a flop, though the problem did not appear to be one of taste. The drivers were disappointed by the lack of a "kick" and, more interestingly, they were confused as to how they should behave.

Commercial influences on alcohol and its use in Japan are nothing new. Commercial sake production dates as far back as the Heian period (794–1185), when the nobility commissioned court brewers. Living within the court compound and using techniques imported from China, the brewers produced numerous forms of sake intended for consumption by different classes of courtiers on diverse ceremonial occasions. The true commercial production of sake began in the Middle Ages (1185–1573). Families that were formerly court sake brewers petitioned the shogunate for permission to establish independent breweries affiliated with shrines and temples. On market days brewers sold sake at the temple gates and began to compete for sales by improving quality through steadily advancing technology. Development and elaboration were further stimulated during the Tokugawa period (1600–1868) by the growth of a rich urban merchant (chōnin) culture: a culture of the practical and worldly, a legally restricted class with large amounts of money and a consuming desire to show off its financial success. Under pressure from the ever-demanding merchant class (Kondo 1984), sake producers fine-tuned their art—and assured their fortunes—by discovering such secrets as the use of special water (for example, miyamizu), highly milled rice, and winter brewing (kanzukuri).

Commercial production of alcohol in Japan continued to expand from the middle of the nineteenth century until just prior to World War II, during which time commercial beer production began.[3] The Japanese are thought to have been introduced to beer at the Dutch compound in Nagasaki during the Tokugawa period (Sapporo n.d., 32), but it was not until 1873 that Japan had its own beer brewery. The Spring Valley Brewery was established in Yokohama by William Copeland (1832–1902), a naturalized American born in Norway (Inagaki 1978, 13–14). Domestic production of whiskey became commercially viable in the late 1930s as whiskey became popular among military personnel and international trade became problematic (Minai 1986, 44 n. 12).

In a provocative article on international alcohol trends, Pekka Sulkunen (1976) observes that the growth in alcohol consumption since World War II is a worldwide phenomenon.[4] Sulkunen correlates this growth with the homogenization of "use value," arguing that the consumption of alcohol was once limited by regional drinking customs. In grape-rich nations such as France and Italy, wine, which was considered food or nutriment, almost always accompanied meals and was drunk by young and old, male and female alike. In grain cultures, such as Great Britain and northern Germany, beer was thought of as an accompaniment to leisure activities, although not usually to eating, and was drunk regularly by male and female adults. In spirit cultures, such as Finland, a narrow segment of adult males used distilled alcohol as an intoxicant for binges. Since World War II, each of these narrow patterns has broken down as drinking practices from other cultures have been introduced. Italians now hold cocktail parties in addition to drinking wine with meals. More Finns now drink with meals, including those who still go on lost weekends.

The same pattern of expanded use value is true for postwar Japan. Sake, shōchū, and unrefined home brew (*doburoku*) in premodern Japan were drunk for a number of purposes (as medicine, sacrament, an accompaniment to meals), but alcohol was associated most closely with community parties and festivals. Yanagita (1956, 30, 32) argues that drinking in rural communities in late premodern and early modern Japan was limited to special celebrations. For these occasions villagers brewed alcohol in large quantities and drank until it was gone.

The diversification of Japanese drinking occasions—which producers have been quick to exploit—has worked to deritualize drinking customs and to dilute the exchange and social-bonding functions of alcohol. There was once a strong positive correlation among alcohol, drinking rituals, and public events that reinforced social solidarity. The meaning of alcohol now encompasses utilitarian functions (such as quenching one's thirst at a sporting event), privatized functions (solitary drinking by housewives), and status-oriented functions (ordering wine with a meal).

NEW DRINKS

The etiquette of cup exchange (and the practice of using fewer cups than drinkers) developed under circumstances in which drinkers shared the same beverage. At a village celebration (*matsuri*), for example, everyone partook of the same unrefined brew made from rice, perhaps all from the same batch.

There is still a strong tendency for Japanese drinkers in groups to choose the same drink. In part this reflects a cultural disinclination to set oneself apart from the group. Americans are far more likely to make personal statements by ordering drinks that are different from what others are drinking; Japanese will regularly decide collectively what to drink so as to minimize differences.[5]

The likelihood that Japanese drinkers would choose the same drink was once greater because the alternatives were fewer than in the West. There was only a choice between sake and shōchū until beer and whiskey were added as possibilities. Mixed drinks are not popular; the elaborate cocktails found in Western cultures are still seldom available. But varieties of alcoholic beverages and beverage packaging are being rapidly expanded and diversified by producers, causing as well as reflecting an individualization of consumer tastes and drinking practices.

Japanese beer brewers have expanded their product lines from standard draft and bottled lager to include bottled draft, high malt, and "dry" beer (which is fermented longer to remove more sugar). The elaboration has occurred so quickly that between 1975 and 1985, the number of beer labels increased fivefold, from 32 to 164.[6] In similar fashion many variants of sake are promoted: a cloudy, less refined sake (*nigorizake*), sake tasting of the wooden cask (*taruzake*), unpasteurized sake (*namazake*), and brown rice sake (*genmaishu*). The rising popularity of small independent breweries with limited production—after years of market domination by a few major manufacturers—has led to the creation of sake bars that offer scores of local labels (*jizake*), much like wine bars. Imported wines have gained cachet among Japanese yuppies, and although these imports account for only a small percentage of all alcohol consumed, they are widely available both as vintage varietals and as table wines bottled in Japan under Japanese labels.

The nature of a beverage can have consequences for the way it is drunk; thus, diversifying liquor tastes can directly influence drinking etiquette. The most dramatic change in Japanese tastes in alcohol has been the shift from sake to beer. The standard size of a bottle of beer at a bar is 633 ml. (21.4 oz.) and the glasses are relatively small (5–6 oz.). (Smaller bottles may sometimes be available for single orders, but two or more drinkers ordering beer would ordinarily be given a larger bottle to share.) As with sake, a beer glass is raised and then filled to the rim. Sake cups may or may not be exchanged, but beer glasses rarely change hands.

There are two reasons why beer glasses do not circulate. First, it is much more difficult for the recipient to quickly finish and return a six-ounce glass of beer than it is a one-ounce sake cup. Another reason has to do with the Japanese concern with cleanliness and purity (Norbeck 1952; Ohnuki-Tierney 1984).[7] As indicated above, until recently sake cups were swished in a bowl of water before being passed on to the next drinker. A quick shake upside down or a flick to the side now serves as the symbolic equivalent. Sake is clear and hot sake is ordinarily served in opaque ceramic cups. Beer, on the other hand, is amber, leaves a residue of bubbles, and is served in clear glasses that show finger smudges. A used beer glass does not look pristine like a sake cup does. Beer glasses do not, therefore, change hands, and thus one important element of traditional drinking etiquette is lost.

The social drinking of whiskey has produced an interesting twist on the ritual of pouring and exchange. Whiskey is almost always diluted with water and served over ice (*mizuwari*). In public drinking establishments, whiskey can be ordered by the glass (a nonexchangeable presentation), but by far the most common way to purchase whiskey is by the "keep" (*kiipu*). Bar patrons buy bottles that are labeled with their names. When a man goes to a bar, he asks for his own bottle and may pay a small fee for the setup (water, ice, glasses). In most of these keep establishments, customers do not pour their own but are served by a hostess or by someone in their party—either a woman or, less often, a younger man. The server constantly refills the customer's glass, never letting it become empty, regularly adding a chunk of ice, a dollop of whiskey, and a splash of water. In this way, drinking establishments exploit traditional exchange forms to enhance sales. Customers relinquish control of their drinks to assertive hostesses who aggressively refill glasses, thus stimulating a great deal of consumption; her repeated pouring (giving) necessitates his drinking (receiving).

The expansion of beer and whiskey in the liquor market has led the industry to cross-fertilize with older products to create new ways of drinking. Shōchū is traditionally heated and drunk straight or, more often, mixed with hot water. The whiskey distillers have had major advertising campaigns for "hot whiskey" (that is, whiskey and hot water), a copycat drinking style. Conversely, low-class eateries serving shōchū often serve it with cold water and *hoppu,* a hops flavoring, to make it taste like expensive beer. More recently, there has been a craze for drinking sake and shōchū over ice, reflecting a Western influence.

Except for whiskey and shōchū, distilled spirits have not become popular in Japan. There is a small market for brandy and a recent fad for bourbon, each served like whiskey, over ice and diluted with water. The Japanese do not generally drink mixed drinks. A recent change in the marketing of shōchū, however, may be the beginning of a significant shift in liquor sales. In 1983, a shōchū company introduced Can Chu-Hi, or generically, *chūhai* (for shōchū highball), simply an extrarefined (and essentially flavorless) shōchū mixed with fruit juice and sold in cans. Shōchū sales jumped 30 percent in 1983 and another 40 percent in 1984 (Haberman 1985, 3) The drinkers attribute its popularity to the taste or, more exactly, the lack thereof. A survey of the youth market indicated that young people are seeking lighter-tasting drinks, which are thought to be healthier ("Fight of the Century" 1988, 5). Industry spokesmen say that shōchū is part of a worldwide "white revolution" favoring liquors that are perceived as light: white wine, vodka, and gin. Variable taxation practices in Japan have benefited sales by helping to keep the cost of shōchū relatively low.[8] I would suggest that the premixing and packaging may also be profoundly important to the shōchū boom.

I believe that the reason mixed drinks have not done well in the past is not that people did not like the taste or found the drinks too heavy or prohibitively expensive, but rather that Japanese social drinking traditionally emphasizes the sublimation and unification of individuals into community. Mixed drinks, by definition, are mixed and thus require special preparation that focuses undesirable attention on the individualistic demands of the drinker's order. Japan is a culture in which diners frequently seek consensus as to what they should order, a culture in which guests are automatically given sugar and cream in their coffee so as to save them from socially awkward decisions and the expression of individual demands.

Premixed drinks served in individual portions (can, bottle, or paper box) preempt any issue of sharing the beverage or of special preparation, thus freeing the drinker to choose on the basis of personal taste. It is reported that the chūhai boom has ended ("Fight of the Century" 1988, 5), but with the introduction of premixed alcoholic beverages, there may yet be a market in Japan for mixed drinks made with gin, vodka, or tequila.

The packaging of chūhai in individual servings reflects a major industry response to changing social behavior and at the same time exacerbates the change. Increasing numbers of Japanese are drinking at home and in nontraditional contexts (for example, office parties) where convenience is a consideration. Alcoholic beverages are now packaged in a plethora of sizes, clearly intended to provide an appropriate volume for any conceivable drinking situation. Suntory industries, for example, produces thirty-four different beer containers (Koren 1988, 93), ranging in size from 5 liters to 150 ml. The Kirin Beer Company produces a variety of gimmick containers, such as those made to look like spaceships, eggs, bamboo stalks, and robots (92).

The sake industry has gone through a similar transformation in packaging. The traditional sake bottle is 1 *shō* (1.8 l., or .48 U.S. gal.), cumbersomely large. Sake is now also available in a 900-ml. (.5 shō) paper container (like a 1-qt. milk carton), as well as in sizes that are multiples of the standard one-person serving of 1 *gō* (180 ml., or 6.1 oz.).

The sake maker Ozeki created an individual-size container of sake called the One Cup (*wankappu*) that has transformed the industry. Not only does the One Cup hold 1 gō (the traditional unit for one serving of sake), but the container is a widemouthed glass cup—like a jelly glass—with a pop-off lid. Other sake producers were quick to devise their own individual-portion containers, like the Hakutsuru-brand "Tanburā" (tumbler). The beer industry responded as well with its equivalent to the One Cup. Sapporo Beer, for example, introduced its own 300-ml. (10.1-oz.) widemouthed bottle, the Gui. (*Gui-gui* means to drink in gulps and is reminiscent of the onomatopoeically similar *chug-a-lug*.)

I see the commercial transformation of alcohol packaging as potentially the most disruptive influence on traditional drinking etiquette. The implications of the widemouthed bottle for drink exchange should be clear. In the traditional pattern of using a sake flask or big beer bottle, one repeatedly filled a cup from the container. Individual-portion packaging eliminates the exchange of pouring altogether; a One Cup container *is* the cup, and it is already filled. Each drinker is alone and self-sufficient.

Another recent change in the Japanese alcohol market is that liquor is now sold in vending machines. The machines began to appear around 1965, and by 1981 there were 170,000 (Shokuhin Sangyō Sentā 1982, 240). Almost every liquor store has at least one machine in front dispensing not only cold beer but also whiskey bottles and hot One Cups of sake. The commercial merits of a vending machine outside the store are obvious. It facilitates the most common and simplest transactions and remains open for business when the store is closed, although vending machines are, by law, turned off between 11:00 P.M. and 5:00 A.M. to discourage drunk driving ("Bad News" 1980, 30).

Vending machines, if not the original impetus, may once have encouraged the development of small containers for purely logistical reasons. Such reasons are no longer relevant, because the machines now dispense full-size bottles of whiskey and wine and multiliter kegs of beer. These machines also contribute to the decline of drinking as a social activity. People who might otherwise have dropped in at a bar for a drink or sought out a social context for drinking can now pick up a nightcap to drink alone at home or while standing in front of the machine.

In the past, alcohol was primarily associated with ceremonies, parties, and other public occasions, which reinforced social solidarity. To this day, most social drinking turns on a number of ritual expectations, including the fact that within a group the Japanese tend to drink the same beverage and are actively involved in keeping their companions' glasses filled while relying on them to reciprocate. The pouring and receiving establish a bond, even between individuals of significantly different social rank. Commercial influences on the beverage alcohol trade are not necessarily directly causal in changing the postwar market. By facilitating the diversification of alcohol use values, the liquor industry contributes to the disruption of drinking customs and to the dilution of the connection between alcohol, ritual exchange, and social solidarity.

In sum, one finds that there are more drinking contexts and more ways to drink, making drinking a more individualized, less ritualized experience; new beverages (such as, "dirty" beer) and new packaging (the One Cup) discourage the old etiquette of mutual pouring and reciprocation; and innovations of convenience (individual-portion packaging and vending machines) that facilitate the spontaneous, utilitarian consumption of alcohol diminish the probability that the inchoate desire to drink will be translated into an act of ritual unity or social exchange.

Where is all this headed? One could argue that the Japanese have domesticated the alcoholic beverages they have imported and borrowed from the West. Beer and whiskey in Japan have different social functions, different modes of being served and consumed, and different cultural capital than they have in Western cultures. But this domestication of foreign spirits has been accompanied by a profound westernization of Japanese drinking tastes and customs. Beer and whiskey dominate the market, over their traditional counterparts, sake and shō-chū. There has been a gradual but inexorable shift in drinking practices, from rituals of reciprocity to autonomy and individuality. This evolution is consistent with other domains of a modernization process that disrupts patterns of interactions previously enjoyed in integrated, personalized communities and replaces them with an atomistic, contractually organized society. The westernization and commercialization of alcoholic beverage production and marketing represents a trend in Japan, resonant with other social trends, away from group orientation and toward individualism.

NOTES

1. I have, however, experienced drinking with fewer cups than drinkers in Korea, where the practice is common.
2. In Japanese usage *sake* is the generic term for alcoholic beverages; the terms *nihonshu* (Japanese liquor) and *osake* (honorable sake) are used to indicate the specific beverage we think of as rice wine and call *saki* in English.
3. Japan's steady increase in alcohol production contrasts with a general decrease in consumption in the industrialized West from the 1870s to World War II (Sulkunen 1976, 229).
4. Sulkunen's sample is, unfortunately, limited to twenty-six nations, mostly in Western Europe and North and South America.
5. Doi Takeo contrasts American and Japanese drinking practices in a well-known passage

from his book *The Anatomy of Dependence:* "Another thing that made me nervous was the custom whereby an American host will ask a guest, before the meal, whether he would prefer a strong or a soft drink. Then, if the guest asks for liquor, he will ask him whether, for example, he prefers scotch or bourbon. When the guest has made this decision, he next has to give instructions as to how much he wishes to drink, and how he wants it served. . . . I soon realized that this was only the American's way of showing politeness to his guest, but in my own mind I had a strong feeling that I couldn't care less. What a lot of trivial choices they were obliging one to make—I sometimes felt—almost as though they were doing it to reassure themselves of their own freedom" (1973, 12).

6. These statistics are attributed to the Association of Beer Producers in a paper by Iwai Sumiko, "Recent Changes in Japanese Attitudes," originally presented at the Ōiso Conference on Social Changes, Ōiso, Japan, December 10–11, 1988 (p. 17, fig. 3). This paper cannot be cited without the permission of the Council on Foreign Relations, but I mention it as a source of other data.

7. Sake, like salt and water, is a ritually purifying substance in Shinto.

8. In 1980, a standard bottle (1,800 ml.) of special-class (16 percent) sake retailed for 2,200 yen, of which 738 yen, or 33.6 percent, was tax. A bottle (1,800 ml.) of special-class (at least 20 percent) shōchū cost 790 yen, of which 96 yen, or 12.2 percent, was tax (Kokuzeichō 1981, 15).

REFERENCES

Bad news for late-night imbibers. 1980. *Asahi Evening News,* February 8, p. 3.

Befu, Harumi. 1968. Gift giving in modernizing Japan. *Monumenta Nipponica* 23(3–4):445–456.

———. 1974. Power in exchange. *Asian Profile* 2(6):601–622.

———. 1980. The group model of Japanese society and its alternatives. *Rice University Studies* 66(1):169–187.

Bestor, Theodore C. 1989. *Neighborhood Tokyo.* Stanford: Stanford University Press.

Dixon, J. M. 1885. Japanese etiquette. *Transactions of the Asiatic Society of Japan* 13:1–21.

Doi Takeo. 1973. *The anatomy of dependence.* Tokyo: Kodansha International.

Edwards, Walter. 1989. *Modern Japan through its weddings.* Stanford: Stanford University Press.

Fight of the century: Battle of the dry beers in the season of suds. 1988. *Discover Kinki!* July, p. 5.

Haberman, Clyde. 1985. In Japan, a new cachet for an old drink. *New York Times,* 5 June 1985, sec. C, p. 3.

Hendry, Joy. 1981. *Marriage in changing Japan.* Rutland, Vt.: Charles E. Tuttle.

Inagaki, Masami. 1978. *Nippon no biiru (Japanese beer).* Tokyo: Chūōkōronsha.

Ishino Iwao. 1953. The *oyabun-kobun:* A ritualized kinship institution. *American Anthropologist* 55:695–707.

Iwai Hiroaki. 1974. Delinquent groups and organized crime. In Takie Sugiyama Lebra and William P. Lebra (eds.), *Japanese culture and behavior,* 383–395. Honolulu: University of Hawaii Press.

Kokuzeichō. 1981. *Dai 107 kai Kokuzeichō Tōkei Nenpōsho* (The 107th National Tax Office annual statistical report). Tokyo: Kokuzeichō Kanzeibu Shuzeika (National Tax Office, Indirect Tax Bureau, Alcohol Tax Section).

Kondō Hiroshi. 1984. *Sake: A drinker's guide*. Tokyo: Kodansha International.

Kono, H., J. Nakagawa, S. Saito, K. Shimada, and A. Tanaka. 1977. *Nihonjin no inshu kōdō* (Japanese drinking behavior). Tokyo: Yoka Kaihatsu Sentā (Leisure Development Center).

Koren, Leonard. 1988. *283 useful ideas from Japan*. San Francisco: Chronicle.

Lebra, Takie Sugiyama. 1974. Reciprocity and the asymmetric principle: An analytical reappraisal of the Japanese concept of *on*. In Takie Sugiyama Lebra and William P. Lebra (eds.), *Japanese culture and behavior*, 155–173. Honolulu: University of Hawaii Press.

Lévi-Strauss, Claude. 1949. *Les structures élémentaires de la parenté*. Paris: Presses Universitaires de France.

Mauss, Marcel. 1967. *The gift*. Translated by Ian Cunnison. New York: W. W. Norton.

Minai Keiko. 1986. Trends in alcoholic beverage consumption in postwar Japan: An analysis and interpretation of aggregate data. Occasional Paper Series, no. 4 (July), Department of Japanese Studies, National University of Singapore.

Nakane Chie. 1970. *Japanese society*. Berkeley: University of California Press.

Norbeck, Edward. 1952. Pollution and taboo in contemporary Japan. *Southwest Journal of Anthropology* 8(3):269–285.

Nukada Akira. 1981. Nihon ni okeru arukōru inryō shōhi no dōkō oyobi kenkō shōgai no jōkyō (Trends in alcohol consumption and health problems in Japan). In *Teisei inshu gaidobukku* (Guidebook to proper drinking), Kōseisho Kōshueiseikyoku Seishineiseika (Ministry of Health and Welfare, Public Health Bureau, Mental Health Division). Tokyo: Arukōru Kenkō Igaku Kyōkai.

Ohnuki-Tierney, Emiko. 1984. *Illness and culture in contemporary Japan*. Cambridge: Cambridge University Press.

Sapporo. n.d. *Sapporo beer guide* (A Sapporo Beer Company brochure, 36 pp., in Japanese. Contains no publication information).

Shokuhin Sangyō Sentā. 1982. *Shokuhin sangyō tōkei nenpō* (Annual statistical report of the foodstuffs industry). Tokyo: Shokuhin Sangyō Sentā.

Sulkunen, Pekka. 1976. Drinking patterns and the level of alcohol consumption: An international overview. In Robert J. Gibbins, Yedy Israel, Harold Kalant, Robert E. Popham, Wolfgang Schmidt, and Reginald Smart (eds.), *Research advances in alcohol and drug problems*, vol. 3, 223–281. New York: John Wiley.

World Fellowship Committee of the Young Women's Christian Association of Tokyo, Japan. 1955. *Japanese etiquette: An introduction*. Rutland, Vt.: Charles E. Tuttle

Yanagita Kunio. 1956. *Japanese manners and customs in the Meiji era*. Tokyo: Obansha.

• • • • •

9

A JAPANESE-FRENCH RESTAURANT
IN HAWAI'I

JEFFREY TOBIN

Washizu, chef of the Honolulu restaurant Papadore, was even more high-strung than usual, because Ōhashi, president of the parent company in Japan, was paying one of his rare visits. For months business had been good, but Washizu was uneasy. The customers were almost exclusively Japanese honeymooners who ordered only the tourist menu. At six o'clock every evening, the tour buses and stretch limousines would zero in on Papadore, depositing as many as one hundred customers in a half hour. So many Japanese honeymooners were appearing that the American waiters had taken to announcing their arrival with the call "*Tora! Tora! Tora!*"—the Japanese battlecry during the attack on Pearl Harbor. Toshi, the president of the local company, was happy to show a steady profit from selling to tour groups. But Washizu considered himself an artist, a highly trained chef capable of creativity. He had gone to Paris to learn how to prepare *nouvelle cuisine*. Feeding the same meal to hundreds of tourists a week was taking a toll on his professional self-image.

Tonight Washizu would introduce his new cuisine, the cuisine that would attract a more sophisticated clientele to the restaurant. Ōhashi was not an accountant, like Toshi, but a man of taste and class who would appreciate Washizu's innovative cooking. Tonight would mark the beginning of a new era at Papadore, the birth of a fine French restaurant. Ōhashi would be the first to taste Washizu's rendition of French-style Japanese food. He would be dining *à la japonaise*—that is, in the style of the Japanese as evoked by the French or, more precisely, as Washizu imagined that the French evoked the food of his own Japan.

Washizu planned to serve carpaccio for the first course, but in a Japanese style. Though originally an Italian dish, carpaccio, like many other dishes from around the world, has been adapted by French chefs. In its French form, seasoned beef tenderloin is cut into thin slices and served raw with mixed greens in a vinaigrette dressing. Washizu added a Japanese twist to the French version of this Italian dish by using shoyu (soy sauce) in the vinaigrette.

Washizu instructed one of the cooks, an American, to prepare the carpaccio. Having gone out for sushi with Washizu many times, the American knew something about this Japanese specialty and about Washizu's ideas for the new cuisine. Following the chef's lead, he decided to prepare the carpaccio sushi-style. He began by making a fine julienne of endive, tossed with chopped watercress and parsley in a lemon vinaigrette dressing. He then cut thin slices of raw beef tenderloin and coated them on one side with the chef's special shōyu dressing. He formed the salad into little bundles, each one wrapped in a piece of beef, with the dressing on the inside. He placed two of the beef-wrapped bundles on each plate along with a fanned cornichon and a clamshell filled with extra sauce. Chef Washizu was generally pleased with the preparation, though he removed the clamshell. Voilà, a new dish: *carpaccio nigiri* (sushi).

As I prepared that first order of carpaccio nigiri, I anticipated that some day I would include it in an ethnography of the restaurant. When I started working at Papadore, I did not know that I would ever be writing about the experience. I had already spent nine years working in restaurants and bakeries, so at first, working at Papadore was just another job, not a research endeavor. But by the time I made the first carpaccio nigiri, I knew I would be leaving the kitchen to study anthropology. Perceiving my kitchen work as fieldwork, I started observing my fellow workers and myself, looking for interesting phenomena. And, as in the case of carpaccio nigiri, I even participated in creating data that I thought would be especially rich. I had gone from being a participant to being a participant-observer.

The ethnographer's dual role as a participant-observer can be highly reflexive. As an observer, the ethnographer is a Self observing Others. But as a participant, the ethnographer is one of the observed. Thus, doing ethnography can involve seeing one's Self as an Other (Kondo 1986). As a participant, the ethnographer might even perform Otherness for his observing Self. The relationship between participant and observer is thus reproduced within the single participant-observer. The observer observes his Self as a participant in the Other's culture. Just so, I observed my Self as a participant in Chef Washizu's kitchen. The power relations in the kitchen are such that a cook cannot stray far from the chef's culinary system. Washizu was the boss, and I the employee. But with me as ethnographer and him as my subject, the power relations are reversed. Being the ethnographer permits me a superior stance in relation to my ethnographic Others (Crapanzano 1980, x). The ethnographer's disengagement is an empowering strategy. Chef Washizu is no longer supervising me; I am now viewing him. As the chef, Washizu was looking over my shoulder, but as the ethnographer, I am looking over his (Geertz 1973, 452). As the chef, he had power to determine what happened in the kitchen. But as the ethnographer, I have power to represent those happenings.

My role as an ethnographer is similar to Washizu's role as chef. I have represented my Self as an American cook in the Japanese chef's kitchen: an anthropology student including himself as a cook in his ethnography of a Japanese restaurant serving Japanese food as it is found in France. In Washizu's cuisine, as in my ethnography, the Self is represented as an Other. Washizu's cuisine, like my ethnography, is a narrative in which the author is also a character. Washizu is not simply a Japanese chef making Japanese food. He is a Japanese chef making a French version of Japanese food. He did not serve sashimi; he made French-style sashimi, as only a Japanese could make it. His cuisine was not a Japanese presentation of Japanese food, nor was it a French representation of Japanese food. Rather, Washizu's cuisine was a re-representation: a Japanese representation of a French representation of Japanese cuisine. Washizu was engaged in a highly reflexive cuisine in which he represented his Japanese Self as a French chef's Other. He saw himself, as a Japanese, reflected in a French mirror. Washizu reproduced a world order in which his Self was an Other.

Jean Baudrillard tells a story: "Once there lived in the Ardennes an old cook, to whom the molding of buildings out of cakes and the science of plastic patisserie had given the ambition to take up the creation of the world where God had left it, in its natural phase, so as to eliminate its organic spontaneity and substitute for it a single, unique and polymorphous matter" (1983, 90).

The whole world is constituted in the French culinary discourse, the preeminent ordering of things to eat. "The table seems like a lexicon of the universe, of lands far and near, of Europe conquered and France integrated, with Paris as the capital" (Aron 1975, 124). Anthelme Brillat-Savarin wrote in 1825, "A meal such as can be ordered in Paris is a cosmopolitan whole in which every part of the world is represented by one or many of its products" (1972, 317). And Philéas Gilbert, writing in 1884, envisioned a French school of professional cookery:

> The populations of the five continents would find their native foods there, and each department of France would watch over the preparation of its own individual dishes. In this way, it would be possible to take a course in world geography in terms of the alimentary products of all nations. The products of our French restaurants and foodshops, which are exported all over Europe, would be represented on a vast scale, and the alimentary riches of the entire world would flood into the school, just as they once did into Rome. Our national culinary experts would, in their turn, imprint the seal of their genius upon these products, as they do with everything that passes through their hands, and redistribute them to the greater happiness of our modern gastronomes. (quoted in Aron 1975, 128)

The French kitchen is at the center of a world culinary system in which wealth is accumulated and influence is spread. Thus cuisine is an arena of cultural imperialism. Like fashion, cuisine is used to extend French order in the world; as Jean-Baptiste Colbert advised Louis XIV, "With our taste, let us make war on Europe, and through fashion conquer the world" (quoted in Ewen 1988, 30). A French journalist wrote a century later, "It is, therefore, a question of centralizing the art of the table, just as we have already centralized transport, furniture, fashions, all the everyday things of life" (quoted in Aron 1975, 127). French cuisine can thus be seen as a totalizing, imperialist discourse, a country's "will to power." French chefs have constructed an order of things to eat. They conspire to create a world out of animals and fish, fruits and vegetables, nuts and grains. The world is their oyster; society is constituted in a grain of rice.

Until recently, the Japanese place in this discourse has been peripheral. Consider the garnishes included in Auguste Escoffier's 1921 *Guide culinaire* (1979), from *à l'algérienne, alsacienne,* and *américaine,* through *à la marseillaise, mexicaine,* and *milanaise,* to *à la tyrolienne, Vichy,* and *Zingara.* Escoffier's garnish à la japonaise is distinguished by the presence of either rice croquettes or *crosnes du Japon,* in English commonly known as Chinese (or Japanese) artichokes. *Filet de boeuf japonaise, tournedos japonaise,* and *poulet sauté japonaise* are all prepared with crosnes du Japon, a vegetable introduced to Europe from Beijing in 1882 (Simon 1981, 77). Similarly, Le Divan Japonais, a café in Paris at the end of the nineteenth century, was special because "everything there is Chinese" (Grand-Cateret quoted in Oberthur 1984, 85). There is little that is Japanese in classical japonaise cuisine, though much that is Chinese. Rather, japonaise is an almost purely orientalist category, relating only to Far Eastern exotica—tea, rice, chopsticks, as well as Chinese artichokes.

The representation of Japan is vague and operates at the level of the ingredients that go into the dish. Less peripheral regions are represented with greater specificity. Provence, for example, occurs among Escoffier's garnishes as the general *à la provençale,* as well as the specific *arlésienne* and *marseillaise,* and is joined by its neighbors, *à la dauphinoise, niçoise,* and *italienne.* Such regions, which are close to the Parisian core, tend to be represented by methods of preparation as well as ingredients. As Kondo (this volume) notices in the world of high fashion, core status corresponds with producing styles, whereas the periphery provides material and labor; and, as Savigliano (this volume) observes of tango styles, core nations are granted brand names, while the periphery provides only labels. But *crème anglaise* is a brand name, referring to an English way of making custard (not to English eggs or cream), and *escargots à la bourguignonne* refers to a Burgundian recipe for snails (not to Burgundian garlic or butter). In the culinary discourse, as codified during *la belle époque,* England and Burgundy were of the recipe-producing, brand name core, but Japan was a mere label for exotic ingredients produced at the periphery.

The world constituted in French cuisine is not stable; the French culinary discourse is in flux. Changing world orders are produced and reproduced in this discourse. The French are always at the center, but the positions of others vary greatly. Traditional histories of French cuisine, for example, credit Italian chefs with introducing haute cuisine to France. In the sixteenth century Catherine and Marie de Médicis brought their own chefs with them from Florence to Paris and thus taught the French how to eat well. But such histories are now being revised (for example, Revel 1982, 117), and Italian chefs are being demoted in importance. Inversely, the cuisines of the United States and Japan have gained influence since the age of Escoffier. California cuisine, with its English-language menus and emphasis on California wines, is nothing less than a direct challenge to French hegemony over international cuisine. So far, few French chefs recognize the culinary contributions of North American chefs, but some European experts have made concessions for California wines. Meanwhile, Japan has risen to the heady peaks of the French culinary discourse. Japonaise has come to refer not just to ingredients but to recipes and methods. Paul Bocuse, the current king of *nouveaux cuisiniers,* even wrote about teaching French cooking in Osaka: "I think that I also learned as much there as I taught" (1977, xiii). Japanese, along with Chinese, are being credited with influencing French cuisine, not just by providing new raw materials but by teaching the French new ways to prepare food.

Various world orders are discernible in the evolution of the menu at Papadore. When the restaurant first opened—in December 1987—the classic French discourse was reproduced. Paris was at the center, and the United States and Japan were peripheral. Hawai'i, in this menu, appeared only as a surrogate Mediterranean resort. Neither Japanese nor Americans were granted any special status. By June 1988, Hawai'i's tourist economy had come to influence the cuisine. Relations between Japan and the United States dominated Papadore's menu, reproducing the balance of trade discourse. As a result, Papadore's Frenchness was greatly deemphasized. By the time I left Papadore, in June 1989, the cuisine was again being redefined. Chef Washizu's new cuisine reintroduced the centrality of France to Papadore, but now the Japaneseness of the restaurant also became a significant factor in the menu.

The logo features the name "Papadore" embellished with a radiating sun and the descriptive phrase *la cuisine méditerranéene.* In accordance with the invocation in French of the Mediterranean, Papadore's first menu offered French Mediterranean dishes, including bouillabaisse and fish sautéed with saffron sauce or grilled with tomato and basil. Other such specialties included lamb with pasta and herbs, cold tomato soup, and carpaccio de boeuf. At this stage, the carpaccio was made not with shoyu but with a more traditional red wine and mustard vinaigrette. The cuisine was French Mediterranean to the extent that these dishes are attributed to Provence and Nice or to neighboring provinces in France and Italy.

In the parlance of haute cuisine, any dish based on olive oil, garlic, aromatic herbs, and tomatoes is likely to be labeled provençale, or something more specific, such as niçoise or marseillaise. The cuisine at Papadore was true to this nomenclature. But provençale cuisine is not uncontested territory. Bouillabaisse is ultimately at the center of all battles to define authentic provençale cuisine. Escoffier even offered two different recipes, one for bouillabaisse à la marseillaise, the other for bouillabaisse à la parisienne, and asserted that the bread "should not be fried or toasted for a real bouillabaisse à la marseillaise." These days, the controversies surrounding bouillabaisse seem to depend more on the use of lobster than on toasting the bread. Lobster is the focus of the Parisian version, but in Marseilles, where the dish is said to have originated, lobster is included only for the tourists—and their money. Robert Courtine (1974) adds to the controversy by implying that the only true bouillabaisse à la marseillaise is found not in Marseilles but in Toulon.

Papadore was not a provençale restaurant. Rather, it was supposed to be a Parisian restaurant that featured provençale cuisine. Washizu's bouillabaisse was clearly Parisian, as was his entire cuisine. In addition, the decor, china, silver, and crystal indicated haute cuisine as opposed to a provincial (or ethnic) restaurant. At Papadore, la cuisine méditerranéenne indicated provençale cuisine as found not on the docks of Nice but in the expensive restaurants of Paris. After all, Washizu had trained in Paris, not in Marseilles. Rather than try to reproduce the cuisine of Provence, he tried to reproduce the Parisian representation of provençale cuisine. There are correlations between the Parisian representation and the provençale cuisine. Parisian chefs do not construct their version of provençale cuisine from scratch but pick and choose among the bounties of real provençale tables. So, too, Provence has been affected by its place in the Parisian system. The demands of the Parisian market influence what is grown in Provence, and Parisian representations are reproduced by the internally colonized people of Provence. But the Parisian and original versions of provençale cuisine are still distinguishable.

La cuisine méditerranéenne arrived in Hawai'i as part of a larger colonizing practice, which I call tropicalism. Chef Washizu explained that Mediterranean food should be successful in Hawai'i because Hawai'i has a Mediterranean climate. Also, Hawai'i is supposed to be to Tokyo what the Riviera is to Paris. Mixing the Pacific and the Mediterranean is characteristic of tropical culture. The Mediterranean serves as an archetype according to which other parts of the world are constructed. In an earlier age, sugar dominated the economy of the tropics, but now tourism does. As tropical tourist destinations, the Caribbean and the Pacific are thus patterned after the Mediterranean. All three regions have warm climates, islands inhabited by dark-skinned people, and plantation crops. Cooking Mediterranean food in Hawai'i contributes to this construction of the tropics.

Toshi and Washizu were disappointed with the response to la cuisine méditerranéenne in Hawai'i. As the financial officer and the chef responsible for the restaurant, they worried about low repeat business. Judging from the waiters' remarks, few of the customers (or waiters) appreciated the distinction between a French restaurant and a French Mediterranean restaurant—much less the distinction between a Parisian Mediterranean restaurant and a real Mediterranean restaurant. Honolulu is not a city of fancy French restaurants. The customers did not expect or accept garlic, olive oil, and herbs—much less pasta—at a French restaurant. More than one asked, "What do you mean by Mediterranean, isn't this a French restaurant?" The concept of the restaurant was not meaningful to its potential customers. The French context, in which la cuisine méditerranéenne has meaning, was too far removed from Hawai'i. From his training to be a French chef, Washizu had internalized the French culinary view of the world; for him, the equation of the Mediterranean and the Pacific was logical. But few of the tourists and fewer still of the local customers were sufficiently francocentric to accept the restaurant's Parisian perspective. The menu had to change.

Toshi turned to Japanese travel agencies to bolster business. He was clearly more comfortable doing business in Japanese with Japanese than trying to figure out what the local clientele wanted. But he was also attending to the increasing importance of Japanese tourists in the local market. Toshi and Washizu met with Japanese travel agents and designed a tourist menu directed at pleasing Japanese in Hawai'i. Toshi abandoned the goal of selling to local diners and geared the restaurant to attracting the Japanese honeymoon trade.

On the new menu, French-American food replaced French Mediterranean. It had not occurred to me or to other Americans in the kitchen that Japanese tourists would seek American food in the middle of the Pacific. But for Japanese, a Hawaiian vacation is a trip to the United States, and a trip to the United States includes dining on beef and lobster.

It is not significant that Hawai'i is over three thousand miles from Des Moines, Iowa, and five thousand miles from Kittery, Maine. Many American tourists, after all, would order bouillabaisse in Paris because it is a French dish, not thinking that Marseilles is several hundred miles away. So, too, Japanese began to come to Papadore for American specialties.[1]

Papadore's Japanese tourist menu has gone through several metamorphoses since its introduction in spring 1988, though it has always been a French variation on American "surf and turf." The first incarnation began with a crab and avocado terrine, followed by shellfish bouillon and a Maine lobster, split and arranged around fettucine with a lobster cream sauce. The next offering was a salad of mixed greens with the meat from the lobster claws. The main course was beef tenderloin, served with a port sauce, potatoes, and mixed vegetables. Dessert was my contribution. As a newcomer, my images of Hawai'i were tropical, so I made a Bavarian custard with tropical fruits—kiwi, papaya, and pineapple. The tropicalisms have persisted. When I left, the dessert was Kona coffee ice cream with chocolate sauce, and since then it has changed to mango custard. The appetizer has also varied, evolving from the original terrine to a traditional French pâté to prosciutto with papaya. But lobster and beef remain.

The abundance of American industrialism is represented not only by the prototypical fare but also by the chauffeur-driven stretch Cadillacs in which the Japanese tourists arrive. Once inside, they are served by American waiters dressed in tuxedos. The grand automobile, the tuxedoed waiters, and the lobster and beef combination bespeak the excesses and the conspicuousness of American consumption. As Hayashi Mariko (1988) observed in a similar situation, "The yen must really have gained in value since we have these good-looking blue-eyed waiters serving us." Thus the Americanness of Papadore's employees became part of the restaurant's fare. Routinely, Japanese customers would ask to be photographed with their American waiter, who, like the lobster and beef, was a valued commodity. Luxuries that are available only at great cost in Japan are easily afforded in this Pacific island paradise. The middle class of Japan is transformed into the rich of Hawai'i. Golf for only eight thousand yen! A hotel room overlooking the beach for only thirty thousand! And sumptuous dinner for two at a French restaurant for only twelve thousand yen!

Japanese and American relations are similarly enacted in Papadore as a place to work. The orders that separate kitchen from dining room, *haole* (white) from local (nonwhite), *kama'aina* (long-time resident) from *malahini* (newcomer), American from immigrant, all disintegrate under the pressure of Japanese and American labor relations. At Papadore, all the workers who are not from Japan are constituted as Americans, bound together in opposition to the Japanese. Even (especially?) local Japanese are radically separate from the Japanese-from-Japan. The division between Japanese managers and American workers corresponds to the division between the customers and the products and services consumed. The managers and customers are Japanese, the workers and the food American. The menu reproduced the discourse of "Japan as Number One," having displaced the United States from the center of the world economy. The once-consumed Japanese have become the consumers.

The response to the tourist menu has been strong. Every week, hundreds of Japanese honeymooners have flocked (been herded) to Papadore. Toshi, at least, has been thoroughly pleased with the steady business. But the number of local customers has dwindled even further. Americans seem to dislike dining in a French restaurant with a large crowd of Japanese. The Japanese honeymooners and their popping flashes do not conform to American customers' ideas about the proper ambience for a French restaurant. Washizu, too, became dissatisfied with the Japanese trade. The Frenchness of Papadore had been downplayed, if not altogether forgotten. Surf and turf was not Washizu's idea of haute cuisine. French cooking, with its emphasis on sauces and styles, was not compatible with a touristic emphasis on quantity and value. For Chef Washizu, Papadore is high-class because it is French. Never simply Mediterranean or American, the cooking is, first and foremost, French, and its Frenchness is what makes it special.[2] But the honeymooners were too bourgeois to appreciate the chef's fine French sauces; for them, only steak and lobster were significant. The class of customer the restaurant was attracting was concerned with quantity, not quality.

As with the schools of tango in Japan (Savigliano, this volume), Anglo-American and French cuisines correspond to Japanese class differences. An Anglo-American version of haute cuisine attracted middle-class Japanese to Papadore. So to attract a more sophisticated clientele, Washizu turned to a more French form of fine dining that would also salvage the Frenchness that Toshi had sacrificed for the tourist trade. But Washizu was not allowed to make dramatic changes in the cuisine.

The travel agencies had already promised Maine lobster and beef tenderloin, along with an appetizer, salad, and dessert, all for a set price.
Also, Toshi and the travel agents were too pleased with business to care
about Washizu's artistic sensibilities. The tourist menu remained, though
Washizu dreamed of greater glory.

JAPANESE-FRENCH-JAPANESE CUISINE

When Washizu first arrived in Hawai'i, he rejected any suggestion
that his cuisine might in some way be Japanese or Oriental. He mocked
the Japanese customers who asked for shoyu with their fish, much as
French chefs mock Americans who ask for ketchup with their fried
potatoes. Washizu even described himself as more French than Japanese
and confessed that he had felt more comfortable living in Paris than in
his native Hokkaido. Also, all his friends in Hawai'i were French, or at
least French-speaking. A year and a half later, however, Washizu's point
of view had changed: he had rediscovered his Japaneseness.

Washizu designed a new menu for Papadore that featured his own
Japanese version of French cuisine. La cuisine méditerranéenne remained, as did the tourist menu, but with a deliberate Japanese touch
added. Many of the Japanese-influenced dishes derived from sushi. Carpaccio nigiri, as already described, was patterned after *nigirizushi* (classic sushi). *Ahi tartare,* diced fresh tuna mixed with shoyu and herbs,
was another notable dish served raw.[3] Other examples of Washizu's
Japanese-French cuisine included *salade d'algues* (seaweed salad) and
boeuf tetake (rare beef with a ginger sauce). But the Japanese influence
was often less explicit. As a matter of dining custom, no foods were
served in groups of four, a number that the Japanese associated with
death; this was not a stated rule, but in practice a grouping of four
(ravioli, for example) was considered unattractive. Also true to Japanese
aesthetics, as well as to nouvelle cuisine, the food was served in relatively
modest portions on large plates, and the presentation was elegant rather
than elaborate.

Washizu reproduced Western representations of Japanese cuisine.
Such Japanese stereotypes as raw fish and seaweed for breakfast went
unchallenged in Washizu's cuisine. Consider this commentary from *Oddities in Modern Japan:* "They will eat almost anything that lives and
moves—even things like snakes and squids and seaweed, the very

169

thought of which causes most Englishmen to vomit.... Whereas we English dislike the adjective 'raw' as applied to food, the Japanese find in the corresponding adjective *nama* a positive fascination. Here everything is presented, so far as possible, in its raw condition, just as it came from the womb of Mother Nature" (Milward 1980, 139). Similarly, Jean-Pierre Rampal recorded having a breakfast in Japan that included "both raw fish and raw eggs!" (Omae and Tachibana 1981). Washizu seems to have internalized this Western fascination with Japanese rawness. Of all the foods eaten in Japan, raw fish signified for Washizu, as for Westerners, the essence of Japanese cuisine.

Washizu's representation of Japanese food is consistent with other auto-exoticizing practices in Japan. In this volume Kondo records a parallel movement in the world of high fashion. Japanese chefs, like Japanese designers, are ironically self-orientalizing. This auto-exoticism is examined in this volume by Savigliano on a global scale. Washizu found sushi exotic, just as Argentineans find tango exotic. Japanese, like Argentineans, see themselves as Others in the French mirror. For cuisine, as for fashion and dance, Paris is home to the Self, against which all other selves are Others. Marilyn Ivy (1988) observes this Japanese-French auto-exoticism in many areas of contemporary Japanese society. She cites the Japanese term *neo-Japonesuku:*

> It refers to the revived interest, particularly among the Americanized young, in things Japanese. The "Japonesque" refers to the French interest in Japan and the creation of "Japonaiserie"—not necessarily authentic Japanese objects and motifs, but things in the *style* of Japan, citations of "Japan." The "Japonesque" indicates the French appropriation of Japan. The 1980s promoters have given it another twist by affixing the "neo" to the term: not only is Japan looked at with the eyes of the foreigner, but it is presented as merely an ensemble of styles, waiting to be revived as in all those "neo" movements in art history.(27–28)

The cuisine at Papadore is neo-Japonesuku in that it reproduces the French appropriation of Japanese cooking styles. For Chef Washizu, sushi is an exotic style, available for representation in his version of French cuisine.

Once again, France is located at the center of the culinary world, mediating even the relation between the Japanese chef and his Japanese diners. The Japanese who makes a Japanese dish does so from a Parisian point of view. Like Papadore's original cuisine, this Japanese-French cuisine failed to find a sufficient audience. As before, customers did not buy the francocentrism. The Japanese honeymooners appreciated the Japanese-French cuisine even less than they had the French Mediterranean. Bourgeois sensibilities did not accept traveling to the United States to have Japanese food as it might be found in France. And once again, local clientele were less than enthusiastic—or perhaps they had already written off Papadore.[4]

THE POSTMODERN KITCHEN

Postmodernism provides a useful context for understanding Washizu's nouvelle cuisine, which can be seen as a culinary expression of the movement. Washizu and other nouveaux cuisiniers subject food to an elaborate process of "noncooking." Their emphasis on raw dishes entails preparing food in ways that leave the food uncooked. Well-dressed customers sit at elaborately set tables and dine on the freshest, rawest, and most natural food, served on large plates, at very high prices. Dishes often arrive at the table without sauce and without garnish. Nouveaux cuisiniers claim to take away the artifice of haute cuisine. They simultaneously disrupt and profit from the culinary system, as their noncooking is valued more than their predecessors' cooking. Like other postmodernists, nouveaux cuisiniers trade on the deconstruction of capitalism; they make naughty rebelliousness a good business.

And, like other postmodernists, nouveaux cuisiniers are playful. In Roger Verge's *gratin d'huîtres à la coque,* for example, oysters are placed in an eggshell, and eggs in an oyster shell. Washizu's carpaccio nigiri and ahi tartare are similarly playful; beef substitutes for fish in a traditional Japanese dish, and fish replaces beef in a traditional French dish.[5] For Washizu, such postmodern playfulness is empowering. His Japanese-French cuisine gives him mastery of a discourse that once mastered him. Washizu's Japaneseness, which he formerly suppressed, is a source of strength in his new cuisine. Washizu had at one point almost denied being Japanese, especially in his cooking. Being Japanese was a disadvantage within the world of French cooking. Thus he was proud to have tastes that were French as opposed to Japanese, and he mocked his fellow Japanese for being so gauche. Japanese-French cuisine gave Washizu the opportunity to play with his own Japaneseness. Though Washizu often included shoyu in his Japanese-French cuisine, he remained scornful of the Japanese honeymooners who asked for shoyu to put on their food. He still considered use of shoyu in the dining room to be bourgeois, but shoyu in the kitchen was a sign of sophistication. The Japanese honeymooners used shōyu parochially, but Washizu used shoyu with a wink and thereby transformed bourgeois naïveté into international hipness. Similarly, nouveaux cuisiniers in France have succeeded in making "home cooking" sophisticated. When a nouveau cuisinier prepares a traditional dish *à la mère,* he is credited with an extra degree of sophistication that his mother could never merit. Serving the humble dish in the fancy dining room is considered a creative coup.

Japan has a special place in nouvelle cuisine and in other postmodernisms. French nouveaux cuisiniers routinely locate their inspiration in the Orient. The indigenous cuisines of Japan and China are perceived as intrinsically "nouvelle." The West's new cuisine turns out to be the timeless cuisine of the East. Sushi is only part of the story. M. F. K. Fisher (1988), for example, finds the origins for much of nouvelle cuisine in Japan. She notes the influence of *ryōri* (Japanese cuisine) on "the high priests of *nouvelle cuisine* and *cuisine minceur*": "Perhaps it started for us with Whistler and the 'Japanese' simplicity of his mother's portrait? The fact remains that Zen austerity now intrudes on our old dreams of pastry shaped laboriously into towers of caramel and whipped cream and candied violets" (60). Again there are signs that the current Western interest in Japan is a "neo-" movement. Japanese style is being rediscovered at the end of this century much as it was at the end of the last. We are "turning Japanese," or at least our cuisine is being simplified "according to Japanese teachings" (ibid.).

As Fisher finds that Japanese cuisine is intrinsically nouvelle, postmodernists have discussed "whether or not Japan's indigenous thought is deconstructive or postmodern before the fact" (Ivy 1989, 440). Roland Barthes (1982) implies that Japan and its cuisine are intrinsically postmodern. Thus he writes that sukiyaki is "decentered, like an uninterrupted text."

> No Japanese dish is endowed with a *center* (the alimentary center implied in the West by the rite which consists of arranging the meal, of surrounding or covering the article of food); here everything is the ornament of another ornament: first of all because on the table, on the tray, food is never anything but a collection of fragments, none of which appears privileged by an order of ingestion; to eat is not to respect a menu (an itinerary of

dishes), but to select, with a light touch of the chopsticks, sometimes one color, sometimes another, depending on a kind of inspiration which appears in its slowness as the detached, indirect accompaniment of the conversation (which itself may be extremely silent); and then because this food—and this is its originality—unites in a single time that of its fabrication and that of its consumption. (22)

Barthes finds in traditional Japan many of the elements of contemporary France: the crisis of the sign, the elimination of critical distance, the decentering of authority, the conflation of production and consumption. Thus Japan is constructed as a postmodern promised land, the place where people truly are unimpeded by remnants of modernity.

Asada Akira (1988) refers to postmodernism in Japan as a "fairy tale." Citing a conversation he had with Félix Guattari, Asada relates Japan's postmodernism to "infantile capitalism." Modern "adult" capitalism is located in the United States, and premodern "elderly" capitalism is at home in "countries like Italy and France." Elderly capitalism exists by decapitating the feudal aristocracy, that is, by decodifying the ancient régime, by creating and consuming new distinctions. In adult capitalism, the system is internalized, as entrepreneurs construct their own controlling structures. Infantile capitalists are unimpeded by ancient or new systems, as they simply play at producing and consuming. These infants float freely in the currents of capitalism, whereas the adults attempt to steer a way in their own little boats, and the old people's grand ships are carried along by current, with anchors dragging behind. Infantile capitalists have neither *ancien* ships nor modern boats; they get wet. With time, the location of capitalism moves westward, from Europe across the Atlantic to America, and from there, across the Pacific to Japan. Meanwhile capitalism de-develops, from elderly to infantile. The end of history is marked by having traveled so far West as to have reached the East, and by having regressed to the beginning.

Further progress seems impossible, unless another generation of scholars can locate fetal capitalism, perhaps in India. The fetal capitalist will not be a distinguishable body, carried by the currents of capitalism. The symbiosis of the self and the system will mean the end of the history of bodies. The fetus is not released into the flow, but the flow pulses through the fetus. The subject and object are unified. No ships, no boats, no bodies, just currents and flows: capitalism at last. Then, too, maybe curries will be rediscovered by French chefs. Cuisine will dare to be flavorful, to satisfy and satiate. But until this chapter in history is written, until this territory is mapped, postmodernism and Japan mark the frontiers of capitalism and our scholarship.

Asada thus mocks the Westerners who locate postmodernism in Japan. He calls attention to the logic by which French history is translated into world geography. Japan represents across space what France has achieved over time. That is, Japan is where France has been heading. Accordingly, traditional Japanese cuisine is located within contemporary French cuisine. The Japonesuku is transformed from a style to an epoch. For nouveaux cuisiniers, Japan provides the current answer to a French historical problem. In the French mirror, Japanese even see their own cuisine and their own thought as French discoveries. Thus Japanese cuisine is constituted in its appropriation by the French. Even Japanese success is a French invention, because cultural success is still—as always—determined by the French. Washizu's Japanese representation of French representation of Japanese cuisine is still essentially French. As in other postmodernisms, Others can play the game, but the game remains French.

NOTES

1. Hawai'i is thus constituted as part of America. Featuring American food in Hawai'i naturalizes the inclusion of Pacific islands in the United States of America.
2. As in Itami Juzo's *Tampopo* (a *rāmen* Western), Washizu participates in the Japanese valorization of French culture. Thus when Tampopo has been remade, she is told, "You look like a movie star—a French movie star," and the greatest connoisseurs in the film comment knowingly on Château Pichon-Lalande and the finest French restaurants of Tokyo.
3. The dish happens to be very similar to *ahi poki*, a Hawaiian dish that was introduced to the Islands by Japanese plantation workers.
4. In fall 1989, two years after coming to Hawai'i, Washizu returned to Japan to work in another Papadore restaurant. A non-Japanese succeeded him as chef. Thus the Japanese-French cuisine came to an end, as did the francocentric perspective. Papadore continues to feature a Japanese tourist menu, and the tourist trade remains steady.
5. A modernist commitment to authenticity would require me to note that tartare originated in Russia and that nigiri came from Thailand. But Washizu's play is on the surface.

REFERENCES

Aron, Jean-Paul. 1975. *The art of eating in France: Manners and menus in the nineteenth century.* New York: Harper and Row.

Asada Akira. 1988. Infantile capitalism and Japan's postmodernism: A fairy tale. *South Atlantic Quarterly* 87(3):629–634.

Barthes, Roland. 1982. Translated by Richard Howard. *Empire of signs.* New York: Hill and Wang.

Baudrillard, Jean. Translated by Paul Foss, Paul Patton, and Philip Beitchman. 1983. *Simulations.* New York: Semiotext(e).

Bocuse, Paul. 1977. *Paul Bocuse's French cooking.* New York: Pantheon.

Brillat-Savarin, Anthelme. 1972. *The physiology of taste, or meditations on transcendental gastronomy.* New York: Alfred A. Knopf.

Courtine, Robert. 1974. *Feasts of a militant gastronome.* New York: William Morrow.

Crapanzano, Vincent. 1980. *Tuhami: Portrait of a Moroccan.* Chicago: University of Chicago Press.

Escoffier, Auguste. 1979. *Le guide culinaire: The complete guide to the art of modern cookery.* New York: Mayflower.

Ewen, Stuart. 1988. *All consuming images: The politics of style in contemporary culture.* New York: Basic.

Fisher, M. F. K. 1988. Introduction to Japanese cooking: A simple art by Shizou Tsuji. In *Dubious Honors,* 50–63. San Francisco: North Point Press.

Geertz, Clifford. 1973. Deep play: Notes on the Balinese cockfight. In *The interpretation of cultures: Selected essays,* 412–453. New York: Basic.

Hayashi Mariko. 1988. *Shūkon Bunshun,* June 30.

Ivy, Marilyn. 1988. Tradition and difference in the Japanese mass media. *Public Culture Bulletin* 1(1):21–29.

——. 1989. Critical texts, mass artifacts: The consumption of knowledge in postmodern Japan. *South Atlantic Quarterly* 87(3):419–444.

Kondo, Dorinne K. 1986. Dissolution and reconstruction of the self: Implications for anthropological epistemology. *Cultural Anthropology* 1(1):74–88.

Milward, Peter. 1980. *Oddities in modern Japan: Observations of an outsider.* Tokyo: Hokuseido Press.

Oberthur, Mariel. 1984. *Cafés and cabarets of Montmartre.* Salt Lake City: Gibbs M. Smith.

Omae Kinjiro, and Tachibana Yuzuru. 1981. *The book of sushi.* Tokyo: Kodansha International.

Revel, Jean-François. 1982. *Culture and cuisine: A journey through the history of food.* Garden City: Doubleday.

Simon, André L. 1981. *A concise encyclopedia of gastronomy.* Woodstock: Overlook Press.

. . . . .

10

THE AESTHETICS AND POLITICS OF JAPANESE IDENTITY IN THE FASHION INDUSTRY

DORINNE KONDO

In the early 1980s Japanese fashion exploded onto the international scene. The work of such designers as Issey Miyake, Yohji Yamamoto, and Rei Kawakubo was predicated on a revolutionary aesthetic vision—loose, architectural shapes, uneven hemlines, unusual textures, somber colors, "lace" made of rips or holes in the fabric. These garments articulated different ideas about what counts as fashion and how clothing relates to human bodies. The fashion world reacted strongly. Some dismissed the new styles as the Hiroshima bag-lady look, too avant-garde and depressing to be a serious competitor for global markets. Yet in the past eight or nine years the Japanese fashion industry has become an international presence. Japanese designers forced Paris and New York to take them into account, if sometimes grudgingly, and to recognize Tokyo as a center of creative fashion design—not merely of production, a role Asia continues to fulfill globally in the garment industry.

Fashion, garments, and textiles define a critically important arena

Research for this work was funded by the Rockefeller Foundation, through the Center for Cultural Studies at Rice University, and by the MacArthur Research Fund at Pomona College. Comments from Elizabeth Long, George Marcus, and Matthews Hamabata have been helpful in formulating my argument.

where global economic power and cultural authority are contested. Keen economic competition is paralleled by competition for cultural recognition, and here Japan is assuming a place at the forefront of design, the meeting point of high tech and aesthetic. Fashion, graphic design, photography, industrial design, furniture, and architecture, among other forms, index Japanese participation in a world culture of functional objects that provoke aesthetic pleasure and presumably stimulate the desire to buy. Japanese fashion is one of the sites where the workings of "commodity aesthetics" are most visible (Haugh 1986).

In this context, what counts as Japanese is a vexed, troubling, and always problematic question for Japanese designers. For them, the fashion world is an arena of contestation and reinscription of power, where contradictory and complex identities are asserted. What is at stake in these questions of identity is politics in a broad sense—economic power, cultural authority, world recognition, place in a world order—at a historical moment when boundaries among nations are contested and highly charged. "Nation" and "culture" are problematized as fashion industries participate in a global Fashion Industry, for how does one speak of "Japanese" design when flows of creative talent and capital are truly transnational and when "Japanese" designer garments are consumed not just in Japan but throughout the world? Indeed, what counts as Japanese clothing when "Western" clothing has been on the Japanese scene at least since the 1860s and when today's designers grew up with blue jeans more than with kimono?

As these questions construct a transnational space, essentializing gestures and geopolitical relations simultaneously refabricate national boundaries. The imagined communities of developed nations and, more specifically, major urban centers in those nations assert hegemony as the sites of creation.[1] The accession of Japanese designers to these ranks is in one sense a gesture of parity, a sign that Japan's creative and artistic powers are commensurate with its economic strength. Yet for Japanese designers, the competition in the fashion industry is always on someone else's ground, for they must work in an idiom and a tradition developed elsewhere. And even when some designers see themselves as operating within a postmodern, transcultural narrative field, the sedimented histories of nation-states and recirculated tropes of nationality resituate them in terms of their national identities.

These unravelings and reweavings of identities are always already political and occur in a multiplicity of sites in the terrain of fashion: in the industry's complex relationship to Paris; in the construction of Japanese and cosmopolitan identities, including gender; in garments created by Japanese designers; in the international reception of those garments. My concern here is not how "Japanese fashion" reflects "Japanese culture" but what signifying practices produce "culture effects," fabricating the essence of "Japaneseness" or "cosmopolitanism." Investigating the material practices through which essences are fabricated and rent asunder should allow us to explore the possibilities for what Linda Hutcheon (1989) termed "complicitous critique": in the case of the fashion industry, the potential for contesting received meanings and for oppositional practice in a domain suffused, indeed constituted, by commodification.

Questions of cosmopolitan and national identities are articulated in paradigmatic form in the fashion world's complex relationship to Paris. In recent years, New York, Milan, London, and, to a lesser extent, Tokyo have risen as strong contending sites of fashion design. Yet as the fashion world proliferates and disperses, a strong centripetal force draws designers to Paris, for it is still the case that only "the designer who has made it in Paris has *really* made it" (Brubach 1989, 101). Continuing Parisian hegemony has been symbolized by the recent pilgrimages of Italian designers Romeo Gigli, Gianni Versace, and Valentino Garavani and British designers John Galliano and Katherine Hamnett to show their collections in the French capital.[2] Certainly, of the Japanese designers, only the handful who regularly show in Paris can be said to have achieved worldwide recognition: Hanae Mori, Issey Miyake, Rei Kawakubo, Yohji Yamamoto, and Mitsuhiro Matsuda. With the scheduled building of a permanent facility to host the Paris collections, the continuing dominance of Paris should be assured.

To address the question of Parisian hegemony, however, one must also problematize what counts as French. Multinational financing, licensing, and the hiring of foreign designers have wrought dramatic changes in French design houses, refiguring the boundaries of "Paris." For years, Chanel has been the domain of the German Karl Lagerfeld. Milanese designer Gianfranco Ferre now heads the House of Dior, replacing long-regnant Marc Bohan. Where Japan is concerned, the multicultural mixings are equally significant. The venerable House of Grès, the epitome of French elegance, was purchased by the Japanese textile and apparel company Yagi Tsusho in 1988, and the ailing eighty-

six-year-old Mme. Alix Grès was replaced by thirty-nine-year-old Ta-
kashi Sasaki, who worked for fifteen years at Pierre Cardin. In an interesting recent development, the House of Cacharel, symbol of soft
French femininity, hired a new head designer, Atsuro Tayama, the chief
of the Japanese fashion atelier A.T.[3] Romeo Gigli recently opened his
first Paris boutique, owned by the Japanese department store Takashimaya—which also has the exclusive right to produce and market Gigli
clothes in Japan. The Japanese firm Onward Kashiyama finances some
of the most talented avant-garde designers around the world, including
fashion's brilliant bad boy, Jean-Paul Gaultier. If Paris is hegemonic, it
is no longer the Paris reigned exclusively by the French.

Given this context of an industry defined by cosmopolitanism, global
dispersion, and a contested European cultural hegemony, what counts
as Japanese is a vexed issue for the Japanese designers—a label many
themselves eschew, preferring not to be lumped with others or to be
seen as designing out of a culture. Fashion, they say, should transcend
nationality (*mukokuseki*). Issey Miyake's well-documented career and
his thoughtful disquisitions on the subject eloquently illustrate these
complex ambivalences. After graduating from Tama Art University in
1964, he went to Paris to work at the houses of Lanvin and Givenchy
for four years. He describes his awakening to possibilities for the synthesis of "Japanese" and "Western" forms:

> Away from the home country, living and working in Paris, I looked at
> myself very hard and asked, "what could I do as a Japanese fashion
> designer?" Then I realized that my very disadvantage, lack of Western
> heritage, would also be my advantage. I was free of Western tradition or
> convention. I thought, "I can try anything new. I cannot go back to the
> past because there is no past in me as far as Western clothing is concerned.
> There was no other way for me but to go forward." The lack of Western
> tradition was the very thing I needed to create contemporary and universal
> fashion. But as a Japanese I come from a heritage rich in tradition. . . . I
> realized these two wonderful advantages I enjoy, and that was when I
> started to experiment creating a new genre of clothing, neither Western
> nor Japanese but beyond nationality. I hoped to create a new universal
> clothing which is challenging to our time. (Miyake 1984)

Predictably, Miyake feels uncomfortable with the label "Japanese
designer" precisely because it enforces stereotyped limits to his vision
of a design with universal appeal and will make the interest in his clothing
simply a fad. Miyake wryly and poignantly stated: "I have been trying

to create something more than Japanese or Western for over ten years and, ironically, I find myself as one of the leaders of the new Japanese craze. I hope I will be around a lot longer than this sudden interest."

REFIGURING EAST AND WEST

To understand how Miyake and others could claim a universal—that is, transnational—aesthetic requires some examination of the clothing itself. The creative multiplicity of their designs transcends the binary opposition of Japanese and Western. Hanae Mori, the first Japanese to become an international force and the only Japanese allowed by the Chambre Syndicale de la Couture to design haute couture, is the trail-blazer. Known since the mid–1960s for her feminine, classic garments with an unmistakably upper-class air, she designs for the elegant, well-heeled woman. The shapes of her clothing draw from classic draping and tailoring. The "Japanese" elements in her work are in the patterns of the fabric she uses: the butterfly (the company logo), for instance, or motifs from kimono on her luxurious evening gowns.

The second generation of Japanese designers includes Miyake, Kansai Yamamoto, and Kenzo, who won international acclaim in the early 1970s. Kansai Yamamoto is renowned for his exuberant designs and the equally exuberant staging for his fashion shows. His work has drawn on the stylishness of Edo (now Tokyo) townsmen's culture. Understated aestheticism has no place here; instead, Kansai boldly appropriated Edo stripes and Edo firemen's gear, among other motifs, to create wildly patterned tops, bright, multicolored sweaters with padded shoulders reminiscent of samurai armor, and dramatic combinations of strong colors and bold graphics in his space-age, Edo-retro look. Kenzo, now considered essentially a French designer by the Japanese, has lived in France for over twenty years. His colorful, folkloric styles, his re-creations of boxy kimono shapes in quilted and flowered fabrics in the 1970s, and his sporadic references to kimono in later collections allude to regional costume even as they modify it. Mitsuhiro Matsuda, and to some extent Takeo Kikuchi of Bigi, both well known in Japan, claim a different cosmopolitan identity, recalling the Japanese appropriation of Western clothing in earlier parts of this century. One of Bigi's labels, Moga, explicitly invokes the heritage of the flapper, the *mo(dan) ga(aru)* (modern girl) of the 1920s. Matsuda stresses the romantic aspects of fashion in his work, through nostalgic evocations of prewar elegance in tailored suits, rich patterns and colors, embroidery, and passementerie. He was Kenzo's classmate at Bunka Fukusō, the design school that produces most of today's well-known young designers. Instead of going to Paris initially, Matsuda first chose to build his following in Japan and in the United States.

It is the avant-garde of Japanese fashion that is usually grouped together under the label "Japanese designers," and these three—Miyake, Kawakubo, Yohji Yamamoto—are engaged in the most radical experimentation, most creative synthesis, and greatest subversion of clothing conventions, both Japanese and European. Generationally, Miyake is one rung above the other two, because he went to Paris and New York during the late 1960s. The experiments of these three have provoked worldwide acclaim as well as virulent condemnation. Though the designers themselves might protest, fashion commentators pinpoint certain commonly shared characteristics among the three.

First is the importance of the cloth as a point of departure for design. The fabrics are often in-house designs, specially commissioned, artisanally produced textiles, or startling synthetics that draw on the best available technology. Yohji Yamamoto speaks of *nuno no hyōjō,* the expression of the cloth: "displaying what is inherent in the cloth: wrinkles in linen, puckers along a seam, the texture of handwashed silk satin" (Stinchecum 1983, 74). Miyake explicitly likens fabric to the "grain in wood. You can't go against it. I close my eyes and let the fabric tell me what to do" (Cocks 1986a, 70). All three designers appreciate the playful and innovative use of unexpected materials. Barbara Weiser of the boutique Charivari, who discovered Yamamoto's clothing in Paris and introduced it to New York, voiced her delight at finding Yohji working with, among other things, the fabric used to cover tennis balls! Kawakubo is inspired by "different types of fabric she has seen in her lifetime—not necessarily clothing, but perhaps a piece of paper or carpeting" (Sidorsky 1983, 18). In 1986 she used thick fabric of bonded cotton, rayon, and polyurethane to create a work that sculpted the space around the body.

Similarly, Issey Miyake both draws on artisanal production from Japan and other sites and explores the technologies of synthetic fabrics.[4] In recent collections, he has pursued the technology of pleats in garments gently reminiscent of Fortuny. A recent Yamamoto collection challenged the notion that clothing should be made from any material even

Off-white bonded cotton/rayon/polyurethane asymmetric dress. Comme des Garçons fall-winter collection, 1986. (Photo by Steven Meisel; reproduced by permission.)

remotely resembling cloth. Instead, he offered garments made of wooden slats, held together by hinges.

Interviews with Harold Koda, costume curator at the Fashion Institute of Technology (FIT), revealed another common feature in the designers most closely associated with the Japanese avant-garde, a tendency he labeled "terse expression"—that is, a respect for the integrity of the material and an aversion to cutting into the cloth. He linked this aesthetic principle to the use of cloth in kimono and regional costume, where virtually the entire bolt is used, with relatively little waste and little cutting. He further points out that if one looks at the pattern pieces of, say, a Kawakubo garment in a poncholike shape, the tendency will be to use one piece of fabric rather than two or more pieces cut and stitched together. Richard Martin of FIT (1987) characterizes the aesthetic underlying Miyake's *East Meets West* volume as the "capacity to wrap." In photograph after photograph, we see layered cloth wrapped in various configurations around Japanese models, highlighting an aesthetic strikingly different from the classic French notion of cutting and tailoring garments close to the body.[5]

In addition to playing off culturally specific aesthetics and creating ironic new forms and visions, Kawakubo, Miyake, and others are rethinking what counts as fashion. In an exhibit called "Three Women," focusing on the radical clothing of Madeleine Vionnet, Claire McCardell, and Kawakubo, Harold Koda argues that for all three designers, decoration was adjunct to function, so that, for example, a bow would be cut and formed of the same piece of fabric as the collar. In Kawakubo's case, the finishing on a garment often serves as decoration. In a modernist sense, for her form follows function. But she goes beyond the modernist aesthetic, challenging us to examine our assumptions about what counts as functional—collars are attached to nothing, jackets appear with four arms, what looks like a coat is a collar and lapel, but there is a gaping void where the shoulders, front, and back should be. Such a coat surely offers almost no functional protection from the elements. Kawakubo is deconstructing garments by making the functional decorative and vice versa, thereby subverting the distinctions between categories.

Holly Brubach of the *New Yorker* puts these garments in perspective by comparing Kawakubo's menswear for the Comme des Garçons collections with the styles of Jean-Paul Gaultier:

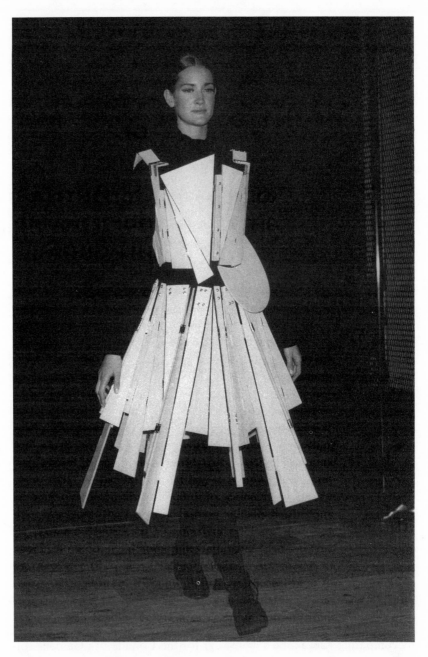

Dress of wooden slats. Yohji Yamamoto autumn-winter collection, 1991–1992.
(Photo by Kiyomatsu Hideyuki; reproduced by permission.)

Both are engaged in a process of dismantling clothes and recombining the component parts in astonishing, sometimes ironic ways. This season, the models at Comme des Garçons wore detachable collars draped around their necks but fastened to nothing, and mystifying jacket combinations— one looked like a sleeveless blouson over a suit—that were in fact all one piece. . . . If every piece in their collections isn't what the fashion press calls "wearable," and if the things that are sold aren't worn as they were shown on the runway, that's beside the point. Both Kawakubo and Gaultier are forcing us to look at clothes in new ways, disrupting the habits of thinking we've fallen into. (Brubach 1989, 107)

It is this aesthetic disruption, leading us to confront our assumptions, that constitutes the challenge of much of Japanese fashion. As Amanda Mayer Stinchecum tells us: "Perhaps the most valuable thing about this group of designers is that they make us question the assumptions we have about what clothes are like. For example, must we tolerate tight clothing to be beautiful? They raise the consideration of comfort and practicality to a new level of importance. . . . Finally, they make us realize that the designs we take for granted are merely conventions that fashion has been following and reinterpreting for the last 50 years. The Japanese have stepped outside these conventions and made something new, something of their own" (1983, 76).

This making of the new extends to postmodernist, ironic appropriation of standard clothing forms. Quotations abound but are transposed into other, avant-garde registers. Jeff Weinstein likens the design techniques of Yohji Yamamoto, Kawakubo, and others to postmodernist notions of *"displacement,* slight changes in expected scale, shape, or type that pay homage to, yet supersede old modes" (Weinstein 1983, 80). Herein lies the creative genius of the Japanese avant-garde: a postmodernist recombination of forms in an aesthetic domain where nothing is created entirely de novo. For example, this sweater filled with holes— one of the garments that elicited allusions to bag ladies and the homeless—was Kawakubo's 1980s version of lace. And reappropriations of styles associated with particular moments in recent history also appear, but with a distinctively Comme des Garçons twist. The Comme des Garçons showings of 1991 included an evening collection reminiscent of Paco Rabanne's disco dresses of the 1960s, made of plastic or metal pieces linked together into chain mail. But instead of round or square pieces configured in recognizably symmetrical dresses, Kawakubo's chain mail dripped into jagged, irregular shapes. The bits of plastic were

Black hand-knit wool "lace" sweater coordinated with a black cotton jersey padded skirt. Comme des Garçons fall-winter collection, 1982–1983. (Photo by Peter Lindbergh; reproduced by permission.)

themselves irregular, so that the effect of the "vests" draped over characteristically smocked black or white knit dresses and jackets was of a Paco Rabanne gone awry, thrown off balance, an embodied contradiction—structured and hard, yet flowing and graceful.

Miyake, too, enjoys the play with forms, describing his activities in utterances such as "I will challenge the tuxedo" (quoted in Knaufo 1988, 108). The tuxedo will be unlike any seen before, while remaining recognizable as a tuxedo. Challenge to convention is part of this aesthetic stance: "It's irritating in a way when someone comes up to me and says

Black wool jersey dress with pieced mirror attachment. Comme des Garçons spring-summer collection, 1990. (Photo by Tominaga Minsei for Six 5 1990; reproduced by permission.)

a design was very understandable. That means it's not good enough, that it's not challenging enough. I don't want to do decoration. I believe in questioning" (Miyake Design Studio 1988, 24). Yohji Yamamoto echoes these sentiments: "My way of working is an independent, egoistic way. Such people like to work against the existing way. I design *against*. I struggle *against*. If I lose this feeling, if my work is too accepted, perhaps I will lose my energy and my meaning of designing clothes" (Koren 1984, 98).

This sort of radical questioning participates in the antifoundational critiques of received categories that defines this historical moment. I see in the work of the avant-garde designers a parallel, in another medium, to what is occurring in the world of social theory, a laying bare of the equivalent of fashion's narrative conventions, just as anthropologists might interrogate narrative and rhetoric in conventional ethnography or deconstructionist critics might interrogate language. But like all reconsiderations, challenge and contestation do not occur in a historical vacuum. The emergence of heterodoxy is always dependent on the forms of the orthodoxies against which it reacts, and no pristine space of resistance to convention is possible. Moreover, designers are engaged in the *business* of fashion, and their creation must be creation for a market. In any collection there may be a few "image pieces" that the designer's boutique will carry, knowing that the garments are unlikely to sell; but by and large clothing cannot be so revolutionary that no one will buy it. As Yohji Yamamoto noted in "Carnet de notes sur vêtements et villes," the Wim Wenders film in which Yamamoto is protagonist, his life negotiates a tension between being respected and making enough money to support himself and his sizeable staff. Contestation, then, is constantly compromised and recuperated. Indeed, what does an aesthetic contestation mean in a sphere that is, by definition, thoroughly, utterly commodified? Further, as Jeff Weinstein points out, nothing totally new is ever created; rather, in this domain of the postmodern, everything is transformed, ironically appropriated, reinterpreted, quoted, mocked, enshrined. The spaces for creativity and for resistance are always embedded in their cultural and historical discursive contexts—yet I would argue that the work of the Japanese avant-garde shows us that spaces and fissures and possibilities for recombination and resistance *do* matter, that recuperation need not be total recuperation, that aesthetic contestations and interventions are possible, even as conventions are re-inscribed.

CRAFTING GENDERED SELVES

Perhaps the prime oppositional gesture in the clothing of Japanese avant-garde designers lies in their figurations of gender. Here, their work—and indeed, the notion of fashion itself—highlights the non-essentialist performance of identities, where selves or subjects are not bounded, whole essences but rather shifting subject-positions, created through gesture and through everyday practices such as choosing what we wear.[6] Fashion is a way of crafting selves (see Kondo 1990). Such a figuration of identity would fly in the face of persistent tropes such as surface and depth metaphors, where there is a sharp division between the superficiality of appearance and the interior space of true selfhood and true feelings. Especially in urban, capitalist societies, decisions about what to wear and how to present ourselves are, in fact, constitutive of ourselves. Our everyday choices and the work of fashion designers are meaningful practices that deploy and resignify the socially constructed meanings of gender, class, and nation, as those forces and meanings intersect in the nodes we call identity.

The high-fashion industry at one level participates enthusiastically in the relentless reproduction of the gender binary. The industry itself is predicated on the division between men's and women's clothing, both in showing the collections and in the organization of retailing, with departments or boutiques specializing in men's or women's sections. The imperative to reproduce these dualisms is apparent in a recent exhibition at the Musée des Arts Décoratifs, commemorating the fortieth anniversary of Snoopy, the famous beagle of the Charles Schulz comic strips. A sister, Belle, was invented for Snoopy, and the museum curators asked designers to create costumes for Snoopy and Belle, which most did, obligingly. Seeing hundreds of men's and women's fashions worn by two anthropomorphized stuffed animals demonstrated the pervasive stubbornness of the gender binary, even as the exhibit also produced a bemused irony in some, where the very absurdity of "men's" and "women's" clothing in this context could act to destabilize the categories.

Even within the binary organizational strictures of the fashion industry, the work of avant-garde designers in Japan offers a different way of crafting gendered selves, based on a different relationship between clothing and bodies. In the early 1980s the garments of Miyake, Yamamoto, and Kawakubo made strong statements about a different aesthetic of shape, where the garments do not cling but define a space around the body. Yamamoto and Kawakubo have spoken specifically of a blurring of gender categories, freeing the wearer from familiar gender conventions. Yamamoto himself commented on the arbitrariness of men's and women's clothing in 1983: "I think that my men's clothes look as good on women as my women's clothing. . . . And more and more women are buying my men's clothes. It's happening everywhere, and not just with my clothing. . . . When I started designing, I wanted to make men's clothes for women. But there were no buyers for it. Now there are. I always wonder who decided that there should be a difference in the clothes of men and women. Perhaps men decided this" (quoted in Duka 1983, 63).

Further, Yamamoto comes up with this enigmatic—and, one suspects, self-consciously parodic—version of attractiveness: "I don't feel sexuality at all in the normal meaning. A fantasy of mine is a woman, 40 or 50 years old. She is very skinny with grey hair and smoking a cigarette. She is neither a woman nor a man but she is very attractive. She is sexy for me. She is walking away from me and as I walk after her she calls out, 'Do not follow' " (Koren 1984, 96).

It is precisely this ambiguous gender imagery that has puzzled many a Western observer. A male editor at a fashion magazine told me of his bewilderment in the face of the "shapeless" Japanese clothing, which tends not to reveal a woman's body. He said that he would never want *his* girlfriend to wear Japanese fashions; rather, he preferred the form-fitting styles of designers like Thierry Mugler and Azzedine Alaia—whose clothing has curves, even if there is no one in them. But it is precisely this different notion of gender, sexuality, and sensuality that constitutes the critical gesture in the thoroughly commodified realm of fashion, creating potential for refiguring conventional gender images. And although recent Miyake, Yamamoto, and Kawakubo collections have sometimes shown work that draws on the present rage for tight bodysuits or clinging knits, by and large they are still associated with loose, somewhat androgynous clothing, as a recent *Elle* (March 19, 1990) feature entitled "Over Size" underlined. The young, boyish-looking model wore sometimes slender, sometimes voluminous pants, overalls or shorts, teamed up with loose-fitting tops and jackets; at least half the work featured was from Miyake, Kawakubo, Yamamoto, or Akira "Zucca" Onozuka, a Miyake protégé. Designers like Kawakubo talk of the sensuality of the clothing coming not from the way a person (woman) looks but from the feel of the clothing. An ideal customer is in fact someone who would buy an ensemble based on how a garment feels— its textures, its weight, the way it drapes and flows around the body.

The radical subversion of prettiness and conventional gendered imagery reaches its most uncompromised expression in Kawakubo's aptly named line, Comme des Garçons—like the boys.

> As a woman, she is aware of the expectations of not only men, but women as well, that women look and act pretty, and that this prettiness conforms to accepted norms. The lips should be red, the eyelids blue, the waist narrow, the hips curved, and so on. To be appealing, clothing too is supposed to meet certain expectations: symmetry, neatness, sexiness (suggesting if not revealing—Kawakubo's clothes do neither). Her designs express both a reaction against these expectations, and an interest in pure form. She doesn't work with pattern pieces, but with an abstract idea of shape. Her sample-hand makes up a model from a sketch; if it isn't right, she says, "add a little volume here," and this produces the bulging, curved and twisting seams that are found in many of her designs. Kawakubo's clothes are the most extreme because she, more than the others, refuses to meet the expectations we have of clothing and of women. (Stinchecum 1983, 76)

If makeup is used at all, it, too, is intended to disrupt convention. Neither Kawakubo nor her staff use any makeup, and her models also appear to be largely makeup-free. But in the 1982 Paris collections, Kawakubo employed a makeup artist who put "blotches of color on their faces, suggesting that the designer had battered women or the victims of Hiroshima in mind. Nothing of the sort." It was, in fact, done to subvert aesthetic conventions. Kawakubo said, "If you are to put color on the face, it need not be on the lips. It can be anywhere" (Morris 1982, C10).

I had not appreciated the degree of this contestation until I saw the Paris collections of designers such as Hanae Mori, Japan's equivalent of Bill Blass or Oscar de la Renta: that is, someone who designs conventionally feminine clothes. The look is tailored, soigné, close to the body, the kind of fashion designed "for eating lunch at a French restaurant where the walls are painted some flattering shade of pink" (Brubach 1988, 92). In the Miyake, Kawakubo, and Yamamoto shows, the models wore little, if any, makeup and simply walked out onto the runway—striding vigorously at Miyake, walking energetically, with an almost perky air, at Comme des Garçons, ambling slowly and with stateliness in the Yamamoto shows. This contrasted starkly with the sashaying of the Mori models, who simpered and tossed their hair, flirting with the audience and the video cameras at the end of the runway.[7] The designs of the avant-grade threesome are striking, unusual, and strong; even when the garments cling, the lines are clean, and the effect is sometimes tough, even intimidating, rather than sexy in a soft, feminine sense. The Miyake collection, for example, shown in March 1990 featured a series of skin tightblack bodysuits, worn with sunglasses, visored caps, gauntlets, and holsters strapped onto the models' thighs—space-age macho for the woman of the 1990s. The clothing, the models, the staging of the shows among the avant-garde designers, make conventional prettiness and femininity seem not only outdated but politically retrograde and downright embarrassing.

Equally surely, fashion is shaped by larger historical trends and the movement of women into the world of work in Japan, Europe, and the United States. Clothing is increasingly designed with strong, independent working women in mind, designed for a world where traditional gender boundaries are breaking down. Tokio Kumagai links clothing to these dramatic social changes: "Men and women are crossing over. There's no longer a notion that because you're a man, you have to do this, or because you're a woman you have to do this. Putting the physical functions aside for a minute, even husbands wake up in the middle of the night to take care of the kids; even wives are working, earning money, so from the point of view of everyday life, differences are disappearing. The obstructive view that because you are a woman you have to wear a slim skirt no longer exists" (quoted in Kusunoki 1986, 142; translation mine).[8]

Kawakubo concurs, restating her vision of women's position in society, and the woman for whom she designs: "The goal for all women should be to make her own living and to support herself, to be self-sufficient. That is the philosophy of her clothes. They are working for modern women. Women who do not need to assure their happiness by looking sexy to men, by emphasizing their figures, but who attract them with their minds. Miss Kawakubo says this dream of anonymous self-sufficiency has been her beacon since childhood. She says if she was not a fashion designer she would like to be an explorer, discovering places which no one has ever been to before" (quoted in Coleridge 1988, 89).

Fashion, especially high fashion and the metadiscourses that translate and present garments to the public—that is, advertising and fashion magazines—is instrumental in producing culturally and historically specific ideals of gendered beauty. And just as surely as the fashion industry promotes—and indeed, is premised on—the objectification of women and the enshrinement of dominant cultural ideals, it also offers possibilities for creation of different aesthetics and different ideals. Particularly in the early 1980s, the Kawakubo and Yamamoto collections had a unisex look; even now, though gender differences seem to have reemerged, they are tempered by gestures such as Kawakubo's use of sheer, soft, flowered cottons for her men's collection for the spring and summer of 1990. In his spring and summer collection of 1988 Yamamoto offered a pair of wrapped-waist skirt trousers.

A softening of the gender binary, a refiguration of feminine prettiness, a subversion of the objectifying gaze in favor of an aesthetic based on the sensuality of the *feel* of the clothing to the wearer, a rethinking of sexuality, a construction of an independent, powerful, and daring wearer—these are the challenges posed by the Japanese avant-garde.

FABRICATING ESSENCES

The initial and continuing reception of the work of Japanese designers by fashion journalists in the United States leads us into geopolitical terrains of essence fabrication, where Japanese fashion is often categorized by recirculating tropes of national and cultural identity. Japanese fashion has often provoked strong reaction, celebratory or vituperative. Journalists such as Brubach and Weinstein have pointed to the deconstructive elements of avant-garde designers like Kawakubo in particular, remaining largely appreciative and even laudatory, but traditional fashion gatekeepers have not been so kind. *Women's Wear Daily* is notorious for its publication of a large two-page spread of Japanese avant-garde clothing with Xs dramatically splashed across the page. Racial undertones emerge blatantly, as in the coverage of the Paris collections by the Associated Press in the early 1980s: "Rei Kawakubo for Comme des Garçons proved as usual to be the high priestess of the Jap wrap."[9]

Condescension and dismissal are sometimes shown in subtler ways.

Writer and publisher James Nelson told me of the frequent misspellings of the names of Japanese designers in articles in *Vogue* and in British fashion magazines in the early 1980s. He passionately contends that such mistakes would be neither committed nor tolerated in mentioning European or American designers. The misspellings, though seemingly trivial, tell us who counts and who does not. Moreover, ignorance and misattributions continue to this day. The expensive (three hundred dollars a copy) trade publication *The Fashion Guide* contains numerous errors in information on Japanese designers. Comme des Garçons is listed as French, and Rei Kawakubo's name is given, in the introduction to Japanese fashion, as "Hai Kawakube"! "Harajuku," the trendy Tokyo hangout, referred to as "Harajuka"; Hiromichi Nakano comes across as "Wakano," the Bigi group as "Higi," and so on. American, French, British, and Italian designers are subject to no such acts of violence.

Reception among retailers seems equally mixed. Jeff Weinstein of the *Village Voice* described for me the shabby treatment given the Japanese designers in such meccas of fashion as Bloomingdale's in New York. According to his assessment, the work of Japanese designers is displayed badly, clearly as an unimportant holding of the store. In an interview, Barabara Weiser, one of the retailers who introduced the work of Yamamoto and others to New York, linked the anti-Japanese reaction in the fashion world to wider issues of trade and economic competition at that historical moment, when Japan bashing was in the air (as it continues to be).

Just as the daring of Japanese clothing has provoked virulent negative response, so has it attracted acclaim. Hanae Mori was recently awarded the title of Chevalier des Lettres, and Issey Miyake a comparable honor, from the French government. The Musée des Arts Décoratifs exhibited Miyake's work in the winter of 1988; the costume curator at the museum, Yvonne Deslandres, calls him "the greatest creator of clothing of our time" (Cocks 1986a, 67). Innovative designers Claude Montana and Romeo Gigli acknowledge Issey Miyake as a major influence. The corps of French fashion journalists presented Miyake with an "oscar" of fashion as the best international designer at their first awards ceremony in October 1985. Miyake, in particular, is celebrated for his creations that push fashion into new realms, earning him the greatest accolade the fashion industry can bestow: *"son style dépasse les modes"* ("his style goes beyond fashion"; *Elle,* Feb. 3, 1986, 58).[10]

But praise can construct limits and categories and create a colonizing distance even as it celebrates. Take, for example, the trendy downtown magazine *Details,* which described the 1988 Mori collections with this orientalizing gesture: "Hanae Mori happily returned to her roots with fabulously painted panels on silk crepe, their motif lifted from ancient Japanese art screens. The fabric, uncut, formed flowing kimono evening dresses. What a lovely surprise to see Madame Mori return to her original source of inspiration after years of misguided attempts to imitate European style" (Cunningham 1988, 121). Laudatory though this passage may seem to be, the subtext tells us that East is East and West is West, and attempts to blur the boundaries are misguided. Only when the motifs are ancient and recognizable as kimono are they successful. "Stay Japanese," according to some stereotyped view of Japaneseness, this passage tells us. An editor with American *Elle* told me that many French fashion people are fascinated with Japan, for they consider Japan to be the only country truly to appreciate and to understand French fashion on an aesthetic level. What appears to be a lavish compliment seems less flattering on closer examination. In fact, the utterance reasserts the centrality of French fashion as a standard. Surely the elevation of Japan to the position of France's appreciative audience scarcely constructs the relationship as an equal one; indeed, it is a gesture that constitutes Japan as feminized "Orient," admirer of France's aesthetic prowess. The air of authority with which pronouncements of Western superiority are made gives eloquent testimony to the battles for recognition in which the Japanese designers must engage. For even as Japanese designers work in what they consider to be a postmodern, transnational space, persistent tropes of nation and culture push them back into an essentialized Japanese identity.

The passionate and ambivalent reactions to Japanese fashion from all players suggest that what is at stake goes beyond the purely aesthetic (as though such a realm could exist, beyond history, politics, and economics). At issue are global geopolitical relations, where the historically sedimented terms, "Japan-Europe," "Japan–U.S.," and "East-West" bristle with significance. The recent burgeoning of the Japanese economy engenders both admiration and fear in the fashion industry. The rhetoric of war—invasion, takeover—occurs in fashion trade papers and popular fashion magazines just as it does in the popular press and in business journals. For example, in *Vogue*'s recent retrospective of the major fashion influences of the 1980s, the Japanese designers are grouped together in a series of photos labeled the "Japanese invasion."[11] The use of martial metaphors reminds us of the interpenetration of the world of fashion with the worlds of economics and politics.

The positioning of Japan on the present fashion scene arises directly from historical geopolitical realities. The incorporation of American popular culture and Western clothing as part of Japanese identity arises directly out of Western cultural, economic, and military dominance. The postmodern play of genres and cross-references does not occur in some ludic site beyond power; it is inseparable from the "opening" of Japan in the Meiji period and the outcome of World War II, especially the American Occupation of Japan. Yohji Yamamoto, in "Carnet de nôtes sur vêtements et villes," made the point explicitly. He spoke poignantly of his father, who had been drafted into the imperial army during World War II and who died in Manchuria. He said that when he read his father's letters and the letters of his father's companions in combat, he felt caught up in history. Though his feelings were still inchoate, he somehow perceived a connection between his own work in Paris and their lives, their struggles. For him, involvement in the world of international fashion design is a way of participating in an ongoing history—not necessarily one of militarism and domination but certainly one where larger questions of national power and identity are at stake.

Implicit in these formulations is a sense that the Japanese fashion industry is still in a position of playing catch-up to the West, producing ambivalence, contradictions, resentments, opposition. The late Tokio Kumagai, whose political analysis was unfailingly lucid, offered this view:

I'm working in the "fashion" world, but I also have hopes for political trends to go a certain way. In this present moment, the latter half of the twentieth century, there are many different ways of thinking, different ways of life. But I think it is wrong to invade or to negate another culture or another idea, in other words another way of life, through an economic system or political might, simply because of the fact that one part of the population has more power.[12] I think we have to make a world where different cultures can cooperate and move forward. Even in Japanese fashion, the compelling power of white people has been strong; there's something wrong with thinking that white people's culture created at the end of the 19th century is more beautiful and powerful than any other. "Beauty" is something found in Japanese, and in Chinese, and in people with black skin, in their various ways; the notion that certain proportions are the most beautiful is nothing more than prejudice. (Quoted in Kusunoki 1986, 142; my translation)

In this statement, Kumagai explicitly links the present state of the Japanese fashion world to politics and passionately argues against the enshrinement of white people's culture in the Japanese fashion world, where power and standards of beauty are directly related. In arguing for a multiplicity of definitions of beauty, Kumagai makes an oppositional gesture, contesting hegemonic European and American aesthetic canons.

In an attempt to make room for themselves in world arenas, a consortium of well-known Japanese designers initiated the first Tokyo collections in 1985. The goal of this council, made up of Miyake, Kawakubo, Yohji Yamamoto, Matsuda, Kansai Yamamoto, and Mori, was "to wedge the country's talent into the traditional fashion route: Milan, Paris, New York" (Cocks 1986b, 92). Recently, four international designers were invited to Tokyo for a "Tokyo summit," creating a meeting of "world powers" on the fashion scene. The analogy is taken seriously. The stakes are nothing less than Japan's struggle to establish itself as a peer of the West. "I hope," Miyake remarked toward the end of the Tokyo shows, "that my contemporaries and I will be the last to have to go to Paris" (94).

Japanese desire for world recognition is not limited to gaining equality with the West. In the realm of production quality, Japan is preeminent in the fashion industry—at least in the eyes of its designers. Yamamoto abandoned production in Hong Kong after one year because of his dissatisfaction with what he felt to be inferior workmanship. Europe is considered second-rate as well, though both Yamamoto and Comme des Garçons will sometimes use French manufacturers for their less demanding garments and less expensive lines. For example, Comme des Garçons uses French manufacturers only for Comme des Garçons Shirt, a so-called bridge, or intermediately priced line, costing between $150 and $200 rather than $300 and up. Yamamoto's division of labor was less clear-cut, but their public relations representative told me in their showroom in Paris that only the simple things are made in France. Moreover, although Miyake and Yamamoto sometimes buy fabrics abroad—for example, Miyake has special relationships with artisanal textile producers in India, while Yamamoto has purchased fabrics in

Thailand—production of the garment itself can be entrusted primarily to the Japanese and occasionally to the French.

First World status can be claimed through gestures of parity with, even superiority to, the United States and Europe. It is also gained by differentiating Japan from other Asian countries, and from the Third World generally, recirculating in the fashion industry the tropes of dominance familiar from other domains of Japanese business and politics. The competitive anxieties of businessmen throughout Japan are articulated in the fashion world by Yohji Yamamoto:

> Everyone going the same way, everyone wanting the middle ground. I'm always saying, "No, stop it!" because I feel Tokyo should be apart from the rest. If we don't keep our own spirit we will lose everything. The Koreans are the next runners, they are coming. The Korean designers are eager to overtake us and enthusiasm makes fashion, so they cannot fail. On the other hand, you need your home town's basic culture behind fashion, so maybe they won't make it intellectually. Whenever I travel in Europe, each time I go to Paris, each time I go to London, each time I go to New York, I feel the culture is so big, so deep, I feel it heavy, weighing on me. And in fashion you need that most of all. (Quoted in Coleridge 1988, 93–94)

Here a momentary appreciation of Korea is paired with a sense of inferiority to the West and a fear of not having a culture as big or deep as Britain, France, or the United States. But Korea is not considered the intellectual equal of Japan or the West. Yamamoto articulates a fear of encroachment and allays those fears through a gesture of colonizing distance from Korea. The domain of fashion cannot be isolated from global politics and economics. Tropes of national identity are deployed in service of essence fabrication and jockeyings for relative position in a global hierarchy.

In the Wenders film, on the other hand, Yamamoto speaks eloquently of his cosmopolitan identity in a postmodern landscape of cities around the world. He speaks of his love for cities, where people are scattered, pursuing their different lives; he eloquently describes a sense of growing up, not as "Japanese" but as a Tokyo resident, for whom mass culture, novelty, and cosmopolitan urbanism are a way of life. In this way, he feels at home in cities, most of all in Tokyo, but also in Paris. But it is only when he came to Paris, Yamamoto says, that he first felt Japanese, as reactions to his presence were couched in terms of his Japaneseness— a feeling familiar to tourists, expatriates, and anthropologists. "Japanese designers" like Yamamoto desire to explode the category "Japanese," yet these desires coexist with reassertions of national identity and ethnocentric pride in "Japanese quality" or "Japanese culture." And even as cosmopolites like Yamamoto feel they live in a transcultural space, others push them back into essential Japaneseness, like it or not. Nor should the impact of historical memory and the real consequences of the actions of nation-states be ignored; Yamamoto's linkage of his own enterprise to his father's experiences in World War II attests to the power of national and cultural identity to shape lives. At different moments, then, perhaps at different levels of consciousness, to various audiences, when various issues are at stake, culture effects are produced and undermined.

The cosmopolitan gestures in the Japanese fashion industry, the worship and appropriation of things Western, signify more than a particular moment in the development of late capitalism or the postmodern, whatever that may mean in a Japanese context. The slippery, multiple positionings of the Japanese in the fashion industry articulate in a particular register the slippery positionings of the Japanese nation-state at this historical moment, a moment when economic dominance, growing confidence, enshrinement or denigration of the West, and questions about Western racism are in play, and where global political relations are at stake. The construction of a Japanese identity and the appropriation, domestication, or enshrinement of Western objects must be seen within a particular sedimented history, not simply due to the autochthonous emergence of a "postmodern," "consumer," "information" society.

The question posed at the outset, the possibilities for "complicitous critique," can perhaps best be answered in the domain of gender figuration, where—even though the astronomical price tags relegate the work of these particular designers to elite consumption—the impact of their clothing in the 1980s was widespread.[13] In the United States, the loose, usually black clothing that defined a New York, downtown art scene "trickled down" sufficiently to influence the looser cuts of clothing familiar to most of us during the 1980s, offering to academic women, certainly, a change from conventionally feminine prettiness in professional settings.[14] Given the fashion industry's key position in providing us with the elements from which we can construct our genders, the presence of different choices, based on different visions of bodies, clothing, and proliferations of gender beyond the binary, can only be welcome relief, though closer analysis of the precise ways in which avant-garde

Japanese clothing is or was consumed and resignified in the acts of wearing must await further study.

In the world of Japanese fashion, as in other domains, aesthetic objects do not occupy some pristine space beyond power; they are sites of political contest. The simple act of putting on a piece of clothing immediately implicates us in a nexus of power and meaning, a globally dispersed struggle in which national identity, a semiotics of class distinction, a reproduction and contestation of gender conventions, participation in subcultures, and enmeshment in global capitalism are at stake. In its spectacle of incessant and fetishized change, its thorough commodification, its provocation of desire, fashion gives us a way of understanding the contradictions animating our late twentieth-century worlds: the creation of objects of profound aesthetic beauty and seductive pleasure, inextricable from, indeed produced by, commodification, competition, and an intense semiotics of distinction. Fashion elicits pleasure and disgust; it subverts and reinscribes the essentialist identities of gender and nation; its utopian gesture fabricates a world of beauty and fantasy, a world dependent on the exploitative reach of global capitalism, a world where aesthetics and politics are indissoluble.

NOTES

1. Production, on the other hand, is often the province of Third World women. For the avant-garde Japanese designers who have "made it" internationally, this tends not to be true, as most of their clothing is sewn in Japan or in France from textiles made in Japan or by specially commissioned artisans in other countries. Miyake has used fabrics from Indian artisans, for instance; Yohji Yamamoto has worked with Thai producers. Still, as I later argue, a colonizing gesture of presumed Japanese superiority is also implicit in confining production to Japan.
2. Valentino caused a sensation by announcing that he would show the greater part of his collection—140 pieces—in Paris, while only 20 pieces would be displayed, "in a still-life mode," in Rome (*Women's Wear Daily*, Jan. 17, 1990).
3. Like many Japanese designers, Tayama puts his first name first, Western-style, and uses Roman letters to transliterate his name. Similarly, companies like Yohji Yamamoto and Tokio Kumagai render their names either in the Western alphabet or in katakana and invert the usual Japanese name order, putting their family names last instead of first. (See Stanlaw, this volume.)
4. Miyake was instrumental in helping to mount an exhibition of Indian textile design at the Musée des Arts Décoratifs in Paris in 1985; he also created garments from some of these Indian textiles.
5. For more on the cultural significance on wrapping in Japan, see Eyal Ben-Ari, Brian Moeran, and James Valentine, eds., *Unwrapping Japan* (Honolulu: University of Hawaii Press, 1990).

6. For a performative, nonessentialist theorizing of gender, see Judith Butler, *Gender Trouble* (1990).

7. One of the models, a well-known androgynous-looking African-American woman named Sebastian, injected a refreshing note of subversion into the Mori proceedings. Looking distinctly grim in her silk dresses, pumps, and heavy makeup, she did something unexpected each time she came out on the runway—lifting up her skirt and waggling her exposed leg to the camera, snatching off a silk turban she wore, dramatically dropping a feathery coat in the middle of the runway and snatching it up again as she walked out, throwing it over her shoulder, refusing to stand in the tableau vivant of posing models at the end of each segment. Her small refusals and parodies of gender objectification acted to subvert that very objectification.

8. "Otoko mo onna mo kurosuōbā shiteru. Otoko da kara kō, onna da kara kō to iu kangaekata wa arimasen. Nikutaiteki na kinō wa betsu to shite, danna san datte yonaka ni okite kodomo no sewa o suru shi, okusan datte shigoto shite kaseide iru wake da kara seikatsumen de wa amari sa ga naku natte kite iru. Onna da kara surimu na sukāto to iu kodawari wa mattaku arimasen."

9. Partially because of her more conservative and tailored designs (designated for a market similar to, in the United States, the classicism of a Bill Blass or Oscar de la Renta), and partially, one suspects, because of joint financial ventures with John Fairchild (one of her sons publishes *W Japan,* the Japanese branch of the Fairchild publication), Hanae Mori tends to fare better in *Women's Wear Daily,* and her designs are featured with relative frequency.

10. Oddly, in the fashion world, this emerges time and again as the highest compliment a designer can receive. It appears to mean that the garments are timeless—either so classic that they are not subject to the vicissitudes of this year's "in" look or so avant-garde that they never go out of style because they are never quite "in" style; i.e., they will always look unusual and avant-garde. Because the fashion industry is based on incessant and ceaseless seasonal change, enforced among the top designers and among retailers through the seasonal collections (for the designers who show in Paris, this means at least four collections: women's spring/summer, men's spring/summer, women's fall/winter, men's fall/winter), this may reflect a barely submerged desire to be out of the hectic round of preparing collections. What it more likely indicates, however, is the wish to be recognized as a kind of craftsperson or artist who works in the medium of clothing. Miyake is one of the designers who is rethinking the incessant changes of fashion. His Permanente collection is based on styles from years past, and he claims his goal to be the kind of clothing in which new items can be mixed and matched with items from past collections.

11. The tendency to group all the Japanese designers together (a rhetorical move this chapter makes as well, even as I try to deconstruct this essentializing category) proves understandably frustrating to people who pride themselves on their distinctness and creativity. Certainly, to lump together Hanae Mori's lavishly printed silks, Miyake's technology of pleats, Matsuda's nostalgic retro mode, and Kawakubo's radically deconstructive vision does violence to what is, after all, a highly diverse group. On the other hand, the terms of individual genius and creativity are also products of a constitutive history, and eventually, this inquiry will address the ways the fashion world (and our cultural, linguistic, and historical discourses) circulates the tropes of *both* individual creativity and national identity as the terms of discourse. For the moment, I am highlighting the racial and political elements at work in the construction of a national identity, but eventually, both the trope of individual genius and the trope of national essence must be interrogated.

12. Perhaps telling is the fact that the word *power* is rendered in English transliteration rather than by the Japanese term.
13. Interviews with Jean Drusedow, curator of the Costume Institute at the Metropolitan Museum of Art, and with Barbara Weiser, of the highly successful New York boutique Charivari, attest to the influence of Japanese fashion on the looser cuts of clothing of the 1980s.
14. Professor Patricia Seed relates the story of a recent search at Rice University, where all three female candidates—each from a different part of the country—wore loose-fitting black garments to their interviews and talks, a fact prompting comments from members of the search committee.

REFERENCES

Brubach, Holly. 1988. The rites of spring. *New Yorker,* June 6.
———. 1989. Between times. *New Yorker,* April 24.
Butler, Judith. 1990. *Gender trouble: Feminism and the subversion of identity.* New York: Routledge.
Cocks, Jay. 1986a. A change of clothes. *Time,* January 27.
———. 1986b. Showroom at the top. *Time,* May 19.
Coleridge, Nicholas. 1988. *The fashion conspiracy.* New York: Harper.
Cunningham, Bill. 1988. Couturist class. *Details,* November, 119–135.
Drusedow, Jean. 1989. Curator, Costume Institute, Metropolitan Museum of Art, New York. Interview with author, November.
Duka, John. 1983. Yohji Yamamoto defines his fashion philosophy. *New York Times,* October 23.
Haug, Wolfgang. 1986. *Critique of commodity aesthetics.* Minneapolis: University of Minnesota Press.
Hutcheon, Linda. 1989. *The politics of postmodernism.* New York: Routledge.
Kanai Jun. 1989. Representative, Miyake Design Studio, New York. Interview with author, July.
Knaufo, Robert. 1988. The new Japanese standard. *Connoisseur,* March.
Koda, Harold. 1989. Curator, Fashion Institute of Technology, New York. Interview with author, July.
Kondo, Dorinne. 1990. *Crafting selves: Power, gender, and discourses of identity in a Japanese workplace.* Chicago: University of Chicago Press.
Koren, Leonard. 1984. *New fashion Japan.* Tokyo: Kodansha.
Kusunoki Shizuyo (ed.). 1986. *The Tokyo collection.* Tokyo: Graphic-sha.
Martin, Richard. 1987. Bodyworks: Issey Miyake's design theory, unpublished ms.
Miyake, Issey. 1984. Speech delivered at Japan Today Conference, San Francisco, September.
Miyake Design Studio. 1978. *Issey Miyake: East meets West.* Tokyo: Heibonsha.
———. 1988. *Issey Miyake.* New York: Little, Brown.
Miyoshi, Masao, and Harry Harootunian (eds.). 1989. *Postmodernism and Japan.* Durham: Duke University Press.
Morris, Bernadine. 1982. From Japan, new faces, new shapes. *New York Times,* December 14, C10.
Nelson, James. 1989. Editor, Magazine House, Tokyo; freelance consultant, Honolulu, Hawaii. Interview with author, August.

Servan-Schreiber, Franklin. 1989. Editor, *Elle,* New York. Interview with author, July.

Sidorsky, Gina. 1983. From East to West: A new breed of Japanese designers. *Image NYC,* 17–20.

Stinchecum, Amanda Mayer. 1983. The Japanese aesthetic: A new way for women to dress. *Village Voice,* April 19, 70–76.

Weinstein, Jeff. 1983. The man in the gray flannel kimono. *Village Voice,* April 19.

———. 1989. Editor, *Village Voice,* New York. Interview with author, July.

Weiser, Barbara. 1989. Vice president, Charivari, New York. Interview with author, July.

· · · · ·

11

SHOPPING FOR SOUVENIRS
IN HAWAI'I

FUMITERU NITTA

One consequence of Japan's affluence in this era of globalization and internationalization is the popularity of packaged overseas tours. More than 8.5 million Japanese visited foreign countries in 1985 (Hawaii Visitors Bureau [hereafter HVB] 1989). Japanese tourists are known for their extravagant shopping, spending hundreds or even thousands of dollars on souvenirs and other foreign products during their relatively short stays. Japanese tourist shopping in Hawai'i suggests that the so-called *kaigai ryokō būmu* (overseas tour boom) is fueled not only by curiosity about foreign countries but also by the desire to consume foreign goods. In this chapter, which focuses on the shopping behavior of Japanese tourists in Hawai'i, I argue that Japanese tourists make the foreign products they purchase overseas familiar by transforming them into something Japanese.

Hawai'i is the most popular foreign destination for Japanese tourists, followed by Hong Kong, South Korea, and Taiwan (HVB 1989). In 1988, over 1.3 million Japanese tourists visited Hawai'i, representing nearly one-quarter of the tourist flow to the Islands. Of total expenditures in Hawai'i, however, Japanese visitors accounted for over 40 percent, or approximately $4 billion. In 1989, this increased to about $4.6 billion.

Japanese differ from non-Japanese tourists in their shopping expenditures. Japanese visitors, for example, spent $323 per day per person in Hawai'i in 1989, compared to $127 per day for visitors from the U.S. mainland, Canada, and Europe (HVB 1990). This dramatic difference in spending between Japanese and North American visitors to Hawai'i (and, presumably, to other foreign destinations) is due in part to Japanese purchases of gifts and souvenirs.[1] In 1987, 30 percent of expenditures by Japanese visitors to Hawai'i was on gifts and souvenirs, compared to only 9 percent for visitors from the U.S. mainland (HVB 1987).

Honeymooners are, per capita, the highest-spending Japanese consumers in Hawai'i, ahead of business travelers, families, office workers, married couples, and students. In 1989, Japanese newlyweds spent $2,111 per couple on gifts and souvenirs (HVB 1990).

Why do they spend so much on gifts and souvenirs? Flush with the money they receive as wedding gifts, newlyweds buy goods for themselves and presents for others to reciprocate the generosity of relatives and friends. In 1987, average "wedding expenses were 7.6 million yen (approximately $55,000), and the honeymoon trip was over 1 million yen ($7,200), which includes shopping" (Noda 1988, 2). In Japan, where weddings are an important rite of passage and social occasion (Edwards 1989), parents generally pay for most of the wedding costs. "The only costs actually paid by the newlyweds on honeymoon would most probably be for gifts and souvenirs for their relatives and close friends" (Noda 1988, 2).

An interesting subcategory of honeymoon spending in Hawai'i is the packaged wedding tour. Weddings have become so expensive in Japan that many couples are choosing to get married abroad. Even the most luxurious of these wedding-tour packages costs only a fraction of the cost of a wedding in Japan, where the hosts are expected to rent expensive clothing, purchase elaborate floral displays, serve an elegant meal, and even give high-quality gifts to the guests (Edwards 1989). Couples choosing to get married in Hawai'i purchase a package that typically includes round-trip airfare for two, leis, the rental of traditional (Western) wedding clothes, the use of a church, the services of a minister, transportation to and from the ceremony in a chauffeured limousine, a bridal bouquet, a video tape and photo album of the proceedings, a one-night stay in a hotel bridal suite, a surf and turf dinner at an elegant restaurant (see Jeffrey Tobin, this volume), matching his-and-hers aloha wear, excursions to Pearl Harbor, Sea Life Park,

OLs shopping in Waikiki.

Hilo Hatties, and the Polynesian Cultural Center, a ride in an outrigger canoe, and a luau. Sunburned, jet-lagged, shell-shocked Japanese new-lyweds in matching aloha attire are common sights in Hawaiian shopping malls. Whether their marriages get off to good or rocky starts, these newlyweds spend a good portion of their first few days of married life shopping for souvenirs to take home.

The second group of Japanese visitors who spend a large amount of money on shopping are young single working women, commonly known as office ladies, or OLs. In her work on "The New Female Consumer," Minegishi Machiko (1988, 2) points out that the typical "OL has more spending money than the average working man with a family." The discretionary income of the single OL is $432 a month, compared to $360 a month for a middle-aged businessman. These young women, who live with their parents, generally contribute little or nothing to the house-hold budget and thus have lots of money to spend on themselves. They are also far freer to travel than their male colleagues who rarely dare to use all of their vacation days. Interested in fashion and travel, OLs are well positioned to spend large amounts of money in Hawai'i.

Purchases by Japanese tourists fall into two general categories.[2] The first includes local specialties, such as macadamia-nut chocolates, trop-

ical fruits, and aloha wear.[3] The second is made up of items not associated with Hawai'i—liquor, cigarettes and cigars, perfumes, and fashion goods. Some liquor products are bottled in Europe, some on the
U.S. mainland. Well-known brands of American whiskeys and French
cognacs are always popular (see Smith, this volume). Johnny Walker
was the leading gift beverage in Japan until recently (Morsbach 1977),
when it was replaced by Chivas Regal. Buying foreign-made liquor while
abroad parallels the Japanese practice of purchasing regional brands of
sake (rice wine) as souvenirs within Japan.

American- and European-made sports equipment is an increasingly
popular purchase among leisure-conscious tourists. One of the most
frequent purchases among both female and male tourists is a pair of
Reebok or Nike jogging shoes. Tennis rackets and golf clubs are also
popular with business men and college students.

Expensive perfumes, luggage, clothing, and accessories are prized
among several categories of female shoppers. These goods are available
at both Waikiki, which is in Honolulu, on the island of Oahu, and
at the Ala Moana Shopping Center, the largest in Hawai'i. The popularity of brand name products, with Western or Western-sounding
labels, is changing the face of retailing in Hawai'i. In recent years,
several well-known stores from Europe and elsewhere have opened
branches in Honolulu. At Waikiki, for example, a Chanel boutique
is strategically located at the entrance to the Sheraton Waikiki Hotel.
The Royal Hawaiian Shopping Center has Lancel, another designer
handbag store. In addition, Chanel operates two stores at the Ala
Moana Shopping Center, which also has shops selling Gucci, Christian
Dior, Louis Vuitton, and other famous designers. Some elegant Japanese stores such as Okadaya have outlets in Honolulu that sell European labels.

The presence of these brand name stores is significant in two respects.
First, they provide opportunities for Japanese tourists to purchase designer items at about half the price they would cost in Japan; even at
half-price, these products are expensive. Japanese tourists I interviewed
mentioned that they bought designer handbags costing between two
hundred and eight hundred dollars. Second, because designer items cost
significantly more than the local products, they constitute a major portion of Japanese tourists' expenditures in Hawai'i.

The posh designer stores in Honolulu, such as Chanel, Louis Vuitton,
and Gucci, are unmistakably designed for Japanese visitors rather than
for American tourists or locals, who rarely enter the shops. Most sales-

Shoppers near the chic boutiques of Ala Moana.

people speak Japanese. Interestingly, most of these stores do not display the "Japanese spoken here" sign (in Japanese) in their windows, which one commonly sees at stores in Waikiki and Ala Moana. Apparently, their windows are too fancy for such signs. Or perhaps such information is unnecessary or redundant at these extravagant establishments, where customers take it for granted that Japanese-speaking salesclerks will be at hand. The interiors of these stores are elegantly designed, and customers are greeted by well-dressed salespeople. Americans who venture into these stores in Waikiki or Ala Moana are likely to hear little English spoken.

Expensive designer items are also available at the duty-free shops at the airport and in Waikiki. About 90 percent of the patrons at the Duty Free Shoppers store in Hawai'i are Japanese (Hochi Business Forum 1990). In summer 1990, Duty Free Shoppers opened a new larger store in Waikiki, which Japanese visitors frequent day and night.

During interviews with Japanese visitors at the Ala Moana Shopping Center and at Duty Free Shoppers I was impressed with their knowledge of famous-name items. Perhaps this reflects, at least in small part, the impact of *Nantonaku Kurisutaru* (Somehow, Crystal), a book by Yasuo

Tanaka, which sold approximately 800,000 copies in the early 1980s (Field 1989). Providing extensive information on brand name goods, *Nantonaku Kurisutaru* "is in part a study of the brand-name syndrome" (173). As Norma Field remarked, "The book's cataloging of brand-name goods favored by the affluent young was simultaneously the source of its popularity and its critical rejection" (171).

Most Japanese tourists carry a copy not of *Nantonaku Kurisutaru* but of a guidebook or a special issue of a magazine that features tours and shopping in Hawai'i. One often sees Japanese tourists walking around Waikiki or Ala Moana with colorfully illustrated books containing detailed information on locations of stores and what each store specializes in.

Before ever taking a trip, Japanese consumers learn how and what to buy from such magazines as *Non-No,* which targets young women, and *Popeye,* which targets young men. The consumption of souvenirs, gifts, and other foreign products by Japanese tourists overseas is aided and guided by a parallel consumption of knowledge (Ivy 1989) provided by books and magazines.

THE CULTURAL SIGNIFICANCE OF SOUVENIR SHOPPING

Why do Japanese tourists spend so much money on souvenirs and gifts? For centuries, Japanese travelers have bought *omiyage*—local specialties purchased as gifts for families and friends at home. Although the Japanese word *omiyage* is usually translated as "souvenir," the two words have slightly different meanings. *Souvenir* signifies "something serving as a token of remembrance, as of a place, occasion, or experience" (*American Heritage Dictionary*). Thus, for American tourists, souvenir items are usually something one buys for oneself. On the other hand, omiyage are purchased specifically as gifts. Omiyage are intended as tokens that enable the traveler to share the experience with others (Hayashiya et al. 1973). According to one explanation, the omiyage shopping practice can be traced back to the fifteenth century, when rural villagers started to organize pilgrimage groups. Known as *kō,* the village organizations chose a representative to travel to certain shrines, such as the Ise Grand Shrine. If the village was located in a remote area, the trip could be long and costly for the farmers. Thus, the kō functioned as a supporting and financing organization by providing funds collected as annual fees from its members. The money given to the traveler is called *senbetsu* (sending-off money).

Hidetoshi Kato (n.d.) discusses this historical practice of senbetsu and how it is related to omiyage: "The receipt of *'senbetsu'* established an obligatory relationship; i.e., the representative was obliged to bring something back from his trip. He usually brought some small things bought at the shrine with the *'senbetsu.'* These small items were known as *'miyage,'* which literally means 'shrine box' but is synonymous with 'souvenir.' " Today, regardless of whether or not senbetsu has been received, Japanese tourists buy omiyage for family members, friends, neighbors, and colleagues (Keown 1989).[4]

The practice of souvenir gift giving starts early in Japan. On their *shūgaku ryokō* (school excursions) students visit historically and culturally significant sites such as Nikko, Kamakura, Kyoto, and Nara. Most Japanese have taken three or more of these trips by the time they graduate from high school. These days shūgaku ryokō are not limited to domestic destinations. Japan's affluence has made it possible for some schools groups to travel to Korea, China, and even Hawai'i.

Parents give *okozukai* (spending money) to their children to use on these trips. Although this money is not usually called senbetsu, it functions the same way. Students on a school excursion, like village representatives in former times, bring back small souvenir items for their friends, neighbors, and family. Omiyage shopping consumes a considerable amount of time and thought during these school excursions, preparing the students for a lifetime of souvenir shopping.

Most Japanese visitors to Hawai'i devote as much as half of their vacation solely to shopping. In Honolulu the importance of this phenomenon is fully appreciated. The Duty Free Shoppers store in Waikiki is open from 9:00 A.M. to 11:00 P.M. Several businesses that specialize in selling omiyage make it possible for Japanese customers to shop from their hotel rooms by providing order forms listing such items as New York steaks, live lobsters, Kona coffee, Häagen Dazs ice cream (packed in dry ice), and gourmet popcorn. Orders are then delivered to the Honolulu airport and picked up when the plane lands in Japan.

A variety of free publications are available to tourists in Waikiki in both English and Japanese, though there are many more pages devoted to shopping in the Japanese publications. *Japanese Beach Press,* the most comprehensive magazine available free of charge, has floor plans of several major Honolulu shopping centers. The Japanese publications also provide special checklists for omiyage shopping. The *Japanese Beach Press* checklist includes nineteen categories of recipient, including self, parents, siblings, children, spouses, grandparents, teachers, employer, employees, boss, clients, colleagues, teachers, and marriage go-betweens. A similar form is handed to Japanese customers entering the Duty Free Shoppers stores.

It should be noted that self (*honnin*) is one of the categories on the *Japanese Beach Press* shopping list. Undoubtedly, the purchase of gifts (Befu 1986; Morsbach 1977) is a key factor in the extravagant spending of Japanese tourists overseas. But my interviews with Japanese shoppers in Hawai'i suggest that they also spend a considerable amount of money on themselves. The Duty Free Shoppers checklist has a cartoon on the cover showing a young couple looking over liquor, handbags, and perfume; having saved on gifts for others, they decide to buy for themselves as well.

Another important trend is shopping as a favor to others—commonly referred to as *tanomare mono* (things one is asked to buy). Japanese planning a trip to Hawai'i are frequently given cash by friends and relatives who ask them to purchase cosmetics, purses, and other luxury products that retail for much more in Japan. This obligation can become particularly onerous for an OL who on the final day of a four-day trip finds herself running in and out of stores in Ala Moana looking for particular brands, types, and sizes of items that her co-workers in Tokyo asked her to buy for them.

The diversity of wealth and social class among Japanese tourists in Hawai'i is reflected in their shopping. Just a decade ago, when a trip to Hawai'i was still considered a luxury, most Japanese tourists spent most of their stay in Waikiki. Although Waikiki is still the largest and most popular Japanese tourist destination, many wealthy, sophisticated Japanese are now staying in hotels and condominiums outside Waikiki or skipping Honolulu altogether and spending their vacations in expensive "destination resorts" on one of the outer islands.

Honeymooning couples on inexpensive package tours, working-class tour groups, students, and other first-time Japanese visitors tend to spend most or all of their vacation in Waikiki. Like their American middle-class counterparts, they purchase aloha wear and discounted items at T-shirt and trinket stalls in Waikiki and at Woolworths, Sears, and the less expensive stores in Ala Moana Shopping Center.

Higher-class, wealthier travelers do most of their shopping at brand

The front of the Duty Free Shoppers checklist.

name stores and designer boutiques in Waikiki and Ala Moana and in ritzy hotel gift shops; the majority of these hotels are owned by Japanese. Sophisticated travelers who have been abroad several times may feel little need to buy omiyage for themselves or their friends. As one informant said, "I've been to Hawai'i many times and so have most of my friends. We are all sick of macadamia nuts, aloha shirts, and pineapples. We don't feel that it is necessary to keep bringing each other these gifts. This whole custom has grown tiresome and lost meaning in an age of widespread international travel."

212

Paralleling the tourist shopping described in this chapter, there are similar shifts toward serving Japanese customers in the hotel, entertainment, and dining sectors of the Hawaiian economy. The strong Japanese presence in the development of resorts and golf courses and in the residential real estate market is one of the most highly charged political issues in Hawai'i. During the period of yen inflation in the middle and late 1980s, Japanese purchased large numbers of Hawaiian hotels, condominium units, expensive homes, golf courses, and shopping centers. The effect Japanese investment is perceived to have had on middle-class home prices and on the transformation of land from agricultural to resort and recreational use created a backlash of resentment and led to the accusation that Japan was turning Hawai'i into a colonial economy.

Japanese tourist shopping is far less controversial. Hawai'i's taxpayers are well aware of the economic impact of the over $4.6 billion that Japanese spend annually in the state. Japanese tourist shopping is not entirely benign, however, for this consumer power is changing the space, labor, social relations, and education system of Hawai'i. A symbol of this is the center of the Ala Moana Shopping Center, which over the past few years has been rapidly transformed from a local shopping spot and hangout to a high-priced designer boutique area for Japanese.

People who speak Japanese have a definite employment advantage in retail, hotel, and other service businesses. And doctors, lawyers, realtors, and accountants who know the language are increasingly in demand. In both public and private schools in Hawai'i, Japanese is the most popular language studied. As a result of this demand, there is a shortage of Japanese-language teachers.

Although the state as a whole benefits from Japanese tourist spending, local business people are often frustrated by their inability to attract Japanese customers. Most Japanese tourist shopping occurs in Waikiki, Ala Moana, or in the lobbies of hotels, where the shops are rarely locally owned. Waikiki is a tourist enclave, with few corridors connecting it to the retail districts of Honolulu, which makes it difficult for Japanese shoppers to buy from Honolulu merchants. Armed with Japanese-language guidebooks to shopping in Hawai'i, a few of the younger and more adventurous Japanese tourists make it to the University of Hawaii bookstore, where they buy college sweatshirts, or to the McCully Bike Shop, where they buy tennis rackets and boogie boards. But the majority of Japanese shopping takes place in Waikiki and Ala Moana, creating mostly low-paid salesclerk and stockroom jobs in the Hawaiian economy. Since most of the goods Japanese tourists purchase are made on the U.S. mainland, in Europe, or in Asia, tourist shopping does very little to support jobs in the manufacturing sector of the Hawaiian economy.

Most Japanese tourists are at least dimly aware of these tensions, which is one reason they tend not to venture out into the local communities. The extent to which Japanese tourism depends on larger political events was made very clear during the Persian Gulf crisis, when Japanese tourism to Hawai'i dropped precipitously, causing layoffs at stores and hotels and a shortfall in sales taxes. Many Japanese tourists canceled their trips to Hawai'i out of fear of air terrorism. But many others canceled when Japanese government officials suggested that it would be unseemly for Japanese tourists to be lying on the beach or shopping in Waikiki while young Americans were dying in the Gulf.

NOTES

1. In a previous study (Nitta 1987), I found that Japanese tourists also spend a lot of money in interactions with Hare Krishna devotees, who target Japanese tourists as soft touches for their pitch.
2. Charles Keown (1989) studied Japanese visitors to Hawai'i and generated a model of tourists' propensity to buy. The model includes, as dependent variables, types of products available, levels of domestic tax and import duties, relative value of specific goods, and retailers' strategies.
3. Increasingly, many souvenir items sold in Hawai'i are produced on the U.S. mainland or overseas. Some souvenir items that come from Taiwan, Hong Kong, and Korea are acceptable as souvenirs to Japanese tourists so long as they bear the words *Hawai'i, aloha,* or other Hawaiian emblems.
4. In addition to offering tangible omiyage, the traveler was also expected to make an oral report of his trip to all kō members. Because he visited the shrine as a representative of the whole village, his experience had to be shared by those who believed in the same shrine. The oral presentation was called *miyage banashi* (souvenir story). Perhaps the contemporary version of this tradition is the custom of showing friends and family photos taken during a trip abroad.

REFERENCES

Befu, Harumi. 1986. Gift giving in a modernizing Japan. In Takie Sugiyama Lebra and William P. Lebra (eds.), *Japanese culture and behavior: Selected readings,* rev. ed. Honolulu: University of Hawaii Press.

Edwards, Walter. 1989. *Modern Japan through its weddings.* Stanford: Stanford University Press.

214

Field, Norma. 1989. Somehow: The postmodern as atmosphere. In Masao Miyoshi and H. D. Harootunian (eds.), *Postmodernism and Japan*. Durham: Duke University Press.

Hawaii Visitors Bureau. 1987. *Study of Japanese visitors to Hawaii 1986*. Honolulu.

———. 1988. *Study of Japanese visitors to Hawaii 1987*. Honolulu.

———. 1989. *Study of Japanese visitors to Hawaii 1988*. Honolulu.

———. 1990. *Study of Japanese visitors to Hawaii 1989*. Honolulu.

Hayashiya, Tatsusaburo, Tadao Umesao, Michitaro Tada, and Hidetoshi Kato (eds.). 1973. *Nihonjin no chie* (The wisdom of Japanese). Tokyo: Chuokoronsha.

Hochi Business Forum. 1990. *Hawaii Hochi,* June 29.

Ivy, Marilyn. 1989. Critical texts, mass artifacts: The consumption of knowledge in postmodern Japan. In Masao Miyoshi and H. D. Harootunian (eds.), *Postmodernism and Japan*. Durham: Duke University Press.

Kato Hidetoshi. n.d. America as seen by Japanese travellers. Manuscript submitted to Mutual Image Project sponsored by U.S.–Japan Joint Committee of Educational Cultural Exchange, East West Center, Honolulu.

Keown, Charles. 1989. A model of tourists' propensity to buy: The case of Japanese visitors to Hawaii. *Journal of Travel Research* (Winter 1989):31–34.

Minegishi Machiko. 1988. The new female consumer. Paper presented at the Hawaii Visitors Bureau Seminar, Japan: The New Female Consumer and Honeymoon Travel Market.

Morsbach, Helmuth. 1977. The psychological importance of ritualized gift exchange in modern Japan. *Annals of the New York Academy of Sciences* 293:98–113.

Nitta, F. 1987. "A flower for you": Patterns of interaction between Japanese tourists and Hare Krishna devotees. In S. Thomas (ed.), *Culture and communication: Methodology, behavior, artifacts, and institutions*. Norwood, N. J.: Ablex.

Noda Shozo. 1988. Why do Japanese honeymooners spend so much? Paper presented at the Hawaii Visitors Bureau Seminar, Japan: The New Female Consumer and Honeymoon Travel Market.

215

• • • • •

12

"BWANA MICKEY": CONSTRUCTING CULTURAL CONSUMPTION AT TOKYO DISNEYLAND

MARY YOKO BRANNEN

We really tried to avoid creating a Japanese version of Disneyland.
We wanted the Japanese visitors to feel they were taking a foreign vacation
by coming here, and to us Disneyland represents the best that America
has to offer.
—Toshiharu Akiba, spokesperson, Tokyo Disneyland

Though the Walt Disney Company wished to diversify its first foreign theme park by including some home-country attractions such as a "Samurai Land" or a show based on a Japanese children's tale like "Little Peach Boy," the Japanese owners of Tokyo Disneyland, the Oriental Land Company, insisted that the original park be duplicated as closely as possible. The phenomenal success of the theme park, which opened on April 15, 1984, suggests that the Japanese owners' reading of consumer preference was correct. In 1988 attendance reached 13,382,000, making Tokyo Disneyland one of the most popular diversionary outings

An earlier version of this work was presented in Washington, D.C., at the 1989 meeting of the American Anthropological Association. I am indebted to Richard Burt for critical comments and suggestions on earlier drafts of the chapter. I would also wish to thank Stephen Smith, Linda Lewis, Katsu Yamaguchi, Shu Ogawa, Robert Murray, Stefan Senders, and Joseph Tobin for their insights.

in Japan. The Japanese spend more money at Tokyo Disneyland than do their American counterparts at either Disneyland, in Anaheim, California, or Disney World, in Orlando, Florida—most of it on such souvenirs as Mickey Mouse dolls, pins, T-shirts, and designer accessories.[1] The theme park is not only a sensational hit among Japanese consumers of leisure-time activities but also a favorite destination of students on school pilgrimages (*shūgaku ryokō*). Previously such groups had preferred to visit traditional historical areas such as Kyoto or Nikko, the sites of ancient temples and shrines referred to in their history books and classical literary texts. In 1988, some 1,171,000 of the park visitors were students on such organized school outings.

The Tokyo Disneyland annual report of 1989 attributes these substantial attendance and sales figures in part to Japan's rapid rise in economic status over the last decade, resulting in a significant increase in per capita disposable income and a new attitude toward relaxation and recreation. Another major factor in Tokyo Disneyland's success is that the Disney philosophy of creating a "dream world" coincides with the current consumer trend of *yuttarism* (from *yutarri*, meaning easy, comfortable, and calm), an attitude of attaching importance to relaxation and comfort. According to the Dentsu Advertising Agency, which handles the Tokyo Disneyland account, consumers are "seeking quality in this world rich with things, [and] are starting to pursue affluence of the mind, time and environment."

But these explanations of the success of Tokyo Disneyland fail to take account of the Oriental Land Company's insistence on maintaining the cultural purity of the original American theme park and its efforts to turn the experience of visiting the theme park into a "foreign vacation" for Japanese visitors. What is remarkable about Tokyo Disneyland is that the Japanese owners wanted an exact copy and think of it as an exact copy, even though they have in fact adapted the Anaheim Disneyland to suit the tastes of Japanese consumers.[2] Ultimately, it is the Japanese, not the Americans, who have defined Tokyo Disneyland. That is to say, it is the *importation* of the artifact rather than its *exportation* that begs to be analyzed.[3]

Why do the Japanese prefer a copy of the original Disneyland to a version incorporating their own history and culture? Broadly speaking, there are two ways of answering this question. One I call context-free and the other context-bound, though neither of these explanations alone is adequate. The context-free account derives from a certain discourse of symbolic domination in the West that is put forth by such Marxist theorists as Frederic Jameson and Jean Baudrillard.[4] In this view, the Japanese fascination with representations of American popular culture exemplifies the westernization of Japan. While this account does not explicitly address cross-cultural domination, it implies that the West is the major global power; therefore as it gains power over other cultures, it dominates them in the same way it dominates people in the West—namely, by homogenizing culture. Thus Disneyland, as a product of cultureless world capitalism, means the same thing in Japan as in the United States. In anthropological terms, this view suggests that the transferred popular cultural artifacts have the same meaning for the Other as for the home-country consumers.

The alternative, context-bound account, recently articulated by Yoshimoto Mitsuhiro (1989), argues that Japanese society is based on a postmodern order of mimesis in which incongruous cultural artifacts are a facet of everyday life.[5] In contrast to theorists like Jameson and Baudrillard, who argue that meaning is independent of context, Yoshimoto argues that the meaning of cultural artifacts is context-dependent and therefore nonexportable. The symbolism of Disneyland works only within the greater context of its relationship with American society. The theme parks in Anaheim and Orlando reproduce the hegemonic ideology of Middle America by calling attention to the distinction between the imaginary (Disneyland) and the real (America)—a distinction American customers intuitively understand.[6] Disney cultural simulacra consequently are meaningless in Japan because Tokyo Disneyland is decontextualized, surrounded by a people whose cultural logic is different from that of the originally intended audience.

The problem with these two accounts is their assumption that exported cultural artifacts retain their original cultural symbolism. Either Tokyo Disneyland means the same thing in Japan as in the United States (the context-free account), or it can only mean what it means in the United States and therefore is meaningless when transferred to Japanese culture (the context-bound account). Yet if Western domination of the global economy has produced a singular consumer appetite, thereby creating a homogeneous market for Western symbolic capital in the context-free account, why is it that the Japanese owners themselves asked to import an exact replica? And if the exported cultural artifacts, severed from their contextual meaning in the homeland, become meaningless to the Other, as in the context-bound account, why would millions of Japanese go to an incongruous theme park to participate in activities that mean nothing to them?

In contrast to these views, I argue that the commodified cultural artifacts of Disneyland are recontextualized in Japanese terms at Tokyo Disneyland. This recontextualization of Disneyland is a specifically Japanese construction of cultural consumption and takes two forms: making the exotic familiar and keeping the exotic exotic. The first appears in the many accommodations in service and consumer orientation that have made the park more comfortable and accessible to its primary client base, the Japanese—despite the owners' initial insistence on fashioning an exact replica of the original park.[7] The second, keeping the exotic exotic, is a way of distancing the self from the Other, or, in Japanese terms, a way of maintaining the *uchi-soto* dichotomy—the distinction between inside and out.[8] What is significant about this recontextualization of Disneyland is that it complicates the usual way we understand cross-cultural hegemony. In the Western imperialist model of hegemony, exported cultural artifacts are either imposed intact onto the Other's culture or are domesticated by the Other; in either case the exotic is made familiar. But, in the case of Tokyo Disneyland, the owners have insisted upon constructing an exact copy of the original, thereby keeping the exotic exotic to the point of effectively denying that they have familiarized it. My explanation for this apparent paradox is that it represents a specifically Japanese form of cultural imperialism. The process of assimilation of the West, the recontextualization of Western simulacra, demonstrates not that the Japanese are being dominated by Western ideologies but that they differentiate their identity from the West in a way that reinforces their sense of their own cultural uniqueness and superiority, or what we might call Japanese hegemony.

We can begin to see how this process of assimilation works by looking first at how the Japanese recontextualize Western cultural artifacts to make sense of them in their own terms. A reading of the Anaheim and Tokyo Disneylands as cultural texts reveals the contextual differences in the modes of commodification (Geertz 1973).

The original Disneyland layout follows a distinctly modern progression in which guests may relive the American romantic journey by heading "out West" from Main Street.[9] They first fight their way through the turbulent waters of Adventureland, encountering savages and beasts along the way. They relax for a while in the civilized settlement of New Orleans Square before they push forward on their quest for the American dream through the rough terrain of Frontierland. Finally, they reach Fantasyland, where their dreams come true. Tomorrowland is a fantasized extension of this limitless dream—the new frontier.

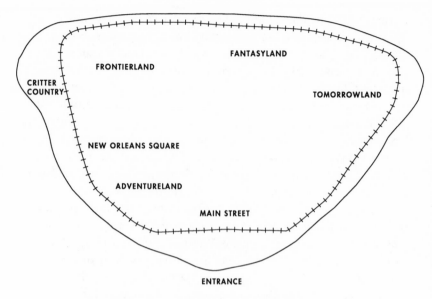

Map of Disneyland, Anaheim, California.

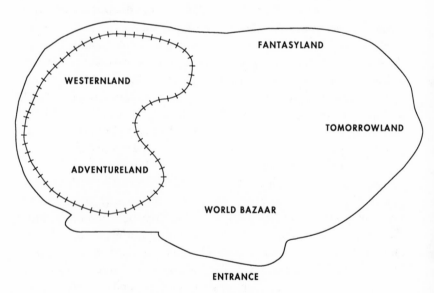

Map of Tokyo Disneyland.

Whereas the original Disneyland can thus be read as a romantic narrative, Tokyo Disneyland yields no such neat reading. Themes nostalgic for Americans but meaningless for the Japanese have been renamed and recontextualized to capture the attention of the new clientele; in the process, the logic of Disneyland's romantic metanarrative is broken.[10] Main Street U.S.A. becomes the World Bazaar; Frontierland becomes Westernland; the Golden Horseshoe Revue becomes the Diamond Horseshoe Revue. Perhaps the most obvious visual break in the Disney metanarrative is the course of the railroad; whereas the original Disneyland's railroad encircles the entire theme park, Tokyo's version cuts off Adventureland and Westernland from the rest of the park.[11]

A Western postmodernist reading, such as the context-bound account put forth by Yoshimoto, would explain this by saying that the decontextualized cultural artifacts have lost their meaning in Japan; therefore, for the Japanese, the Disney metanarrative simply breaks down into meaningless simulacra. I want to show, however, that although the Western metanarrative does break down, the cultural artifacts are recontextualized and function as new mininarratives at Tokyo Disneyland.

Much of the exotica of Disneyland is already familiar to the Japanese. Disney movies and paraphernalia have been a part of the Japanese experience since the late 1940s. Japanese parents I have interviewed say they can relate to the wholesome virtues embodied in the Disney philosophy and therefore feel secure about the positive educative effects the theme park will have on their children. In addition, the park is safe and kept meticulously clean, and the employees are always courteous— all characteristics that fit in with Japanese visitors' own high standards and expectations of service. Disney University, the forty-hour apprenticeship program for those newly hired at Disneyland in the United States, turns out employees (or "cast members," as they are called by insiders) socialized in the Disney corporate culture. Their demeanor is governed by the following three rules: "First, we practice the friendly smile. Second, we use only friendly and courteous phrases. Third, we are not stuffy" (quoted in Van Maanen 1989). The same three rules (among numerous others) can be found in any Japanese training manual for new employees in service-oriented jobs. These are the formulas that have produced the ever-present Japanese "service voice" (a slight adjustment on Disney's version, which involves speaking in a pitch at least one octave higher than one's regular speaking voice) that greets customers as they enter a department store, take a ride on an elevator, or ask for assistance at an information counter. Everyone at Tokyo Disneyland uses the service voice—the guide who leads tours of the park, the crowd-control staff, the food-service people, and of course those in charge of public announcements. Other slight adjustments intended to accommodate Japanese clientele include name tags at Tokyo Disneyland featuring the last name of the employee rather than the first, street signs and signboards with Japanese subtitles, and Japanese sound tracks to all the attractions.

There are also many small but obvious ways in which the owners have made concessions to the Japanese consumer. In spite of Tokyo Disneyland's claim to be a pure copy of the American original, the product has in fact been carefully adjusted to its target market. Looking at these adjustments, we begin to get a sense of the difference between consumer capitalism in Japan and the United States.

Main Street U.S.A. has become the World Bazaar. Although Tokyo's version has retained the quasi-Victorian architecture of the buildings, the storefronts are full-size, as opposed to the three-quarter scale of the original ones, and the facades face Main Street directly, rather than being set at an angle, resulting in a less intimate welcome. The enlarged scale of the buildings, the changes in their angle of placement to the street, plus the covered walkways and glass roof over the entire World Bazaar (a necessary protection against central Japan's often rainy weather) give Tokyo's Main Street the feel of a large suburban shopping mall rather than a quaint town center. In fact, Tokyo Disneyland has more commercial space than the Disney complexes in Anaheim or Orlando, and the owners complain that it still is not enough. There is much more emphasis on shopping; each visitor to Tokyo Disneyland spends an average of six thousand yen (about forty-two dollars) on souvenirs per visit.

Another architectural change reflecting the strong consumer emphasis of Tokyo Disneyland is Cinderella's Castle, situated at the end of the World Bazaar. The original Disneyland features Sleeping Beauty's castle, but in the midst of Japan's newfound economic prosperity, it is no wonder that Tokyo Disneyland chose to feature Cinderella instead, whose rags to riches story relates more directly to the Japanese historical experience.

Whereas stores on the original Disneyland's Main Street sell mostly Americana items, the World Bazaar features gifts from around the world. In addition, the gifts at Tokyo Disneyland are of higher quality and consequently cost more. This is in keeping with what the Dentsu Advertising Company has identified as the key words characterizing Japan's current consumer-product trends: *personal, high function, high quality, global,* and *genuine.*

Rather than appeal to nostalgic sentiment, as Main Street does for Americans, World Bazaar serves the gift-giving needs of the Japanese. The Japanese system of *senbetsu* obliges the traveler to repay this farewell gift of money with a return gift (see Nitta, this volume), which must conform to three rules: it must be worth half the yen value of the original gift; be a specialty of the locale visited on the trip—a *meibutsu;* and have a legitimating mark—a *kinen,* the tag or wrapper proving that it was purchased on site. At the World Bazaar one can buy mementos that serve the functions of both meibutsu and kinen—all Tokyo Disneyland souvenirs have TOKYO DISNEYLAND marked on them, whereas U.S. Disneyland mementos have no such identification. Visitors to Tokyo Disneyland make it a point to mail postcards to family and friends from the Tokyo Disneyland postbox because all mail is stamped with a special Mickey Mouse kinen stamp, reminiscent of the rubber stamps available at virtually all travel sites throughout Japan. Visitors often stamp their travel diaries with these legitimating mementos which feature the name and a picture of a locale.

By far the most popular of legitimating mementos is some commodified form of Mickey Mouse. The cartoon character's popularity in Japan is neither recent nor accidental. Like their American counterparts, many Japanese under the age of forty-five watched the "Mickey Mouse Club" on television as children and when prompted will readily join in a Japanese version of the Mickey Mouse song. In addition to these shared meanings of Mickey, however, the Japanese have other recontextualized meanings for him. For example, whereas in the United States Mickey Mouse is a symbol used predominantly on children's items, in Japan he is a common symbol on items for both adults and children. When an American adult sports Mickey Mouse attire, usually in some form of casual wear, such as a T-shirt or sweatshirt or watch, it can be understood as a nostalgic reference to a childhood experience of sitting in front of the television set with Mickey Mouse ears on, being a part of the Mickey Mouse Club, and wearing one's first watch—a Mickey Mouse watch, of course. Or an American adult may wear a Mickey

Mickey Mouse memorabilia are evident even at traditional religious festivals.

Mouse item in order to be camp or antiestablishment—witness the business person who wears an expensive Mickey Mouse quartz watch.

On the other hand, when a Japanese adult sports Mickey Mouse attire (and this would more likely be a female adult), this can be understood as nostalgia for childhood in general rather than as a reference to a specific experience. Further, Japanese wear Mickey Mouse paraphernalia because they think it is cute (*kawaii*), not as an antiestablishment statement. In addition to adult clothing items, Mickey Mouse can be found on guest towels and adult-size bed and futon sheets; at present he is being used as the mascot for money market accounts because of the similar alliteration of *M*ickey *M*ouse and *m*oney *m*arket. (What sound-minded American would entrust her money to a Mickey Mouse account?)

The restaurants at Tokyo Disneyland originally served only Western food, but there were too many complaints from visitors who were accustomed to enjoying *bentō* (Japanese boxed lunches) on outings. In response, the Hokusai Restaurant on Main Street now serves tempura and sushi, and the Hungry Bear Restaurant in Westernland has added curried rice (a favorite luncheon item for the Japanese) to its menu.

There are not as many food vendors on the streets of Tokyo Disneyland as at the Anaheim Disneyland. Whereas visitors to the original theme park can buy hot dogs, ice cream, snow cones, cotton candy, hot pretzels, and churros, the only option at Tokyo Disneyland is popcorn. The scarcity of food stands in the Tokyo version can probably be explained by the fact that Japanese consider it impolite to eat while walking.

Traveling west from the World Bazaar, one encounters Frontierland, which has been renamed Westernland. A spokesperson for Tokyo Disneyland commented, "We could identify with the Old West, but not with the idea of a frontier."[12] Interviews with Japanese men between the ages of twenty-eight and forty-five help to explain this identification with the West. Each reported growing up with such television Westerns as "The Rifleman," "Laramie," "Wyatt Earp," and "The Lone Ranger." What drew them to these shows, they said, was the simple, nonreligious, yet moral content—the good guy triumphs over evil (*seigi wa katsu*).[13] Many of those interviewed likened the morality in the Western television shows to that of a long-running samurai program called "Mitokōmo."

Disneyland's Golden Horseshoe Review is called the Diamond

Horseshoe Review at Tokyo Disneyland. The original made sense in terms of the Disney metanarrative—the adventuresome American travels West on horseback to find her or his dream—in this case, gold. The renaming upsets this Western narrative, but gold does not have much cultural significance in modern Japan. Traditionally Japanese do not wear wedding rings, but if they do, they favor silver or white gold because they feel it is less ostentatious than yellow gold. In addition, silver is indigenous to Japan (it was formerly mined in northern Japan). Of course, diamonds are generally considered ostentatious, but when pressed with this contradiction, Japanese I have queried have simply responded by saying that "diamonds are a sign of wealth."

Although most of the narrations delivered by ride operators and tour guides at Tokyo Disneyland are direct translations of the original Disneyland versions, there is a substantial amount of ad-libbing by the Japanese facilitators. These adaptations usually take the shape of Japan-specific puns, jokes, and creative explanations. For example, when the trunk of a huge (strategically positioned) African elephant fails to spray the cruise boat's passengers with water, the Tokyo Disneyland ride operator explains that luckily for them the elephant's trunk is stopped up with *hanakuso* (snot). Humorous references to *kuso* (a vulgar generic suffix attached to the names of various bodily orifices from which mucus or excrement is expelled) are commonplace among children and adults in Japan, where people are much less inhibited about bodily functions than in the United States. The American version is that the elephant did not have time enough to get a refill.

A second example of narrative adaptation is the ride operator's explanation that the bwana dressed in safari attire beating an alligator on the river's shore is playing *jan ken pon* (a game of "paper, scissor, rock"—the Japanese equivalent of "eenie, meenie, minie, mo") for his life. "Since we Japanese have legs too short [a common self-deprecating complaint among the Japanese] to facilitate a swift escape, we must use our wits and negotiate for our lives. Everyone knows that an alligator's choice is limited to paper as he can't make a fist [for the rock] or scissors."

KEEPING THE EXOTIC EXOTIC

Western theories of hegemony generally assume that cultural imperialism operates in one way: the dominant West colonizes and subordinates the Other. The following examples, however, show a different type of cultural imperialism at play at Tokyo Disneyland. Here, Japan appropriates a cultural artifact from America (Disneyland) and uses it in relation to its Western and Asian Others in such a way as to retain its own unique identity.[14] This Japanese form of cultural imperialism operates by continually reinforcing the distinction between Japan and the Other, by keeping the exotic exotic. By preserving the experience of Tokyo Disneyland as a foreign vacation the Japanese owners attempt strategically to ward off any threat to their identity from the West. Nevertheless, this strategy is not completely successful, as closer examination of the contradictions in the Japanese response to the exotic will show.[15] The Japanese view the Other dualistically: positive responses include everything from respect to condescending appreciation; negative responses range from ridicule to outright omission.

"Meet the World" is an attraction specific to Tokyo Disneyland. The name of this attraction would seem to suggest that it is about various countries of the world (in the fashion of Disney's "It's a Small World"). On the contrary, "Meet the World" is about the Japanese; more specifically, it is a sixteen-minute crash course on Japanese history.[16]

The show, which combines film and audio-animatronic technologies, begins as a young brother and sister sit on a beach and view the sea. The sister asks her brother a question on the history of Japan. When he cannot answer it, a white crane (a Japanese symbol of longevity) appears and recounts the history of Japan and its relationship to the world. This attraction is really about Japan's relation with the Other. The hidden agenda is to show that the Japanese, despite their numerous encounters with other cultures through trade, remain a unique people.

The first encounter with the Other (according to this history) is with China: Japan's first emissary to China, Shotoku Taishi, returns to Japan with many gifts, which are flashed across the screen. They include pottery, artwork, religious scrolls, artifacts from Persia and India, and the Chinese characters, from which the Japanese develop their unique phonetic symbols—*hiragana*. Then the statue of the Great Buddha (a Japanese architectural treasure in Kamakura) flashes across the screen, and the brother cries out in protest, "You mean that's not really Japanese?" The crane explains that Japan never borrowed cultural artifacts directly but brought back the seeds from other countries to plant in its own soil. "This is how we developed our own unique culture over the years." The crane then narrates, as Yaji-san and Kita-san,[17] the Japanese equivalents of Mutt and Jeff, trace the intensive development of Japanese arts and crafts during Japan's period of isolation from other cultures (1636–1853) by rapidly opening and closing *fusuma* (sliding partitions) on which the artistic treasures are displayed.

The boy's fear that there might be nothing uniquely Japanese is shared by many Japanese. Among the gifts the Japanese received from China, as reported in the narrative, are its writing system, the beginnings of its culture, its political administration, Confucianism, and Buddhism.[18] Having learned culture at the feet of the Chinese, the Japanese have long felt somewhat inferior to them and have therefore strived to distinguish themselves as unique.

This attraction illustrates that Japanese cultural identity is never separate. The entire narrative is framed within the subjectivity of the Asian Other—always in unsettled relations. This is evident from the emphasis on Japan's uniqueness in relationship to China and from the complete absence of any mention of Korea in Japan's history. The attraction treats China positively, paying respect to its role as a source of Japanese culture (in much the same way that the West pays homage to Greece and Rome), but at the same time it distances Japan from China by emphasizing Japan's development of the transplanted cultural seedlings.

This attraction treats Korea negatively by omission.[19] Korea is excluded because it is the Asian country most similar to Japan and therefore the one most difficult for the Japanese to differentiate themselves from. Or, to extend Emiko Ohnuki-Tierney's classification system of outsiders, though the Chinese and Koreans are both "marginal outsiders" and therefore more threatening than the Western Other, Koreans are the closest to the margin and therefore the most problematic. Korea is the Asian country nearest to Japan and is similar in size; Koreans are the largest population of foreigners in Japan and represent the greatest number of aliens who have obtained Japanese citizenship; and archaeological as well as linguistic evidence suggests some common origin for the Japanese and Koreans.[20] Moreover, the Japanese imperial line can be traced to Korea.[21]

Some of the telling omissions in the narrative of "Meet the World" are: (1) Buddhism first came to Japan in 552 from Korea, not China; (2) Korea's role in keeping trade alive with the outside world after Japan closed its doors to trade and travel in 1636 is never mentioned (the crane's version explains that this function was provided by the Chinese and the Dutch alone); and (3) Korea has been exporting goods and culture to Japan intensely since the middle of the ninth century, including such everyday items as rice, beans, cotton, hemp, and handcrafted articles; temple paraphernalia such as Buddhist images and temple bells; smelting, weaving, and pottery techniques; and religious, scientific, and scholarly knowledge.[22]

"Meet the World" deals with Japan's relationship with the West on two occasions. Japan first encountered the West through the Portuguese, who are reported to have introduced guns and Christianity. The second encounter was with the United States; Commodore Matthew Perry arrived in Japan in 1853 and announced to the Japanese that "we didn't come here to fight but to trade." Then, in a cursory treatment of World War II, the screen and theater are completely darkened for thirty seconds; the little boy cries out "*Kurai*" (it's dark); and quickly the crane changes the subject away from the war by saying, "We've been looking at the past—what about the future?" The attraction ends with a slide show of forecasts for the future, accompanied by the theme song "We meet the world with love / *Ai no fune de* [in our love boat] / We meet the world with love."

Westernland features an outdoor show in which a confidence man, Dr. Barker, and his two sidekicks, a dolled-up woman and a male flunky, trick the audience into buying magical healing potions. When I viewed the show, one of the customers asked to come on stage was a Japanese actor dressed up as an American Indian. The confidence man began a hard-sell routine to coerce the Indian to buy a potion. Whereas the doctor and his assistants spoke in the standard Japanese dialect (*hyojungo*), the Indian spoke in a southern Japanese dialect that immediately categorized him as a hick. The doctor, remarking on the Indian's accent, insulted him by asking, "What are you, an Indian or a Chinese?" The comment was met with a round of laughter from the crowd. Here, it is the Chinese Other who is on the wrong end of Asian Orientalism.

Cinderella's castle at Tokyo Disneyland is a repository of all the sinister themes and characters from Walt Disney's stories. The Tokyo Disneyland brochure invites you to this attraction with the question "Can you capture the evil forces of the Disney villains in the castle?" Upon entering the castle, one is surrounded by evil images from such Disney movies as the *Black Cauldron, Fantasia, Sleeping Beauty,* and *Snow White.* As I walked through the castle I had a nagging sense that something was strange but couldn't quite grasp what it was until I ventured upon the "Mirror on the Wall" from Snow White. The image in the mirror was reciting "Mirror mirror on the wall, who's the fairest of them all?" in Japanese, of course, but in a foreign (*gaijin*) accent.[23] Evil is represented as foreign. This is not unlike our custom of giving evil characters in spy movies foreign (usually German or Russian) accents and personae.

The treatment of gaijin at Tokyo Disneyland is complex. The Japanese have wholeheartedly welcomed Disneyland to Japan, praising it as "the best America has to offer," and gaijin employees at Tokyo Disneyland are treated with respect, both of which suggest a positive attitude toward the West. Yet the above example of evil gaijin voices at Cinderella's castle suggests a negative attitude. Although gaijin employees occupy high-status positions at Tokyo Disneyland, they are not integrated into the Disney experience of the customers like their Japanese counterparts. Instead they are treated as exotic specimens.[24]

There are two categories of gaijin employees at Tokyo Disneyland: cast members who dress up as Peter Pan, Snow White, or Cinderella, and authentic craftspersons such as Swiss clock makers, glassblowers, and silversmiths. These gaijin employees function as "authentic artifacts" with whom the Japanese guests can have their pictures taken to legitimate the experience of the foreign vacation. To maintain their distinction as exotic, gaijin employees are asked to speak only in English and not to wear name tags, presumably so that guests do not relate to them as individuals. Rather than function (like their Japanese counterparts) as facilitators of the Disneyland experience, gaijin employees are put on display. Gaijin cast members appear as a group in the place of honor at the front of the daily Disneyland parade, and gaijin craftspersons are displayed throughout the day at their boxed-in workstations, not unlike animals in a zoo.

My account of Tokyo Disneyland allows for difference in the present postmodern moment to show that Western cultural imperialism is neither the only nor the most prevalent form of imperialism at Tokyo Disneyland. Moreover, I have tried to show that cultural imperialism works in a more complicated way than previous theories have allowed. They assume that there is either a systematic encoding of Us by the Other or a totally incoherent reencoding that fractures the American narrative and makes nonsense of it. Both accounts limit our understanding of the way in which the politics of culture works, especially in terms of cultural imperialism.

By contrast, I have undertaken an anthropological cultural critique.[25]

In my account, the process of encoding is neither completely systematic and noncontradictory nor completely unsystematic and contradictory; rather, it is an inconsistent process by which meanings get negotiated. By allowing for inconsistencies in the process of encoding cultural artifacts, I have shown how the Japanese encode (as in the case of the United States and China) or do not encode (as in the case of Korea) other cultures and then reincorporate them for their own purposes, in some cases to stimulate and satisfy consumer desire, in others to advance their own hegemony.

Further inquiry in this area demands a rethinking of the very conception of hegemony that has dominated recent accounts of cultural imperialism. This would, of course, demand that capitalism itself be understood as a nonunified practice, as Japanese versions make clear. Current accounts of hegemony assume that one group is dominant and the other subordinate. In terms of cultural imperialism, they play out a relationship of colonizer and colonized. But the case of Tokyo Disneyland suggests that the opposition between dominant and subordinate groups does not apply to the Japanese and American (or Western) groups. The exported cultural artifacts are not necessarily imposed onto a passive Other. Disney, as colonial emissary for the West, has not succeeded in colonizing and subordinating the Japanese at Tokyo Disneyland. In fact, the selective importation of Disney cultural artifacts works in the service of an ongoing Japanese process of cultural imperialism. Let me formulate this problem as a question: How is the concept of hegemony to be modified to account for the struggle between two dominant powers?[26]

NOTES

1. The Walt Disney Company receives 7 percent of Tokyo Disneyland's profits from admissions, food, and merchandise. Within the first five years of Disneyland's operation, the Japanese had already spent over ten billion yen on Disneyland paraphernalia.
2. The plan for the Paris Disneyland, which will open in 1992, has from the outset incorporated many European adaptations to the Anaheim Disneyland.
3. My point is borne out by the fact that though Tokyo Disneyland started as a joint venture of the Walt Disney Company and the Oriental Land Company, the Japanese company bought out the American interest well before the park opened in 1984.
4. Although Jameson is a classical Marxist and Baudrillard a post-Marxist—which explains their different views of the economy—their theories of cultural domination and the views that they imply of cross-cultural domination are the same. See Frederic Jameson (1984); Jean Baudrillard (1984).
5. For a comprehensive discussion of postmodernism in relation to Japan, see Miyoshi

Masao and H. D. Harootunian (1988). For discussions of the postmodern in Japan by other Japanese commentators, see Karatani Kōjin (1985) and Asada Akira (1985).

6. Jean Baudrillard deconstructs the opposition between "real" America and "imaginary" Disneyland in *Simulations* (1983, 25), by asserting that Disneyland's ideological function as imaginary is to "save the reality principle"—to hide the fact that the rest of America is as imaginary as Disneyland.

7. Although I read this move to make the exotic familiar as an example of good marketing know-how (see my discussion below), it is perhaps also possible to interpret it by means of the group model. If one seeks to understand this type of recontextualization using Doi Takeo's psychobehavioral model, one might see it as fulfilling what he calls the dependency need, or *amae,* of the Japanese people—the expectation of care given to the nurturance of in-group needs. See Doi Takeo (1971).

8. On the uchi-soto dichotomy, see Takie Sugiyama Lebra (1976), 112–113. For a discussion of distinctions between types of outsiders, see Emiko Ohnuki-Tierney (1984), 40–46.

9. I am using Jürgen Habermas's (1987) notion of the modern to mean that there is a connection between the 'self or subject (in this case the guest) and a historical progression and moral improvement.

10. Jean-François Lyotard defines the postmodern as "incredulity toward metanarratives"—breaking up modern metanarratives, which are then replaced by disjoint mini-narratives, is a characteristic of the postmodern era (1984, xxiv, 31–37).

11. A Tokyo Disneyland spokesperson told me that the structural reason for limiting the path of the Tokyo Disneyland railroad involved maintaining the sense of fantasy: if it had been constructed around the entire circumference of the park, the elevation of the tracks at various points along the route would have allowed guests to catch glimpses of the surrounding Chiba area, thereby disrupting their foreign vacation experience.

12. It is understandable that the Japanese, whose borders have always been well defined by water on every side, might not be able to identify with the concept of the American pioneer spirit of expanding a seemingly endless frontier. Nevertheless, the concept of expanding their national border by colonizing other countries is hardly novel to the Japanese experience. See Raymond Myers and Mark Peattie (1984).

13. To understand the extent of the Japanese identification with the American Old West, one need only observe the Japanese "cowhands" on the Japanese-owned cattle ranches in the United States and Australia (a recent area of Japanese foreign investment); they are enthusiastically dressed in chaps, boots, spurs, kerchiefs, and cowboy hats.

14. This penchant for asserting Japan's uniqueness is directly related to a genre of literature called *Nihonjinron* (theories about the Japanese people). For a historical account of nihonjinron, see Kawamura Nozomu (1980). For a comprehensive treatment of the subject see Ross Mouer and Yoshio Sugimoto (1986).

15. I am indebted to Emiko Ohnuki-Tierney's discussion of the inside-outside distinction (1984, 40–46). She argues that in the case of Westerners the inside-outside distinction has a dual nature: Westerners are sometimes seen negatively as the enemy or carrier of germs and sometimes seen positively and received by the Japanese with unsurpassed hospitality. Non-Japanese Asians, on the other hand, are seen as "marginal outsiders toward whom the Japanese feel ambivalent or downright negative." My examples of Japanese hegemony at Tokyo Disneyland add to Ohnuki-Tierney's classifications of treatment of the Other by further breaking down the non-Japanese Asian category to account for specific differences in the treatment of Chinese and Koreans.

16. This sort of confusion between title and content is not a rare occurrence in Japan. A

recent Japanese book entitled *People the Japanese Know,* put out by the Japan *Times* publications department, turns out to be a Who's Who of the Japanese people.

17. These are the popular names of Yajirobe and Kitahachi, characters developed by Juppensha Ikku, a famous comedy writer in the Tokugawa period.

18. Many of these "gifts" were actually received indirectly through Korea. The writing system, for example, was brought to Japan by Korean priests, and the great Daibutsu (statue of Buddha) was constructed by Korean artisans.

19. This negative treatment of the Koreans by omission is not limited to Tokyo Disneyland. An even more poignant example is the fact that the monument for Koreans who died in the August 6, 1945, bombing of Hiroshima (one-fourth of the 100,000 people killed) was not permitted to be constructed inside the Peace Park and therefore lies at a separate location across the river. (Statistics as cited in the *New York Times,* April 29, 1988.)

20. Japanese explain that the Koreans remind the Japanese of their recent past, the bleak period of economic hardship in the wake of the war, and that therefore reference to Koreans is often omitted in popular accounts of Japanese history. Although this explanation awaits empirical confirmation, my hypothesis is reinforced by DeVos and Lee, who report that the "Chinese were always [since the seventh century] given greater deference than their Korean counterparts, since they were thought to be the originators while the Koreans were carrying a borrowed culture." See George DeVos and Changsoo Lee (1980, 15). Again, it is the *shared status* as borrowers of another culture that prejudices the Japanese against the Koreans.

21. Archaeological findings in ancient Japanese tombs, in particular artifacts from Takamatsuzuka's tomb, support the theory that Japan's dynastic line includes Korean rulers. In addition, there is strong evidence that Prince Shōtoku's mother was Korean (DeVos and Lee 1980, 1–14).

22. In fact trade between Japan and Korea was so intense in the ninth century that the Japanese posted Silla interpreters on Tsushima Island (Ki-baik Lee 1984, 95; see also 191–196 for references to items exported from Korea to Japan).

23. Though *gaijin* literally means outsider, in popular usage the meaning has been narrowed to refer more specifically to Caucasian foreigners.

24. This is in keeping with Ohnuki-Tierney's observation that "the Japanese demonstrate [a] favorable attitude [toward Westerners] as long as the Westerners can be kept at a distance" (1984, 42).

25. Here I refer to the notion of cultural critique as put forth by George E. Marcus and Michael M. J. Fisher (1986, ix–x).

26. My notion of hegemony of course assumes the absence of outright conflict, as in the case of Cold War.

REFERENCES

Asada Akira. 1985. *Kōzo to chikara: Kigōron o koete* (Structure and power: Beyond semiotics). Tokyo: Fusanbo.

Baudrillard, Jean. 1983. *Simulations,* translated by Paul Foss, Paul Patton, and Philip Beitchman. New York: Semiotext(e).

———. 1981. *For a critique of the political economy of the sign,* translated by Charles Levin. St. Louis: Telos Press.

DeVos, George, and Changsoo Lee. 1980. *Koreans in Japan.* Berkeley: University of California Press.

Doi Takeo. 1971. *Amae no kōzo* (The structure of *amae*). Tokyo: Kobundo.

Geertz, Clifford. 1973. *The interpretation of cultures.* New York: Basic.

Habermas, Jürgen. 1987. *The philosophical discourse of modernity,* translated by Frederick Lawrence. Cambridge: MIT Press.

Jameson, Frederic. 1984. Postmodernism, or the cultural logic of late capitalism. *New Left Review* 146:53–92.

Karatani Kōjin. 1985. *Hihyō to posutomodan* (Criticism and the postmodern). Tokyo: Fusanbo.

Kawamura Nozomu. 1980. The historical background of arguments emphasizing the uniqueness of the Japanese society. *Social Analysis* 5/6:44–63.

Lebra, Takie Sugiyama. 1976. *Japanese patterns of behavior.* Honolulu: University of Hawaii Press.

Lee, Ki-baik. 1984. *A new history of Korea,* translated by Edward W. Wagner. Cambridge: Harvard University Press.

Lyotard, Jean-François. 1984. *The postmodern condition,* translated by Geoff Bennington and Brian Massumi. Minneapolis: University of Minnesota Press.

Marcus, George E., and Michael M. J. Fisher. 1986. *Anthropology as cultural critique.* Chicago: University of Chicago Press.

Miyoshi, Masao, and H. D. Harootunian. 1988. Postmodernism in Japan. *South Atlantic Quarterly* 87(3):388–444.

Mouer, Ross, and Yoshio Sugimoto. 1986. *Images of Japanese society.* London: Methuen.

Myers, Raymond, and Mark Peattie (eds.). 1984. *The Japanese colonial empire, 1895–1945.* Princeton: Princeton University Press.

Ohnuki-Tierney, Emiko. 1984. *Illness and culture in contemporary Japan.* Cambridge: Cambridge University Press.

Van Maanen, John. 1989. Whistle while you work: On seeing Disneyland as the workers do. Paper presented at the panel on the Magic Kingdom, American Anthropological Association Annual Meetings, Washington, D.C., November 16.

Yoshimoto Mitsuhiro. 1989. The postmodern and mass images in Japan. *Public Culture* (Spring):8–25.

· · · · ·

13

TANGO IN JAPAN AND THE
WORLD ECONOMY OF PASSION

MARTA E. SAVIGLIANO

Japanese-Argentinean relations are uneventful from the point of view
of traditional political science: there are few treaties, little trade,
no conflicts, limited immigration, and only sporadic exchanges of diplomatic courtesies.[1] There is, however, an interesting story of relations between these two distant countries, a story loaded with passion
and marked by surprising twists and turns—the story of the tango in
Japan.

We Argentineans tell a version of this story that is both grandiose
and simplistic, as it exaggerates and decontextualizes the popularity of
the tango in Japan. In this narrative, for example, no one mentions that
the Japanese have an appetite not just for tango but for other Western
music as well—rock, jazz, country, flamenco, classical. This lack of
perspective derives more from a desire for acknowledgment than from
ignorance; Argentineans need to be reassured that we occupy a special
place in the globe and deserve recognition. The tango is our symbol of
national identity. Japan's acceptance and valorization of the tango le-
gitimates our existence as a nation, culture, and people. Japan is, to
Argentineans, the Far East, far away, over there. The tango in Japan
means that our tango is *even* there. It is thrilling, flattering, empowering—our farthest-flung, least likely cultural conquest, a conquest that
gives a needed boost to Argentina's battered national pride. The powers

235

of tango must be so overwhelming that even the enigmatic Japanese fell under its spell.

Argentineans tend to make an epic tale out of the tango's popularity in Japan. Writing in the 1930s, Argentinean journalists reported on the tango's reception in Japan using militaristic metaphors: "In far away JAPAN our Tango wins another battle" (Rivarola and Rivarola 1987, 135). Or, "His majesty 'The Tango' has trespassed the walls of the impenetrable! Defeating the stubborn resistance of the Japanese spirit to all kinds of invasion, Tango conquered with no other weapons than its music" (Ferrer 1980, 255). In the concluding chapter of their *Historia del Tango* (1936), under the heading "Tango in the Orient," Héctor and Luis Bates attempt to explain the tango's unlikely success in Japan:

> What strange seduction [did tango exert] over those fragile wooden houses facing mount Fujiyama? What kind of enchantment emerges from the melancholic notes of "Milonguita" played by the semisen [*sic*] in the delicious hands of the geishas? . . . Those ample kimonos cleaving as they perform a cortada figure; those high hairdresses held by enormous combs, dreamy yellow faces under the spell of "El Entrerriano." . . . It seems impossible to believe! However, there, as well as here, a harakiri must have ended a tormented existence accompanied by the final notes of "No Me Escribas." (73, my translation)

Contemporary Argentinean reports on the fate of the tango in Japan are similarly glowing: Tokyo has become the second capital of the tango (after Buenos Aires, of course). There are more than thirty tango clubs (*tanguerias*) in Tokyo and Osaka. Victor-Japan and Columbia-Japan produce and reissue recordings of famous Argentinean tango musicians. Visiting Argentinean singers, instrumentalists, and dancers perform tango on Japanese stages, and Japanese tango orchestras play in large ballrooms. Each year, a dozen or more books on various aspects of the tango are published in Japanese. *Latina* (formerly *Musica Iberoamericana*), a monthly magazine featuring tango, has a circulation of over eleven thousand. Tango is a featured event in social dancing competitions (Ferrer 1980; Alposta 1987; Cadicamo 1976).

The story I will tell of the tango in Japan is more complex and ambivalent than the epic account. The tango in Japan is not a miracle, nor is it the result of a heroic Argentinean cultural conquest. A variety of tangos have coexisted in Japan since the 1920s, and the "Argentin-eanness" of these tangos has been heavily mediated and compromised by the Europeans and North Americans, who for many years have played major roles in the world circulation of tango. Most of the tango that reaches Japan has been Frenchified, Anglicized, or Americanized once or several times en route.

To make sense of the tango's journey around the world and its arrival in Japan, I find it useful to think in terms of a world economy of passion, an economy intertwined with the more conventional economies grounded in material exchange. Paralleling the extraction of material goods and labor from the Third World, the passion-poor core countries of the capitalist world system have been appropriating emotional and affective practices from their colonies for several centuries. This emotional capital is most often consumed as exotic culture under the sub-categories of "mystery," "untamed wilderness," "the primitive," and "raw passion." The Third World's emotional and expressive practices and arts have been categorized, homogenized, and transformed into commodities suitable for the First World's consumption.

Exotics participate in the reproduction and amplification of these practices and categories as they encounter each other through Western lenses and relate to one another in already exoticized terms: Africans, Arabs, Orientals, Latinos. Exotic people meet in (neo)colonial settings, their relations already shaped by the mediation of the Western mirror into a meeting of Exotic Others. Argentina enjoyed great wealth in the first quarter of this century, and during the past decade Japan has become the model of economic success; yet each country has had to deal with exoticism as a legacy of Western imperialism. The story of the tango in Japan reminds us of the impossibility of Exotics reaching each other outside of the mediation of the West.

TANGO'S TRAVELS

The tango is a dramatic form of dance, music, and lyrics that originated in the Rio de la Plata region of Argentina and Uruguay toward the end of the nineteenth century. From the start, the worldwide reputation of the tango has carried an aura of scandal. Tango is a representation of courtship and seduction, a public display of passion performed by a heterosexual couple locked in a tight embrace with intertwined legs, following an intricate pattern of suggestive footwork. The tango has undergone major adjustments as it was adopted and legitimized by the Argentinean higher classes and then imported by wealthy foreign countries. The form was polished as it made its way from the slums and brothels of the South American harbors to the cabarets and ballrooms of Paris, London, and New York. Once appropriated by high society, the shocking tango became a spicy but acceptable form of entertainment and a commodity suitable for packaging and distribution by the international show business industry, which pumped out tango records, dance handbooks, films, fashion, and stars.

The tango shares with other exotic products the tendency to provoke the strongly ambivalent feelings of repulsion and attraction. But to produce a salable exotic commodity, this ambiguity must be skewed toward the pleasurable, the only slightly disturbingly enjoyable, the acceptably erotic.[2]

Tango steps are the scandalous movements of an alien couple as seen by the colonial gaze. When the Exotics of the tango perform on the stages and screens of Western civilization, they receive no compassion, empathy, or any other sort of reciprocal passionate response from their audience. Otherness is precisely this condition of the absence of emotional connection or mutual identification that opens the necessary space for exploitation to develop. Was this the fate of the tango in Japan?

The tango first appeared in France between 1904 and 1907. Paris quickly became the leading promoter, manager, and curator of the dance, reshaping it in style and exporting it to the rest of the world as an exotic symbol of heterosexual courtship. The tango enjoyed its greatest vogue there during the first half of the 1920s, at the time when the revue was at the height of its popularity. Revues featured the tango in *tableaux de genre,* "where it served as a musical embellishment to representations of luxury . . . and as a mark of the exotic" (Klein 1985, 179).

This glittering, erotic stage rendition of the tango disturbed the social dance instructors who performed and taught a much blander version in their academies. Bothered by the improvisational character of the tango, the Parisian dance masters wrote tango manuals to regiment and normalize the otherwise untamed choreography. One of these dance experts identified seventy-two "attitudes," while another recommended the adoption of nine to twelve set movements (Otterbach 1980, 278–279).

In the production of exotic dances, France was hegemonic but not without contenders. France's struggles with the English codes of social dancing are a well-documented skirmish in their long-standing battle for economic, political, and cultural supremacy (Leppert 1988; Sorell 1981).

This French-English competition to establish the steps and postures of the authentic tango was closely monitored by the Argentineans, who had a great interest in the outcome.

From Paris, the tango made its way to New York, repeating the story: scandal, dance masters and manuals, and a version for the stage.

In 1926, after spending several years in the capitals of Europe, a Baron Megata Tsunumi was called home by his ill father to take care of the family business. He carried back to Japan, among other things, a handful of tango records and a keen knowledge of the dance. In 1956 Megata wrote: "In those days, soon after World War I, dancing the tango argentino was the rage in Paris. One afternoon a friend asked me to go to El Garrón . . . where I saw for the first time an authentic Argentinean band. I was captivated by the music and decided right then to learn the tango. For three years my professor was Master Pradir, in those days the most famous on the European continent" (quoted in Alposta 1987, 27, my translation). Megata later visited London where he took lessons with Victor Silvester. But in his opinion "the tango is danced in a much more beautiful way in Paris than in London."

Back in Tokyo, Megata started a dance academy where he taught his fellow Japanese aristocrats how to tango. His classes were free and limited to friends and acquaintances, but he undertook his role as a dance master very seriously. He tutored his disciples not only in the nuances of the music and dance but also in how to dress, behave, and even eat properly (that is, *à la française*). "Among other things, he would advise his students to avoid eating Japanese sauces before dancing, since these would provoke an abundant and 'strong' perspiration not recommended for coming close to the ladies" (Alposta 1987, 38, my translation).

According to Megata's followers, the tango was not considered scandalous in Japan. The public was ready for it—the aristocratic public, that is. The Japanese aristocracy was working hard to acquire the Western social skills that would allow them to mingle comfortably with foreign diplomats both at home and abroad. At any rate, Megata could get away with almost anything, including the tango, thanks to his charm and aristocratic status.

Megata introduced a particularly stylized tango to his exclusive circle: the Tango *à lo* Megata. Yoneyama Eiko, who learned the tango from Megata thirty years ago, explained Megata's method as well as the circumstances that accompanied his success at introducing the tango to Japan:

> Megata offered private dance classes to the young girls and boys of the aristocracy. Our parents thought that it was important for us to behave properly in Western high circles. There were some young British dance masters around, but our parents didn't trust them. They didn't know them and they were foreigners. Dancing could be tricky, especially for young girls, so Megata was a perfect choice. His hour-long coaching usually started with fox-trots, then moved on to the waltz and finally came the tango. I wanted to dance only tangos, but he wouldn't let me. He would say that in order to perform the tango correctly our bodies had to be relaxed, soft, ready.

Megata would whisper into his students' ears instructions on what dancing—Western dancing—was all about: "Whenever you dance remember you should feel as though you are in love with your partner, even if you have just met him."

To dance the Tango à lo Megata meant to display elegance and style. The steps should not be too long because of the ladies' fashionably tight cocktail dresses; the dance should be led through chest-to-chest contact, the male's right hand gently holding the female's back, without grabbing or pushing. The woman's left hand should rest relaxed on the man's shoulder; their faces should be close so as to allow eye contact and conversation. Megata's golden rule for the tango was to dance it beautifully. He instructed his male students to take care of the appearance of their partners. "The women should look beautiful, stylized, elegant." All abrupt movements had to be avoided so as not to "distort the female figure." With these instructions, Megata distinguished himself from his contenders: the British dance masters. While living in Europe, Megata had been exposed to the French-English tango war and had taken a side; the Tango à lo Megata was definitely a French-style tango—a tango preoccupied with elegance.

By the 1930s, British dance masters were traveling to Japan to teach the large foreign community in Kobe. Some Japanese had access to these *shakō dansu* (social dance) classes, and many others got a hold of manuals and handbooks. The tango, British-style, was taught as one of a series of modern ballroom dances presented as sportive, competitive activities. The tango of the British dance masters was strictly codified into rigid movements: the faces of the partners should point clearly in opposite directions or, when facing the same direction, be turned completely parallel to the right or left shoulder. The position of the hands helped to reaffirm distance and emotional disengagement between the partners: the lady's left hand, with the palm turned down, must touch the gentleman's shoulder perpendicularly as if in a military salute to the flag. The steps should follow a carefully developed sequence of walks, promenades, sways, swivels, reverse turns, chases, and so on, paying attention to a rhythmic pattern of slow, quick-quick, slow and slow and slow-slow. (The figures and pace were referred to by their English names.)

This English version of the tango is currently the most widely practiced in Japan. Some Japanese shakō dansu teachers I interviewed credit the English influence with helping the tango escape its scandalous roots. The straight and stiff tango encouraged by the British school imposes detachment and erases passion. As one instructor commented, "It is a style suited to dance partners who do not know each other, or who behave that way." Another instructor explained to me that among the Latin dances taught in shakō dansu classes, "the tango comes closest to the Japanese spirit. Perhaps the way tango is danced by foreigners, it is very passionate, but the way we teach it here, tango does not require a physical expression of passion through movements. Passionate feelings are kept inside. Japanese people are not drawn to show affection like the Latinos; we don't hug, kiss, and emote like you guys."

Mori Junzaburo, one of Megata's disciples, expressed his admiration toward his teacher in these terms: "Baron Megata is the only person who knows how to dance the tango in an *authentic* way since he studied it in Paris." Mori, converted by Megata into a fanatic student of the Tango à la française, was the author of the first books on tango published in Japan: *Tango* (1930) and *The Argentino Dance: Tango Dance Method* (1933). In one of his many articles devoted to tango he wrote:

> The main reason for the popularization of Argentinean music has been the shako dansu craze.... Once it [the tango] was accepted as a form of "standard dancing" in England, [Japanese] people started to dance it more and more, resulting in a boom of the so-called authentic English school. The general opinion was that since the dance method was an English one, the music should also be played the English way; the Argentinean style was out of the question. In 1932 when the Dancing Florida [supper club] of Tokyo invited some French tango musicians to play, the taste for the Latin style started to develop.... The French musicians opened up the path for those who could play the *bandoneón* [concertina], among them,

Mr. Kogure from Mitsukoshi, an authentic forerunner who had studied it in Paris. On the other hand, taking Baron Megata as the central figure, the group of fans of the French style, that is, the Latin style, grew both in quantity and quality. (Mori 1936, quoted by Alposta 1987, 49–50, my translation)

In this paragraph Mori reflects the complexity of musical colonialism. "The Argentinean Tango" appeared to the Japanese as a raw, exotic material. The authentic tangos competing for the Japanese market were either the French or the English; the Argentinean style was out of the question until it had undergone the necessary processing in the colonial factories of exoticism. The authentic tango was not the one danced in the places of origin but the one developed as a commodity by the manufacturers of exoticism.

As the Japanese imported tangos produced and exoticized in Europe, they also imported European strategies for appropriating, categorizing, and marketing exotic products. The authentic French and English versions of the tango targeted different sectors of the Japanese market for Western culture. The French tango, or Tango à lo Megata, was a hand-crafted luxury good suited to the Japanese aristocracy, while the British-style tango was a mass-produced, quality-controlled version aimed at the Japanese middle classes. Megata's dance lessons were highly personalized and sophisticated. Whereas he never charged for his classes and taught almost exclusively within his aristocratic circle, the British-style dance masters were launching a business—the social dance industry in Japan; they sold classes and manuals and arranged competitions aimed at opening up a new market. The two enterprises shared the common goal of westernizing Japan, but the uses they made of the tango were very different. To Megata and his aristocratic followers, the Tango à la française represented distinction and class. To the shakō dansu masters who popularized the British style, the tango represented modernity. Shakō dansu masters make a distinction between the controlled, sophisticated European tango and rowdy Latin dances. According to their social dance codes, the tango is included in the category of modern dances (together with the waltz and fox-trot), while the mambo, rumba, and cha-cha belong to a separate Latin cluster. This distinction shows how thoroughly successful the Europeans were at domesticating the once-wild tango and helps explain the appeal the tango held for middle-class Japanese attempting to incorporate and domesticate the West.

Megata and the social dance masters played out parallel processes of westernization, each one in its particular style, for a particular class, mirroring an international division of class by national and cultural identity. France represented to the Japanese the aristocratic center of the empire of taste; the British and, later on, the Americans (a former British colony) represented the core of the industrialized world—including the music and dance industry. Neither of these centers of world power ever completely succeeded in displacing the other; in Japan, as elsewhere, they continue to fight for control of particular markets for increasingly differentiated kinds of consumers.

THE ARGENTINEAN TANGO IN JAPAN

Another member of the international elite who helped to introduce the tango to Japan was an Argentinean diplomat in Tokyo, Arturo Montenegro. Montenegro imported records from Argentina, gave tango lessons, and organized tango contests (Ferrer 1980). Argentinean tango music became available in Japan through recordings, and Japanese musicians were soon playing the tunes. These Japanese instrumentalists and singers were fully aware of the distinctions between the Argentinean tango and its European imitators. The most prestigious Japanese tango performers were those who attempted Argentinean tangos in Spanish, complete with *lunfardo* (the slang of Buenos Aires)—the challenge being one of feeling as well as of pronunciation. Aspiring singers studied with Japanese tango fans who had a sensitive ear for Argentinean lyrics and sensitivity to the Argentinean soul, even if the aficionados could not sing themselves.

World War II played a key role in promoting the Argentinean version of the tango in Japan. With the outbreak of the war, U.S. popular music was banned, and the only foreign musical works allowed were German and Italian classics and the tango. During the war years Argentina (which remained neutral) was clearly differentiated from Japan's Western enemies, and the tango provided an attractive substitute for banned Western culture and entertainment.

Most of the Japanese *tangueros* (tango performers) I interviewed in Tokyo, when asked why the Japanese like tangos, emphasized the compatibility of Japanese and Argentinean culture rather than the attraction of the exotic. Kyotani Koji, a bandoneón player and composer, told me that "tangos are basically sentimental, as are we Japanese. When we play, we try to communicate to our audience the similarity of our feelings [with those of Argentineans] rather than the contrasts between the Latino and the Japanese; it is what we have in common that counts— sentimentality, sadness." Yamazaki Mieko, a singer, explained: "The tango is attractive to me because of the contrast between the rhythm and the strongly sentimental melody. This is a challenging combination for a singer. The Japanese women who sing tango understand these complexities because we are real city girls." Abo Ikuo, a tango singer who has recorded with both Argentinean and Japanese tango orchestras, sees a connection between the lyrics of tango and *enka* (Japanese song).

> Enka and tango share melodramatic themes, themes of love; especially "lost love" [in English] and betrayals. Things that make people cry. There are important differences. In enka it is mostly women who moan the absence of their lovers while in tangos, those betrayed are mostly men. But the emotions are similar. By listening to Misora Hibari [a renowned enka singer], Japanese tango singers learn how to express themselves singing tango. Although the rhythms are very different, the feelings of sadness, separation, and forlornness are shared.

Abo has recently composed a tango entitled "El Zorzal y La Calandria," in which he attempts to express this deep affinity. The lyrics (written by Héctor Negro) suggest a kinship of Japanese and Argentinean souls by pointing out that the most famous Argentinean tango singer, Carlos Gardel ("The Thrush"), and the most recognized enka singer, Misora Hibari ("The Lark"), were each known by birds' names and that they died on the same date. Negro adds a romantic touch by lyrically musing that although they never met in life, death has brought them together in heaven.[3]

Luis Alposta, who, like me, was puzzled by the Japanese-Argentinean tango connection, was given similar explanations by the Japanese tango artists he interviewed:

> *Alposta:* Why is Argentinean popular music so liked in Japan?
> *Koga Masao:* Because our musical feelings are convergent and the topics are extraordinarily similar.
> *Alposta:* Do you also sing about love and betrayal?
> *Koga:* Yes. We like to whine over the women who have abandoned us, just like the old tango. Twenty-three years ago, one of the first waltzes I wrote was called "*Shitaite*" (Rage), which means: "Longing for the one who left." Almost all the tangos that are popular in Argentina are sung in Japan. (1987, 101)

•

Alposta: Why do the Japanese like tango so much?
Kanematsu Yoji, president of the Society for the Study of Iberoamerican
    Music (Chunambei Ongaku Kenkyukai): Because your music
    reaches our hearts very easily. (89)

These opinions of Japanese tango artists committed to the Argentinean tango contradict those of the shakō dansu instructors who are constantly struggling to constrain tango's exoticism. Shakō dansu instructors believe that Europeanized tango is marketable in Japan because the sensuality of the original Argentinean tango has been successfully subdued. In contrast, the Japanese followers of the Argentinean tango stress the sentimental affinities of Japanese and Argentineans as a unique spiritual kinship between seemingly alien cultures.

This loyalty to the authentic Argentinean tango and this belief in the similarity between the Japanese and Argentinean souls are shared only by a small group of tango connoisseurs who seek to distinguish themselves through their taste from the unsophisticated Japanese masses who prefer shako dansu and who are afraid of the tango's passion.

Recently, a new version of the Argentinean tango developed by Argentinean impresarios for the Broadway stage was introduced to Japan. The spectacular style of this *Tango Argentino* is stimulating a new round of desire for the passion of the tango in the capitals of the developed world, including Tokyo. As a result, a new generation of Japanese tango fans has emerged, with a taste for exotic passion reminiscent of the days in *la belle époque* when tango was featured in Parisian revues.

The cultural gap is widening between the still-exotic Argentineans and the no-longer-so-exotic Japanese as Japan moves to the core of the world system. The Japanese public has become quite proficient at reproducing Western practices for consuming the exotic. The Argentinean cast members of *Tango Argentino* are consumed by their Japanese audiences as embodiments of passion who have already been given the seal of approval by the cultural capitals of the West.

The fervor associated with the tango produces complex emotions in Japanese. The shakō dansu instructors say that tango's passion has been effectively subdued in Japan, except, perhaps, in the realm of fantasy: "Couples may hold in their minds the eroticism of a Rudolph Valentino movie when they dance the tango, but they don't show it in their movements in our dance classes." The shakō dansu instructors I interviewed

もう一度、抱かれたい。

あの感動を超えて。もっと切なく、もっと哀しく。
「タンゴ・アルゼンチーノ1989ニュー・エディション」。

LAWSON
TANGO ARGENTINO

黒一色の舞台。歯切れのいいリズム。アクロバティックな足さばき。バンドネオンの哀愁に満ちた音色。妖しい緊張感。見る者をぐいぐい引き寄せて離さない刺激。あの心にしみた感動から2年。「タンゴ・アルゼンチーノ」が

再び日本にやって来る。
前回は、来日前から空前のタンゴブームを巻き起こし、チケット発売と同時にほとんどの席が売り切れるという、大ヒットを記録。バンドネオンの名手ホセ・リベルテーラが率いるオルケスタが奏でるタンゴの名曲を、それぞれのダンスペアが優雅に、セクシーに、そして激しく踊る華麗なブロードウェイショー。本ものだけが持ちうる素晴らし

From the publicity flyer for the touring company of Tango Argentino.

took pains to clarify that the Argentinean tango is never performed at their dance hall (the Odeon of Kabuki-chō, Tokyo). By Argentinean tango, they explained, they meant *ashi no karami* (legs intertwined), suggesting an inappropriate display of sensuality. An instructor told me that Japanese people know the Argentinean tango from television shows, but most of them consider it a bit vulgar and embarrassing. The Argentinean tango these instructors have in mind is clearly the Broadway style popularized in Japan by the touring company in 1987. In their opinion, this tango is so exotically erotic that, for the Japanese, it would only be proper to watch it from afar, as a voyeuristic pleasure.

EROTIC INCOMPATIBILITIES OF SOME EXOTICS

According to cultural stereotypes popular in Japan and Argentina, as well as in Europe and North America, passion separates Japanese and Latino souls. On the Western continuum of world eroticism, Japanese and Latinos are polar opposites: Japanese are cold, detached, and controlled; Latinos, including Argentineans, are expressive, passionate, and sensual. Japanese and Argentineans each use this Western map of passion to make sense of the strange case of the tango in Japan. They (we) all wonder: How can such a famously passionate dance as the tango be practiced and enjoyed by such famously repressed people as the Japanese?

Students I interviewed in an Argentinean tango dance class in Tokyo gave answers that challenge the assumptions behind this question and contradict the views of the shakō dansu instructors:

The idea that Japanese people are cold is all *tatemae* [surface, public appearance]; Japanese people are plenty passionate.

•

Japanese people are very passionate, which is why all this emphasis on politeness, etiquette, and control is necessary.

•

To me, tango is very much like Nō dancing: it is stylized, but the feeling is very strong in both tango and Nō if you know where to look. I have never done any other Western-style dances. They don't appeal to me. But something about the tango is beautiful and passionate; as in Nō, you hold the back very stiff and the movements of the legs are controlled, yet exquisitely expressive in their gestures.

247

Eguchi Yuko, one of the few Japanese dancers who teaches and performs Argentinean tango (as opposed to British- or French-style tango) explains: "Japanese aren't scandalized or offended by males and females dancing together. The concern is rather with the young ones, doing *tatchi dansu* [touch dancing] or *bodii kontakuto dansu* [body-contact dancing]. Japanese are not puritans; they don't have a church, like in the West, telling them that things are evil. It's a question of propriety, not morality. That is why young people dance disco but not the lambada." The teachers of this class, Eguchi Yoko and Kobayashi Taihei, are the leading Japanese proponents of "Tango Argentino"—a version of tango where passion and sensuality are clearly displayed. They have launched a "Tango Argentino" campaign through an association they organized to popularize the authentic Argentinean tango in Japan. Ironically, this enterprise was inspired by their seeing the Broadway show *Tango Argentino* on Japanese television. Captivated, they went to Argentina to train with Gloria and Eduardo, a famous professional tango couple.

Kobayashi and Eguchi's Tango Argentino Dance Academy is challenging the notion of an intrinsically dispassionate Japaneseness. They teach their three hundred students a striking form of tango based on the style produced by Argentineans for the stages of the Western world. Still, to a Western observer, and I suspect to most Japanese, something does not quite work. When Japanese perform the Argentinean tango, incorporating all the techniques of passion they have learned from Argentinean performers, they still look Japanese.

This is attributable not to any lack of feeling or skill on the part of the Japanese dancers but to the power of exoticism. The Western mirror stubbornly reflects Otherness. As the tango performer Maeda Hibari said in a published discussion in 1987: "When I started dancing, I wanted to do tango but people would tell me that it was as ridiculous and silly as when foreigners try to perform *kabuki*. I learned tango from an Argentinean teacher who said he had come to Japan to bring the culture from his country. I thought I was ready to perform a tango in a public concert, but then I decided that it would not be appropriate. . . . Argentineans are so passionate and serious about what they do" (Maeda and Itsuki 1987, 52). Ōiwa Yoshihiro, journalist and president of the Porteña Ongaku Dokokai (Association of Porteña Music), expressed his lack of satisfaction with both Japanese attempts at performing tango and Argentinean tango creations addressed to suit the Japanese: "I don't

タンゴ・リベルタ

伝統の極限に、今「自由」の華が開いた

小林太平・江口祐子

小林太平とアルゼンチンタンゴ舞踊団

公演日 **1990年9月20日(木)** 午後6時30分開場 会場 ヤクルトホール
午後7時00分開演 ☎03-574-7255

Promotional flyer for a performance by Kobayashi and Eguchi.

Cover of Luis Alposta's *El Tango en Japón,* drawn by Sigfredo Pastor.

like to listen to Japanese tango singers or to watch Japanese Argentinean tango performers. We [Japanese] talk and move differently, no matter what. Nor do I enjoy the tangos written by Argentineans inspired by Japanese themes. They lose their original passion and become too mental, too intellectual."

Luis Alposta chose for the cover of his book on tango in Japan a painting showing an Oriental male in traditional Japanese costume and coiffure playing the bandoneón, half-squatting, so as to further Japanize the scene. The message is clear: tango in Japan, of all places! Isn't it strange! Japanese tango performers and aficionados I spoke with wince when they look at the cover of Alposta's book but do not complain out loud. Perhaps they, too, are a bit amazed and feel that there is something strange about Japanese doing the tango; they, too, see a Japanese person playing the bandoneón as an exotic.

Japan has entered the global core of wealth and power but has not displaced former hegemonic Western centers or freed itself from the legacy of its culturally colonized past. Japan is now touted as the heir to the capitalist throne. But in spite of this economic success, the question of whether Japan is controlling or being controlled by westernization is a complex matter. The Japanese have successfully domesticated the English, French, and Argentinean versions of the tangos they have imported, adapting each to a particular use linked to the intricacies of Japanese class relations. But domesticating occidental products and practices is not the same thing as being in control of the process of westernization. Japan has been exoticized by the West for a long time. This exoticization has left its mark on Japanese identity and on Japanese desire, including the desire for the passion of the Other, as represented in Japan by the tango.

NOTES

1. Two events are usually mentioned as highlights in the Japanese-Argentinean diplomatic life. The first took place in 1905, when the Argentinean Navy ceded two warships to Japan for use in the war with Russia. The second occurred at the end of World War II, when Argentina sent two cargo ships of wheat to Japan in response to a food crisis.

2. Exotic places, persons, and things domesticated as commodities by the West generally display the amiable side of the Other: plants, perfumes, clothing, jewelry, food and spices, art, courtship, songs and dances. The threatening side is pushed to the background: violence, dictators, volcanos, disease, polygamy, poverty. The Exotic Other always comes out of this operation as a freak: lacking in something (rationality, control, propriety) and excessive in something else (violence, sensuality, passion).

3. "Un zorzal, / en Buenos Aires se largó a cantar. / Y su voz / abrió las alas y se echó a volar. / Fué Gardel (. . .) / Japón . . . / Donde otro pájaro nació . . . , creció. / Mujer . . . / Y fué calandria que cantó. . . . / El cielo abrazara / calandria con zorzal . . . / Del Plata hasta el Japón, / el canto se alzara. / Ya no habrá muerte ni silencio / que podrá. . . . " (A thrush, / in Buenos Aires lets out a song / And his voice / filled his wings and set him aflight. / He was Gardel . . . / Japan . . . / Where another bird was born . . . reared. / A woman . . . / And she was a singing lark. . . . / The sky will join / Lark with thrush . . . / From the Plata to Japan, / Song will fill the air. / Then neither death nor silence / Will be able [to keep them apart]. . . .)—excerpt from "El Zorzal y La Calandria" (1990). Music by Abo Ikuo, lyrics by Héctor Negro.

REFERENCES

Alposta, Luis A. 1987. *El tango en Japon.* Buenos Aires: Editorial Corregidor.

Bates, Héctor, and Luis Bates. 1936. *La historia del tango.* Buenos Aires: Taller Gráfico de la Compañía.

Cadicamo, Enrique. 1976. *El tango en Paris.* Buenos Aires: Editorial Corregidor.

Ferrer, Horacio. 1980. *El libro del tango: Arte popular de Buenos Aires.* Vol. 1, *Cronica del tango;* vol. 2, *Diccionario A–J.* Barcelona: Antonio Tersol.

Klein, Jean-Claude. 1985. Borrowing, syncretism, hybridization: The Parisian revue of the 1920s. In R. Middleton and D. Horn (eds.), *Popular music 5: Continuity and change.* Cambridge: Cambridge University Press.

Leppert, Richard. 1988. *Music and image: Domesticity, ideology and socio-cultural formation in eighteenth-century England.* Cambridge: Cambridge University Press.

Maeda Hibari and Itsuki Hiroyuki. 1987. Passion por el tango. *Asahi Graph:* 52–55.

Otterbach, Friedemann. 1980. *Die Geschichte der europaischen Tanzmusik.* Wilhelmshaven: Heinrichshofen's Verlag.

Rhys, Hedley H. 1971. Afterword. In George J. Becker and Edith Philips (eds. and trans.), *Paris and the arts, 1851–1896: From the Goncourt journal.* Ithaca: Cornell University Press.

Rivarola, Maria, and Carlos Rivarola. 1987. *Asi se baila el tango.* Tokyo.

Sorell, Walter. 1981. *Dance in its time.* New York: Anchor Press.

CONTRIBUTORS

DIANA BETHEL is a Ph.D. candidate in anthropology and program associate at the Center for Japanese Studies at the University of Hawaii.

MARY YOKO BRANNEN is assistant professor of international business, and organizational behavior and human resource management at the University of Michigan.

SCOTT CLARK is assistant professor of anthropology at Indiana State University.

MILLIE R. CREIGHTON is assistant professor in the anthropology and sociology department at the University of British Columbia.

WILLIAM W. KELLY is professor of anthropology at Yale University.

DORINNE KONDO is MacArthur Associate Professor in women's studies and anthropology at Pomona College.

FUMITERU NITTA is outreach coordinator of the Center for Japanese Studies, University of Hawaii, and a Japanese language instructor at Punahou School.

NANCY ROSENBERGER is assistant professor of anthropology at Oregon State University.

MARTA E. SAVIGLIANO is assistant professor in the department of dance at the University of California, Riverside.

STEPHEN R. SMITH is assistant professor of anthropology in the department of sociology at Wittenberg University.

JAMES STANLAW is assistant professor of anthropology at Illinois State University.

JEFFREY TOBIN is studying anthropology at the University of California, Riverside.

JOSEPH J. TOBIN is associate professor in the College of Education and the Center for Youth Research, Social Science Research Institute, of the University of Hawaii.

INDEX

255